Carolina Piedmont Country

Folklife in the South Series

Cajun Country
by Barry Jean Ancelet, Jay Edwards,
and Glen Pitre

Kentucky Bluegrass Country
by R. Gerald Alvey

Upper Cumberland Country
by William Lynwood Montell

South Florida Folklife
by Tina Bucuvalas, Peggy A. Bulger,
and Stetson Kennedy

Great Smoky Mountains
by Michael Ann Williams

Ozark Country
by W. K. McNeil

William Lynwood Montell, General Editor Folklife in the South Series

Carolina Piedmont Country

John M. Coggeshall

UNIVERSITY PRESS OF MISSISSIPPI *Jackson*

Copyright © 1996 by the University Press of Mississippi
Manufactured in the United States of America
99 98 97 96   4 3 2 1
The paper in this book meets the guidelines for permanence
and durability of the Committee on Production Guidelines for
Book Longevity of the Council on Library Resources.

97-98

Library of Congress Cataloging-in-Publication Data

Coggeshall, John M.
    Carolina Piedmont country / John M. Coggeshall.
    271 p.   cm.—(Folklore in the South series)
    Includes bibliographical references and index.
    ISBN 0-87805-766-8 (cloth : alk. paper).—ISBN 0-87805-767-6
(paper : alk. paper)
    1. Folklore—Piedmont (U.S. : Region)   2. Piedmont (U.S. :
Region)—Social life and customs.   I. Title.   II. Series.
GR108.C56   1996
390'.09756'5091734—dc20   95-49438
                                                      CIP

97-98

British Library Cataloging-in-Publication data available

CONTENTS

Folklife, a familiar concept in European scholarship for over a century, is the sum of a community's traditional forms of expression and behavior. It has claimed the attention of American folklorists since the 1950s. Each volume in the Folklife in the South Series focuses on the shared traditions that link people with their past and provide meaning and continuity for them in the present, and sets these traditions in the social contexts in which they flourish. Prepared by recognized scholars in various academic disciplines, these volumes are designed to be read separately. Each contains a vivid description of one region's traditional cultural element—ethnic and mainstream, rural and urban—that, in concert with those of other recognizable southern regions, lend a unique interpretation to the complex social structure of the South.

This extensive study of the Piedmont region of North and South Carolina focuses upon Carolina cotton country—the area roughly between Charlotte, North Carolina, and Greenville, South Carolina. While the folklife of this area has deep and diverse roots, its heritage was principally shaped by cotton production and processing, beginning after the Civil War with the Anglo and African Americans who lived on small farms and in quiet crossroads towns. In the wake of Reconstruction the Piedmont sprouted a number of industrial towns whose cotton mills utilized the area's inexpensive power, labor, and materials. This book examines the early folkways and reviews the process by which these evolved into contemporary Piedmont folklife—the customs, values, beliefs, stories, social and religious activities, foodways, architecture and other traditions that give the region its distinctive character.

William Lynwood Montell
SERIES EDITOR

This book has taken quite a long time from initial idea to final edition, and so there are numerous people who have helped me along the way. I would like to thank all of them in turn.

In October 1988, Lynwood Montell first approached me about the possibility of writing this book. It is to him that I owe my first debt of gratitude, for offering me the chance and for encouraging me to write. I sincerely appreciate Lynwood's continuing faith in my ability.

In June 1991 I first entered the field, and I owe an even greater debt of gratitude to all the Piedmont folks who have shared their lives and their memories with me. Marjorie Peden introduced me to her parents, Raymond and Anne, who in turn introduced me to Don Roper, who then provided numerous names for further interviewing. Dan Ezell and Steve Odum, with the Clemson Agricultural Extension Service, also provided me with valuable contacts and suggestions. I sincerely wish to thank all of my informants for their generosity and kindness over the years.

The staffs at several libraries also deserve special mention. Dr. Richard Shrader and Mike Casey in the Manuscripts Department at Wilson Library, UNC-Chapel Hill, have been extremely helpful in opening the extensive folklife collections there. The staff at USC's Caroliniana Library have been helpful in introducing me to the old WPA files. Donna Roper, at the Pendleton District Historical Commission, has been quite generous with her time and expertise as well. Mike Kohl and the Special Collections staff at Clemson's Cooper Library also deserve thanks.

Financial support came in small but welcome amounts from a Provost's Research Award (1990–1991) and a Faculty Development Award (1992–1993), both through Richard Larson (then Head, Department of Sociology) and Robert Waller (then Dean, College of Liberal Arts). These individuals have helped me both professionally and personally, and I wish to thank them sincerely for their continuing support.

Several graduate students in Clemson's Applied Sociology program have helped in various ways to prepare the manuscript for publication. Ms. Kristen Biestman-Craig dutifully coded data, inventoried field tapes, and kept me focused on the ultimate goal, while Kory Coonen input Kristen's handwritten notes. Lisa Faulkenberry, Donna Sedgwick, Amy Klumas, and Amy Garland volunteered to proofread several editions of the manuscript. My special thanks to all of you.

The editorial staff at the University Press of Mississippi has been patient and understanding during the past several years, especially as various deadlines came and went. JoAnne Prichard, Anne Stascavage, Ginger Tucker, and the manuscript editors deserve special thanks. I would also like to thank the anonymous reviewer of the original manuscript for several helpful suggestions.

Finally, I would like to thank Cathy Robison and Meredith Walker for reading earlier versions of this manuscript, for offering helpful suggestions, and for encouraging me throughout the years of my research and writing of this book.

I would like to dedicate this book to the people of the Piedmont, past and present, black and white, rich and poor, male and female—this region is special because of you. Thank you for allowing me to discover the beauty and richness of your lives.

The drive through the beautiful autumn-tinted countryside was a welcome relief from the intense interview I had just conducted. Rounding a bend in the blacktop, I suddenly saw a rare sight in the Carolina Piedmont today. There, glittering in the late afternoon sun, was a small field of cotton. The contrast of colors immediately struck me: the shimmering white cotton bolls, the brownish-black plants, the reddish-orange soil, the pale green pines beyond, and the clear blue sky above. The colors blended together like strands in cloth: a cloth spun from cotton and woven through time.

While the folklife of the Carolina Piedmont has deep and diverse roots, cotton production has significantly influenced it for the past century, forming a frame upon which to weave more recent threads of tradition. Following the Civil War, the loom consisted of small cotton farms near quiet crossroads towns, with a warp of cultural groups and social interaction, through which have been woven fibers of behaviors and beliefs from both Anglo and African Americans. Later, the introduction of cotton mills modified the weaving process by adding new industries to the loom and new groups to the warp. After World War II came contrasting materials such as those of northerners, further changing the texture of the cloth. Today, the folklife of the Carolina Piedmont consists of a tapestry of overlaid traditions from a variety of fibers, which yet retains the older pattern. This book examines the way in which the loom of Carolina folklife became established after the Civil War and then reviews the process that, through the course of time, blended a variety of traditions into contemporary Piedmont folklife.

Beginning with the post–Reconstruction period about 1880, Anglo-American Piedmonters invigorated cotton production with an antebellum set of values and behaviors. At the same time, the recently freed African-American slaves retained their own separate traditions, which, because of legally and socially reinforced racism, remained somewhat separate from those of their white neighbors. These groups' beliefs and practices became irretrievably interwoven, as black and white sharecroppers worked side by side, as white townspeople hired black cooks, and as black midwives delivered babies alongside white doctors. Despite overt and covert racism, in fact, this commingling of African- and Anglo-American folklife traditions has continued to this day. While it is thus possible to separate some specific group beliefs and behaviors, in order to appreciate Piedmont folklife in general, one must recognize the thorough blending of black and white ideas that has today created an extremely rich and colorful fabric.

The "things" of the folk, folklorist John Vlach argued, are typical, commonplace, ordinary, and familiar; they are also patterned and duplicated over and over again. In short, folklife reflects the common views and behaviors of ordinary people. Specifically, folklorist William Ferris wrote, southern folklife includes oral lore such as sermons, tales, and music; customary behaviors such as planting and harvesting, food preparation and consumption, family reunions, rites of passage, and religious meetings; and material culture such as folk architecture, folk arts and crafts, and folk medicine and healing.

These practices, of course, are not exclusive to the South or to the Piedmont region. However, the region itself gives a special meaning to these traditions by defining the boundaries within which these customs and ideas have taken shape. The South, geographer Carl Sauer stated, "is a major cultural division of the United States, perhaps its most strikingly outstanding cultural unit." Sociologist Rupert Vance continued: "Common traditions, a similar ancestry, common economic interests, and similar climate help to account for its unity." More specifically, as educator Carl Epting explained, "the climate of Maine will never produce cotton, neigher [sic] will the environment of South Carolina produce a Yankee."

In less deterministic words, residents within the Carolina Piedmont share what folklorist Barbara Allen termed "a sense of place," a distinctive regional identity expressed through cultural elements such as folklife. Others as well have noted the essential connection between a regional sense of place and the folk expressions of those in that place. Regional culture, Allen suggested, "provides the vehicle for inhabitants to express both personally and collectively their sense of regional identity and regional consciousness." In this way, regional folklife reflects the thoughts, views, and behaviors of those within that region.

Regional culture, Allen continued, is formed by the geographical features of the place and shaped by the inhabitants, whose lives are in part influenced by the land's physiology. Of course, as Sauer cautioned, people also transform the landscapes that they occupy. Since conditions change, Allen noted, regional cultures are also shaped by the area's history, including migrations, wars, and innovations. Finally, she added, residents of folk regions must possess a distinctive self-identity and see themselves apart from those in adjacent regions. Together, the cultures plus time plus the natural landscape create a distinct region with characteristic folklife traditions.

Since change is constant, however, the presentation of folklife inevitably means establishing parameters around which to base a discussion. In effect, this book represents a segment of the entirety of Piedmont folklife, opening in the late nineteenth century and ending in the present. I recognize that the creation of the region's folklife began some time earlier and that traditions described in this book will continue to evolve as well.

As Ferris's general overview of southern folklife suggested, the traditions of the Carolina Piedmont involve an intricate mesh of interrelated ideas: those involving verbal behavior and folk knowledge systems (chapters 5, 6, and 7); those dealing with social activities (chapters 8, 9, 10, and 11); and those examining material items and the cultural use of space (chapters 12 and 13). None of these general categories is exclusive, but by separating Piedmont traditions into these broad groupings the discussion becomes easier to discern and to appreciate.

Verbal genres of Piedmont folklife include, first of all, an introduction to the regional "southern" accent as well as regional variations. In this dialect exist folktales of various types, and storytelling is an art that local residents greatly enjoy. These stories involve topics such as local characters and supernatural phenomena and their manifestations. This category also includes customary beliefs typical of the region, such as the relationship between astronomical and terrestrial events and traditional methods of healing.

Characteristic types of human social interaction form the second major division of Piedmont folklife to be addressed. These behaviors involve traditional forms of family entertainment such as visiting between neighbors. Family-related gatherings such as reunions and Sunday dinners are also important, as are more formal holidays such as New Year's Day and Christmas and significant religious activities such as revivals and camp meetings. Folklife examples of regional recreation involve children's games, adult relaxation, and shopping at the area flea markets. Typical gender-segregated activities include hunting and fishing for males and quilting and canning for females. At virtually all of these social activities, traditional foods are prepared and consumed.

The third major division of Piedmont folklife is that of material culture, the human modifications to the landscape that characterize the region today. Farming constitutes the base of these transformations, and for the past century those farms have generally produced cotton. Second in development but equal in importance are the mill villages, for textile work frequently appears in the histories of many families in the area today. In local communities both blacks and whites shopped, paid taxes, and marketed crops. In these towns as well, many African Americans found employment as craftspeople, cooks, and child-care providers, for they were segregated from mill work for generations. Finally, there are the cemeteries, where all eventually ended, but (until recently) in different locations and often with racially characteristic epitaphs.

All of these ideas and behaviors are interconnected; and while it is possible to examine each one, the pattern emerges only when all are recombined. In much the same way, a detailed analysis of varied aspects of Carolina Piedmont folklife may cause one to lose sight of the fact that these traditions are completely intertwined in everyday life. For example, while chapters require the separate discussion of family reunions, anecdotes, and traditional foods, each category makes little sense without the others. As will be seen, it is families who provide the food (as well as create the reason for the gathering in the first place), family recipes that are exchanged, and family stories that are told. For clarity's sake, the diverse ideas that characterize the overall pattern have had to be separated, but these will be blended to restore the overall view.

While numerous categories of Piedmont folklife will be examined in the following chapters, not every one will be. In other words, this book highlights many of the region's characteristic traditions; it does not contain an encyclopedic listing of all existing genres. Owing primarily to limitations of space, I have had to restrict my discussion to those categories of folklife that my informants felt to be most significant or distinctive. Other researchers are welcome to expand this study.

Helping shape the general pattern of Piedmont folklife is a continuity of social interaction performed on a background of temporal transformations. Through time, various social groups have settled in the Piedmont; in a sense, each group defined itself in relation to others, drawing a separate identity from the interaction. For example, Scots-Irish farmers perceived real and stereotypical distinctions between themselves and their African-American neighbors, and both groups in turn influenced, and were influenced by, the town elites, mill villagers, Yankees, and other groups who evolved from or settled next to earlier ones. Through all of these groups wind folklife traditions, sometimes linking and sometimes separating them. Over time, change has modified the geographical and social landscape, adding new elements, widening the gaps between others, or affecting the speed of cultural blending.

Similarly, historical transformation has influenced the ongoing production of Piedmont folklife. Folk traditions, based in human interaction, are thus subject to alterations, as these interactions metamorphose through time because of new in-migrants, inventions, political or economic developments, and social changes. For example, as the Piedmont shifted slowly and painfully from cotton agriculture to mill work and from textiles to manufacturing, the traditions reinforced by these occupations shifted as well. Yankees exacerbated stereotypes, poverty increased social distance, and modernization hurried the pace of life. Despite these modifications, folklife persists.

Because of increasing pressure in American culture toward assimilation, scholars such as Gary Stanton have argued that Carolina Piedmont folklife is disappearing in favor of a homogenized "American" culture. While it is true that lay-by time no longer has the social significance it once had, and little boys no longer play mumble peg, for example, Piedmont folklife will not disappear. While some elements fade or wear out, others remain strong; still others are created to fill the gaps. As folklorists Daniel Patterson and Charles Zug argue (of North Carolina folklife): "We see . . . negotiations that little-noticed people from four different continents are carrying on here with the state's varied terrains, with changing economies and social balances, with each other, with the arts and ideas of their own forebears, and with the common crises of human life."

As Stanton warned, though, "each change . . . must be met with an increased effort to document what went before." Change to folklife is inevitable; it then becomes critical to describe folklife at various stages of the production process. This will enable future generations "to keep a sense of place" by learning what makes that place special, Stanton added. The traditions that make the Carolina Piedmont special are the subject of this book.

Methodology

Like virtually all other fieldwork experiences, this one developed partly through planning and partly through serendipity. The geographical area of the Carolina Piedmont encompasses a huge territory, one that could not possibly be covered by participant observation and in-depth interviewing by one researcher. Nevertheless, the area contains enough regularities to permit a logical and reasonable sampling of communities and residents.

Probably the single most noticeable type of community scattered throughout the landscape of the Piedmont is the mill town. Since cotton production and processing have played a significant role in the development of the area for the past century, the selection of a typical mill town and associated farming areas established the starting point of the research. This typical community has been given the pseudonym of Hammondville, South Carolina. The detailed examination of this and similar towns permits the investigation of the background upon which the past century of Piedmont folklife had been formed: a farming tradition, the development and subsequent decline of mill villages, and the complex interactions among mill, town, and farm residents.

For other reasons, too, the town of Hammondville seemed ideal. Although not directly connected to either interstate or U.S. highways, the town sits within ten miles of both, surrounded by farmland and suburban sprawl. It also lies within fifty miles of Greenville, the self-styled "Textile Capital of the World" and the heart of the Cotton Piedmont (and in fact one of the targeted communities for the study by historian Jacquelyn Hall et al.). While formerly quite productive, the corporate descendant of the original Hammondville mill no longer serves as the social or commercial core of the town. Adjacent to this community lies a smaller, traditionally black neighborhood, geographically segregated from but socially intertwined with the mill town. This complex relationship of mutual need and mistrust has permitted the study of the interweaving of African- and Anglo-American traditions within the same community, another major goal of the research.

The other community studied in some depth has been the town of "Kent," about a hundred miles to the north and east of Hammondville. This community shifts the focus of the study much closer to North Carolina (the border lies about fifteen miles north of Kent). A mill town like Hammondville (in fact containing several still-producing mills), Kent is also the county seat and thus has a more thriving commercial center. Using participant observation and interviews from several visits, I obtained the perspectives of contemporary merchants and local politicians. This additional work thus expanded the geographical range of the study as well as incorporated several more examples of traditions.

Kent was also of interest because it had been the site of an in-depth research project conducted by the University of North Carolina in the late 1940s. According to John Morland (the project director), Kent "was chosen as a good example of the mode of life found in the Piedmont area." Thus Kent represents mill towns in the southern Piedmont section of North Carolina as well. To conduct the project, several anthropologists lived in the town for about a year, gathering notes from interviews and observations of town residents (both black and white) and mill workers. The goal, as Morland explained, was to "delineate at least the principal patterns of the subculture."

From these detailed observations were to come three books, one for each segment of the population; only two finally appeared. The unpublished field notes of the researchers, typed on hundreds of index cards and filed with the University of North Carolina at Chapel Hill, provide invaluable glimpses into small-town Carolina Piedmont life just after World War II. These observations have then been updated by my more recent visits.

Besides participant observation and informal interviews in these two communities, another major source of information has come from more in-depth interviewing of informants. These have included residents of both Kent and Hammondville, people in adjacent, unincorporated areas, and still others in more distant communities within the Carolina Piedmont. Formal interviewing began in June 1991 and resulted in more than seventy-five hours of taped recordings from thirty individuals. These interviews have provided the bulk of contemporary views of Piedmont folklife. Brief biographies of all informants appear at the end of this book, along with information about the means by which they were contacted.

During the two years of fieldwork, I also took other trips in order to expand the area of study, to contact informally other participants, and to test assumptions and observations from the core study area. These travels encompassed both North and South Carolina roads and usually were done in association with photographic documentation of buildings and landscapes. Thus, when asking permission to photograph private homes, I would sometimes interview local residents briefly and informally about specific aspects of folklife.

Throughout fieldwork I have been conscious of my Euro-American background, male gender, and northern origin, and how these factors may (or may not) have influenced both my data collection and informant selection. Consequently, a deliberate attempt has been made to balance gender and racial representation. Most of the early informants were white, but not all were. Both black and white informants then introduced me to friends and spouses, in effect expanding the direction of contacts in two quite different directions and into two distinct social groups. A Clemson University County Extension Service agent introduced me to two African-American farmers, who further balanced the sample. Contacts with a local women's organization helped even out gender representation. Despite the cautions of one woman who warned that "southern pride" might prevent locals from offering me their "true feelings," I believe I have obtained accurate information.

Library and archival materials greatly expanded the range of the study. Knowing that in-depth interviewing of North Carolina informants would be impossible because of financial, temporal, and spacial constraints, I utilized the extensive interview collections of folklife materials in the Southern Historical Collection and the Southern Folklife Collection at the University of North Carolina-Chapel Hill (UNC). These excellent collections represented just over one-third of the recordings I used for the study, thus greatly widening the diachronic and demographic scope of fieldwork and providing parallels for and checks against the South Carolina information. Since many of the specific contributors were African American and/or female, this information from UNC also helped to balance the general sample of informants.

Another valuable archival source was that at the Pendleton District Historical Society. Many of these interview tapes were collected as part of an oral history project in the early 1980s from area residents then of retirement age, and only a portion are available for public examination. Since almost all of the interviews are of African Americans in the upper Piedmont region of South Carolina, they greatly increase the numbers of blacks in the study sample. Likewise, several are women, further helping to equalize gender representation.

To trace the evolution of Piedmont folklife over the past century, I also consulted historical materials, primarily the archival collections of the Works Progress Administration (WPA). In both the University of South Carolina's (USC) Caroliniana Library and UNC's Southern Historical Collection are stored dozens of unpublished vignettes of Carolina residents collected in the late 1930s by WPA workers. Both mill hands and farmers (tenant and owner), males and females, blacks (some former slaves) and whites, and young and old are represented. About one-fifth were North Carolina residents. While usually only five or six pages long and somewhat biased, the interviews are still extremely useful. They provide glimpses of life in the Carolinas during the Depression and extend back into the 1880s through recollections. These interviews effectively expand the range of the study back to the end of Reconstruction and to the origins of cotton mill organization, thereby covering an entire century of the development of Carolina Piedmont folklife.

A final area for information has been more general library materials. Unpublished sources include personal or family documents, church or community histories, and theses or scholarly papers in libraries or archives. Published materials include collections of interviews of Piedmont residents (some from WPA sources, such as former slaves from North Carolina) as well as direct recollections of area residents, sometimes nostalgic memories and sometimes humorous exaggeration. Some secondary sources, though, utilized relatively sophisticated qualitative methods while others did not. Secondary sources provide the background and generalizations to support the primary materials.

Carolina Piedmont Country

CHAPTER I

The Piedmont Region

The Piedmont geographical region extends from the Hudson River in New York to central Alabama—technically serving as the foothills of the Appalachians. More specifically, encyclopedist Karen McDearman observed, "the term *Piedmont* refers to the Piedmont 'crescent' of North and South Carolina, continuing into parts of Georgia and Alabama." Here, as will be seen, the underlying geological strata have affected the resultant topographical features, which in turn have shaped the types and distribution of land use.

From this large region, smaller subregions may be differentiated. In 1936, sociologist Howard Odum perceived a distinction between what he termed the "Cotton Piedmont" and other subsections such as the "Tobacco Piedmont" of central North Carolina and Virginia. While the northern and southern boundaries are somewhat vague, Odum's map cleaves the two areas somewhere in central North Carolina, extends through central South Carolina, and spills over the border into central Georgia and a small section of east-central Alabama. This book examines Odum's Carolina Cotton Piedmont.

Even this subregion is large and diverse. It is readily acknowledged that state, county, and even community traditions might vary within this area. Nevertheless, there remains an overall commonality of beliefs and behaviors among long-term residents throughout the region. As noted in the Introduction, for the previous century this heritage has been shaped by the production and processing of cotton. The study concentrates on the center of Odum's Cotton Piedmont, the area roughly between Charlotte, North Carolina, and Greenville, South Carolina—Carolina cotton country.

The Piedmont Plateau, as described in the North Carolina state guidebook, "consists of rolling hill country, with stiff clay soils and numerous swift streams capable of producing great power for industrial and urban development." As prehistoric oceans retreated, these streams cut deeper and wider into the plateau, thereby forming fertile river bottom land interspersed with relatively flat plateaus, both capable of being farmed. The area averages about eighty miles in width in South Carolina but broadens to about two hundred miles wide in North Carolina, and varies in elevation from about five hundred to one thousand feet.

Piedmont soils are typical of forested, humid, subtropical areas, and are generally below average in fertility because of leaching, where plant nutrients percolate through the soil or run off by rain. As the South Carolina state guidebook noted, "these clay lands will produce good crops of corn, cotton, and vegetables if the missing humus is supplied and conserved," conditions that were not always followed. The remaining insoluble minerals and clays thus concentrate in the upper zones, "and their oxidation gives the soils a characteristic red or red-yellow color." Because of this permeability, Piedmont soils remained highly susceptible to erosion, which, together with intensive planting practices after the Civil War, produced devastating soil losses and contributed eventually to the virtual elimination of cotton production in the region.

Historically, changing agricultural practices have modified the area's original oak-hickory forest cover. As farmers cleared the land for crop production and as subsequent soil and price erosion modified these plans, new plant species entered the region. Many abandoned cotton fields have more recently been planted in loblolly pine for the timber industry. Other vacant fields have been overwhelmed by the kudzu vine, introduced to combat erosion. Today, however, kudzu creates a green wave in many open areas, seeming to wash over vacant houses, buildings, and all other vegetation. Sensitive to frost, the vines lose their leaves in late fall, leaving extensive patches of tangled brown thickets cluttering up the landscape. Kudzu, scrub pines, and near bare areas of bright orange clay soils characterize the landscape of the Piedmont today.

While the northern and southern boundaries of the Carolina Cotton Piedmont may be somewhat vague, those borders to the west and east are much clearer. To the west, running approximately southwest to northeast from northern Alabama and Georgia through the Carolinas into Virginia abruptly rise the Blue Ridge Mountains. Formed by the colossal forces of plate tectonics about 470 million years ago, the mountains create a steep barrier dividing two quite distinct geophysical features. The Blue Ridge creates a cultural boundary as well.

To the east lies another easily distinguishable physiographical boundary, the Fall Line. The North Carolina state guidebook explained: "The fall line, at the head of river navigation, marks the western edge of the Coastal Plain." Paralleling the Blue Ridge, the Fall Line continues through South

The Piedmont Plateau from the Blue Ridge Mountains
(Photo by John M. Coggeshall)

Carolina "along a diagonal between the North Carolina boundary . . . and the Georgia boundary in Aiken County. It separates two regions commonly known as the Up Country and the Low Country—regions differing in customs, history, and livelihood," according to the South Carolina state guidebook.

A clear geophysical distinction separates these two regions, as geographers Charles Kovacik and John Winberry explained: "The line of separation between the Low-Country and the Upland Country is marked by a belt of sand-hills. . . . These stretch across the State [of South Carolina] nearly parallel to the coast." The hills continue into North Carolina, paralleling the Blue Ridge. They developed because of a Cenozoic-era invasion of the sea, which left extensive deposits of marine sand that now lie much further inland.

The Sand Hills of the Carolinas, despite a large amount of annual rainfall, cannot retain moisture well, since it all drains immediately through the sandy soil. As might be expected, farming in this area was difficult at best, as Emanuel Schumpert reported to a WPA fieldworker in 1939: "The land around Dixiana [South Carolina] was, and still is, so poor that the only use we Lexingtonians can find for it is a sort of space filler, or just so much poor sand put there to hold the world together. . . . Dixiana is one of the few places where one can be out of sight of land and water all at the same time." The region historically provided poor settlement conditions, thereby forming an effective geographical and cultural barrier between the peoples of the coast and those of the Carolina interior.

In both the Carolinas, the division between the Piedmont and the coast has long been extremely important. In the South Carolina state guidebook, the editor argued that, second to one's state allegiance comes one's regional identity, equivalent to the "Roundhead-Cavalier antagonism in England." Benjamin Dunlap recalled: "Somewhere in my boyhood I distinguished up-country from low-country as Freudians separate ego from id. . . . In-stinctively I seized upon Cash's opposition of Scotch-Irish yeoman and English aristocrat and extended it to connote the conflict of all that is ratio-nal, lurid and progressive with that which is dark, unfathomable and doomed."

Settlement patterns largely account for the distinctions between Low Country and Up Country, differences that easily degenerate into stereo-types. For example, the North Carolina guidebook observed: "The Pied-mont . . . has always been a more serious-minded land. . . . The plantations disappeared at the fall line. Labor became increasingly white. . . . Hard-working, hard-headed men . . . took the Carolina Piedmont into the direct streams of modern mechanical America." Even African Americans in the 1940s Piedmont region noted differences between themselves and blacks in the Low Country, ethnographers Ralph Patrick and John Morland ob-served. Piedmont blacks, they wrote, "feel something of disdain for the downstate (Charleston) Negro; there is a feeling that they are a little more cowed and perhaps cruder." As will be seen, differences between dialects, customs, and stereotypes persist.

The Low Countryman, typically, may live in Charleston (the "New Jeru-salem"), thinks in terms of ease, and remembers proudly the "War Between the States," the South Carolina guidebook remarked. One Upstate woman described Charlestonians as "just plain snootier." "In fact," another woman sniffed, "the lower state considered the Upstate backwoodsy and ignoramuses, mostly. I mean, Charleston—the Upstate was just not as proper as they were." Dale Garroway added that "with Charleston you got to have that blue blood, or you'll *never* be accepted in that place."

Perhaps these impressions might explain what John Edmunds termed the Upstate's "acute case of paranoia," often foundering "in the wake made by the tidewater region." To counterattack, the common joke told in the South Carolina Upstate asks in what ways are Charlestonians like the Chi-nese? The answer: they both eat rice, worship their ancestors, and speak in a foreign language. For whatever reasons they developed, the cultural divisions between Low Country and Up Country persist.

Another cultural distinction (partly historical, partly stereotypical) persists as well between the residents of the Upstate and those of the mountains. Sociologist Jennings Rhyne argued that the mountaineer, beyond the reach of slavery, was economically disadvantaged and traditionally backward because of the geographic barrier of the mountains. This "traditional backwardness" supported stereotypes of "our contemporary ancestors," as Marjorie Potwin (a mill management employee) described these mountain residents. She also characterized them as being strongly individualistic but having poor sanitation and work habits.

Mountain residents, who formed a sizable percentage of the cotton mill labor pool by the early twentieth century, felt uncomfortable when moving to the Up Country because of these stereotypes about them held by their new Piedmont neighbors. This feeling of initial discomfort was described by an anonymous mill worker in 1939, whose family had just moved from the mountains of North Carolina to a mill town: "The people dressed differently than we had up in the mountains. Why, when we went to church up there all we needed was a clean pair of overalls and that was good enough, but we sorta felt out of place in a city church with everybody dressed up in store-bought clothes." Compounding that embarrassment, of course, would have been all those disquieting stares from the "civilized" congregation.

These differences persist. "There's mostly good people" in the mountains, one woman stated; her companion added "and some with no education . . . just as ignorant as a weed."

A final distinction, political rather than geographical in origin, consists of the state boundaries separating the constituent elements. In a sense, this division represents an alternate form of identity alongside one's geographical region. For example, at times being a North Carolinian might outweigh a mountain heritage, thereby separating Blue Ridge residents from the Carolinas. But at other times, a Piedmont heritage shared by mill workers in both Carolinas might more completely link them than their state origins might separate them.

Both of the Carolinas take great pride in their separate histories. Ben Robertson, a South Carolinian, reported that his grandmother considered North Carolina to be "just nothing but new and rich . . . [;] it practically did not exist." North Carolinians, in their WPA state guidebook, countered with the old story that they consider themselves to be a vale of humility between two mountains of conceit: Virginia and South Carolina. While this attitude may no longer be true, North Carolinians try to ignore the "haughty, aristocratic superiority" often assumed by Charleston-bred South Carolinians, and many Tar Heels still hold their southern neighbors in humorous contempt.

Settlement History

The groups that entered what eventually became the states of the Carolinas, and those that specifically entered the Piedmont section, both shaped and were shaped by the land they occupied and by earlier groups they displaced. Euro-American immigrants, avoiding the Low Country elites and seeking (or being granted) "unoccupied" interior territory, pushed the Native-American inhabitants from the Carolinas and staked their claims in the Up Country. Almost from the beginning of European occupation, of course, African Americans also entered the region, both as freepersons and as slaves. The agricultural qualities (or lack thereof) of the land in part determined why these groups settled the area and how they made their living. As these groups interacted with each other and the land they inhabited, the basis of Carolina Piedmont folklife became established.

NATIVE-AMERICAN SETTLEMENT

Native Americans have inhabited the Carolina Piedmont for thousands of years, probably since the Paleo-Indian period about twelve thousand years ago. Questions about dates of occupation persist because these first Native Americans were nomadic foragers who left no long-term campsites. Longer-term settlement occurred during the Archaic period about eight thousand years ago. During this time groups in the Upstate began to utilize more intensively the wild resources available, such as deer, fish, wildfowl, nuts, and wild plant foods, in an extremely successful lifestyle adaptation. Beginning about 1000 B.C., different cultural elaborations appeared, indicating a new cultural period—the Woodland. Probably forced by increasing population, Native Americans by this time emphasized low-intensity squash and corn agriculture in order to supplement foraging for wild foods. As a consequence of early farming, settled life in villages became much more widespread as well.

Sometime around 1100 A.D., a new cultural tradition, the Mississippian, entered the Carolinas, most likely from Georgia. Mississippian peoples probably coexisted somewhat uneasily with their Woodland neighbors, living in large villages of mound-based public buildings surrounded by symbolically and realistically protective palisades. This cultural period persisted into historic times, because Spanish explorers of the 1500s described farming communities of sizable populations, with elites living in "palaces" atop mounds in fortified towns. Most of the coastal and inland villages had disappeared by the mid-1600s because of disease and depradation by Europeans.

EURO-AMERICAN SETTLEMENT

While some of the earliest European contacts with Native Americans occurred in the Sea Islands of South Carolina, Upstate Indian groups such as the Cherokee and Catawba (most likely descendants of prehistoric Mississippian-era peoples) remained relatively untouched for more than a century. Eventual European contact came from two directions: up from the Low Country, as explorers and settlers marched out of Charles Town (later Charleston) and followed the rivers upstream to the Fall Line and beyond; and southwestward, along the foothills of the Blue Ridge, down forest trails from pioneer communities in Virginia and Pennsylvania. The Upstate was relatively attractive for settlement, a WPA historian noted, because the climate was cooler than the Low Country. However, because of the Fall Line, the Piedmont was also more isolated from military protection and economic contact with other Euro-American towns.

During the mid-eighteenth century, most of the settlers entering the Piedmont region were Scots-Irish and some Germans, whom journalist W. J. Cash described as "yeoman farmers" of the Upland South. These immigrants remained farmers of small holdings for several reasons. First, because the reddish clay soil of the Uplands was not as fertile as the dark soil of the Low Country, yields and fields remained smaller. Second, these farmers lived across the relatively barren Sand Hills, far from the coast and shipping ports. Finally, since their landholdings were small, few held sizable numbers of slaves who typically worked large plantation holdings such as in the Low Country.

Max Revelise, a WPA writer, believed that the Scots-Irish and German immigrants settled in the Upstate only partly to escape the humidity and heat of the Low Country; he also believed it had been "because of their dislike of the treatment accorded them in the unfair assignment of [land] grants." For example, Emanuel Schumpert, a farmer in Lexington County, told a WPA worker in 1939 that his German ancestors "had been pushed back into the poorer sandhills by the old landed aristocracy in the early days of the State."

The traditional belief has been that these upstanding Upstate pioneers had been expelled from, excluded from, or consciously avoided the "high society" and large slaveholding plantations of the Low Country. Ben Robertson explained: "We did not call our farms plantations in the Upcountry, and we did not call ourselves old Southern planters—we were old Southern farmers. . . . Charleston was a symbol to us—it represented luxury and easy soft living and all the evils of Egypt. Charleston . . . was Cavalier from the start; we were Puritan. . . . Charlestonians had come to the colony of South Carolina with money and china dishes and English silver. We had come down along the mountains from Pennsylvania with nothing—we had walked."

Thus, the traditions continue, the Scots-Irish and Germans of the Piedmont contrasting markedly in heritage and character with the English elites of Low Country Charleston. Robertson, for example, characterized his "Scotch-Irish" ancestors as believing in "self-reliance, in self-improvement, . . . in total abstinence, in total immersion, . . . [and] in honoring our parents." Revelise described these Upstate pioneers as "an industrious people of severe discipline and moderate tastes[;] they induced a much-needed restraint of the easy-going plantation ways as well as the lax morality then prevalent."

As might be imagined, this evolving social differentiation enhanced the already existing geographical boundary between Low and Up Country. By 1804, WPA writer Louise Jones DuBose wrote, "there was as little unity of feeling between the upper and lower country as between any rival States of the Union." This distinction between the thrifty, conservative, God-fearing Piedmont and the elitist, slaveholding Low Country helped establish significant regional boundaries that persist today.

AFRICAN-AMERICAN SETTLEMENT

An equally prominent social boundary existed between the Anglo Americans and their black neighbors, primarily slaves until after the Civil War. As discussed above, the Low Country plantations harbored numerous slaves while the smaller Up Country farms needed fewer hands. Thus, African-American settlement, both forced and free, began with the Carolina Sea Islands and gradually percolated inland.

A few black informants provided secondhand recollections of life during "slavery times." Some recalled stories their grandparents had told them as children, enthralled by narratives of an almost mythical time. Velma Childers, for example, remembered listening to her maternal grandfather, a former slave: "We used to sit on his knee and ask him, 'Grandpa, tell us something about what all happened.' And he was very alert; he would tell us all kind of stories. . . . Now my mother and my father, either one, wasn't born in slavery, and so they took it kind of a wishful thinking, as though it didn't happen. But it did."

Slaves faced tremendous difficulties, Vernon Randle had heard his great-grandfather say: "I used to love to hear my great-granddaddy talk about slavery time. . . . Used to sell us just like mules and cows. . . . He said he knowed he was sold twice, but who he was when he was first born, he didn't know. . . . Said they'd swap you, trade you, and all like a-that. . . . Like I'm married. And me and my wife didn't have no children, they'd take my wife from me and sell her to a man over yonder, so she could have children. . . . You have a child—somebody see your child, your son or your daughter, and they wanted them, they'd go to their white man, he'd sell them. They'd take them all from you—you wouldn't see them no more."

While life for many slave children was as cruel as that for adults, other African-American youngsters lived almost like pets in the master's house. For example, Velma Childers described her grandfather's childhood: "He told us one time about how his old mistress would have all these beautiful, great big table cloths and everything. And he was a little old boy under the table. And if he wanted a biscuit or some bread or something he would pull his old mistress's skirt and she would slip him some bread from the table." This story also reflects the long-established tradition of paternalistic concern that whites believe they have shown to "their" blacks.

Subtle social-class distinctions arose between slaves working in the home and those laboring in the fields. The former tended to have slightly easier lives, as Ms. Childers depicted her grandfather, often because of significant (but forbidden) emotional ties: "He actually was never sold as a slave, because he grew up in the old master's house, you might say. Because his mother . . . didn't work out in the fields like the other slaves. She tended to the house and did things like that. And believe it or not, my grandfather's father was the master of this house."

Other class divisions, Maxine Williams had heard, developed between white owners and white overseers. The latter were "just jealous" of the good treatment the owners reserved for the house slaves, she felt, and so the overseers would retaliate with increased cruelty toward their charges. She continued: "He would try to be overbearing to impress—you understand what I'm trying to say. That's the way they'd tell it, and I kind of believed it." Williams's narrative also suggests the contemporary distinction between owners and nonowners of slaves, a division of rich and poor that by her parents' time had evolved into a recognized social distinction between "good" whites and "white trash," discussed in chapter 3.

Writing in 1939, Louise Jones DuBose felt that this socioeconomic gulf between poor whites and elites was widened even further during Reconstruction. The former Confederate elites, the landholders who had also been the officeholders, tended to be excluded from government, while northern carpetbaggers, poorly educated whites, and freed slaves occupied the capitols and federal positions in the states. This social and political revolution placed blacks and Yankees in positions of power over southern white aristocrats while simultaneously subverting the deeply rooted antebellum attitude of an appropriate white hierarchy.

One disenfranchised and embittered Confederate veteran, Warren Flenniken, offered in his WPA interview a nostalgic, white-tinted, alternative perspective on slavery: "There was a deep abiding affection existing between the slave owners and the slaves. It was manifested all through the [Civil] war and for a while after the war ended. I don't think there would have been any trouble had it not been for the adventurer and carpetbagger, who seized upon the opportunity to inflame the Negro's passionate desire for social equality and the race's power of equal suffrage at the ballot box." This old soldier revealed another significant theme in the Piedmont's traditional belief system: the idea that southerners in general would have been better off without the intervention of these carpetbaggers and their twentieth-century descendants, the Yankees.

After the abolition of slavery and the defeat of the South, Reconstruction seemed to offer African Americans the beginning of a much improved way of life. With little land and few tools of agricultural production, however, freedom often meant increased economic hardship. "I'll tell you—the South was ruined after the war; they didn't have nothing," Lucindy Brown explained. Violet Guntharpe, a former slave in Depression-era Winnsboro, felt the same way: " 'Honey, us wasn't ready for de big change dat come! Us had no education, no land, no mule, no cow, not a pig, nor a chicken, to set up house keeping. . . . Us colored folks was left widout any place to lay our heads.' "

One solution was to resettle freed blacks in small communities with the good intention of providing a new beginning. One such settlement was called "Promised Land," several thousand acres in Greenwood and McCormick Counties, South Carolina. An African-American community still persists in the area.

A far more common solution to the employment of former slaves was that explained by "Granny" Cain, of Newberry County, South Carolina, in 1937: "I don't know nothing about 40 acres of land for the slaves after the war. We just stayed on with the master 'til he died, for wages; then we hired out to other people for wages." " 'The slaves did not expect anything after Freedom,' " Henry Ryan, former slave from Newberry County, South Carolina, commented, " 'for the South was in such a bad fix. They just got jobs where they could find them.' " As "Granny" Cain noted, the system became institutionalized: "Ever since the war was over, the slaves have worked for wages on plantations or moved to town and got little jobs here and there where they could. Some of the slaves would rent small farms from land owners or work the farms on shares." In this way developed two additional themes in Piedmont folklife: the oppressive and persistent tenant/sharecropper system, and the segregated but symbiotic relationship between blacks and whites.

The complexity of this latter relationship was owing to the fact that blacks and whites remained segregated by institutions but integrated by

Former African-American schoolhouse on a large estate
(Photo by John M. Coggeshall)

employment. For example, white and black sharecroppers worked along-side each other but worshiped in different churches and attended separate schools. Consequently, cultural information (such as work songs, food traditions, and weather signs) crossed this highly permeable social boundary. Cash described this relationship "as nothing less than organic. Negro entered into white man as profoundly as white man entered into Negro—subtly influencing every gesture, every word, every emotion and idea, every attitude." As will be seen, this cultural integration persisted into the twentieth century and has thoroughly interwoven the folk traditions of both groups today.

Generally speaking, though, Reconstruction could not erase the deeply ingrained race and class divisions separating whites and blacks, and African Americans noticed only slight differences in their lives before and after the war. Patsy Mitchner, born into slavery and interviewed in 1937 in Raleigh, poetically expressed the hardships of her life: " 'Slavery was a bad thing, and freedom, of the kind we got, with nothing to live on, was bad. Two snakes full of poison. . . . Their names was slavery and freedom. The snake called slavery lay with his head pointed south, and the snake called freedom lay with his head pointed north. Both bit the niggers, and they was both bad.' "

Besides the Scots-Irish, only a few other European immigrant groups left their mark on the Piedmont landscape prior to the Civil War: Moravians in North Carolina and Germans in the "Dutch Fork" area north of Columbia, South Carolina, for example. Generally speaking, though, European immigration to the Carolinas has never been as significant as it has been in other parts of the United States. Consequently, the white population of the Carolinas remained generally homogeneous. Ethnicity in the Piedmont, then, became solely a black and white issue until fairly recently. As one Anglo-American resident explained, before World War II "all you had [in this region] were either the white Caucasian Americans or black people."

Conclusion

By 1865, the fundamental patterns of Carolina Piedmont folklife had already been established. The hardy Scots-Irish settlers had organized small farms in the rolling hills of the Piedmont, culturally and socially separate from the aristocratic English elites of the Low Country. African Americans, primarily slaves, immigrated (or were forcibly imported) to work the estates and farms, often alongside their white owners. Cultural traditions began to blend while social distinctions rigidified. The desperation of the war and the depradation of Reconstruction further modified the general design: the initiation of some core regional values and antagonisms, especially toward northerners; and the development of cotton sharecropping, the agricultural way of life that influenced the political economy of the Piedmont for the next century.

Regional Economy

After the devastation of the Civil War and Reconstruction, the South in general, and the Piedmont in particular, changed dramatically. Huge numbers of recently freed African Americans sought employment. Many white and black farmers, searching for work in a cash-poor economy, surrendered for various reasons to King Cotton. With many marginally employed, these farmers came to share a common desperation of poverty and a hope for improvement. Into this void spilled northern (and later southern) capital, to develop a new industry based on the transformation of cotton to cloth. Today, as different industries invade or are invited, the region has undergone significant changes, with associated modifications to traditions as well.

The Development of Cotton Farming

From the end of the Civil War through 1900, the Carolina Piedmont underwent a slow and painful transformation. Underlying the entire change was the devastation brought about by the war. The loss of human lives had decimated the labor force, but Sherman's calculated march through South Carolina in particular had destroyed much of the state's agricultural and industrial infrastructure as well. By 1865, the Piedmont needed a slow and gradual recovery period.

As any student of southern history knows, however, this restoration did not occur. Instead, carpeting the Piedmont was another army, composed of occupying federal troops, "foreign" (northern) legislators and judges, and others eager to capitalize upon the region's desperation in order to make their fortunes. The era of Reconstruction began—a decade or so of the region's history that so embittered most southern whites toward anything northern that the legacy continues to distinguish social groups and to justify stereotypes today.

The solution proposed for, or imposed upon, the Piedmont (and much of the South) was a revival through agriculture, particularly with the investiture of a new king: cotton. "After the Civil War," Robert Gooding told a WPA worker, "our people had had no money. We became a one-crop people. Cotton was ready money." While antebellum cotton production had already existed, the system became much more widespread after the war. As Ben Thomas (a retired farmer in the 1930s) admitted: " 'I can now look back and see the mistakes I made as a farmer. I depended too much on cotton, and failed to plan for the future. It was a habit of the farmer then to think in terms of cotton bales, and I had the disease.' "

The etiology of this disease, historian Steven Hahn argued, lies in the changing political economy of the Upstate. Following the war and Reconstruction, farmers needed goods and services from town merchants but had no cash to pay. The mercantile class soon received a significant economic boost with the passage in Upstate legislatures of lien laws. These laws allowed merchants to accept a mortgage on future crops (and later land) in exchange for essential supplies such as seeds, fertilizer, clothes, and other household goods. In return, Hahn noted, merchants demanded from farmers that they cease their self-sufficiency and instead produce easily marketable crops such as cotton.

Slowly but inexorably, farmers fell into a deadly trap, Hahn continued. As cotton expanded, less food was homegrown, thereby necessitating increasing debts over store-bought items. As cotton prices eventually fell toward the end of the nineteenth century because of international competition, farmers faced several repugnant options: increase debt even further, abandon the land for the mills (a recourse available only for whites), migrate to another region, or mortgage their farms and join the increasing ranks of landless tenants or sharecroppers.

The sharecropping system, then swelling with thousands of landless farmers, developed from the immediate effects of the Civil War. Landowners needed labor to work their farms but had no capital to pay; most blacks and many whites needed work but had no land to farm. Thus the majority of landowners became landlords, renting their land "on shares" to those with no other recourse.

For both landowner and sharecropper alike, the total dependence on cotton meant that the vagaries of weather or accident might spell utter disaster. Farmer J. M. Pearson, writing to Elizabeth Reeves in Gwinnett County, Georgia, in November 1884, echoed this concern: "Crops are very short in this section of country, Especially cotten [sic]. . . . We may hope for better

Contemporary cotton fields near Kent, South Carolina
(Photo by John M. Coggeshall)

times, but I have my fears." For most farmers, the situation grew worse
with time. The decade of the 1880s was particularly difficult, and by the
depression of 1893, cotton prices had dropped precipitously. Farmers became even more desperate.

Clearing timber from marginal lands, cash-starved farmers planted as
much cotton as possible, even on the easily eroded red clay soils of the
Piedmont. "Cotton was the money crop," John Culberton told a WPA
worker in 1939, but admitted, "I did very little terracing on the hillsides
then, and fertilizer was almost unknown." As educator Eugene Crow noted,
tenants care little for the land since they most likely will soon leave; landowners also care little for the land since their main motive is short-term
profits by using fertilizers. Consequently, soil erosion and fertility decline
continued unabated. The years between 1910 and 1930, Ben Robertson
observed, "were the years that bled us and nearly dried the well of our
faith."

Gradually, historian Allen Tullos felt, "independence and the self-suffi-
cient farming ideal gave way to the fear and the reality of debt and dependence." The Upstate, like the South in general, had an agricultural landscape characterized primarily by cotton tenant farming by the eve of the
Depression. As Robertson described, however, it was difficult to surrender

this traditional way of life: "Our wagon was hitched to cotton's star. . . . Cotton is a state of mind with us, a philosophy. . . . It is never easy for a people to give up a hundred-year-old tradition—our lives and our father's father's lives have been built around cotton."

Thousands of tenants and sharecroppers desperately needed a way out of this trap of tradition. The saving grace, Thomas Dawley argued, appeared to come from "men with enterprise and brains" who recognized "the water-power of the streams in the Up Country" and developed textile mills.

The Development of the Textile Industry

With the explosion of cotton farming across the Carolina Piedmont came a concomitant explosion, that of the textile mill industry. As Tullos noted, the two are intimately associated. At the same time, however, W. J. Cash observed that the South's gradual replacement of agriculture by industrialization did not mean the complete abandonment of an agrarian way of thinking. As will be seen in later chapters, the creation of a "rural industry" has affected settlement patterns, work relationships, unionization, and recreational patterns, among other aspects of Piedmont life.

Although not unknown in the region before the Civil War, textile mills and their associated villages became much more prominent fixtures of the Piedmont landscape after 1880. Within one generation, ethnographer Lois MacDonald noted, a primarily rural population became industrialized. The industry was hailed as a savior that would effectively reconstruct the South, salvage indebted (white) tenant farmers, and restore the pride of a defeated people.

The cotton production industry snowballed throughout the late nineteenth century as northern capital recognized the tremendous benefits of cheap labor coupled with inexpensive water power (from the Fall Line) and adjacent raw materials. Moreover, southern capital and local investors also became increasingly interested in the Piedmont's potential. By 1890, W. G. Cooper rhapsodized, "this region has had the attention of the world." Mills had increased from fourteen to more than one hundred in South Carolina alone, and employment boomed from two thousand to more than thirty thousand. Even before the turn of the century, Melton McLaurin believed, the Carolinas dominated the textile industry.

By 1929, according to a map in Jacquelyn Hall's *Like a Family,* a contiguous area of North and South Carolina far surpassed any other areas in the United States in the number of active spindles. Furthermore, the core of the area (Cabarrus and Gaston Counties in North Carolina and Greenville and Spartanburg Counties in South Carolina) contained more than twice as many spindles for weaving textiles as in the neighboring counties.

From Gastonia, North Carolina, south through Greenville, South Carolina, the expanding textile industry had transfigured the Carolina Piedmont. By the 1920s, Lois MacDonald observed, "a traveller who follows the main line of the Southern Railroad from Lynchburg, Virginia, to Atlanta, Georgia, is hardly out of sight of one cotton mill until he is in sight of another." Mill villages, as many authors since the early twentieth century have noted, differed from urban neighborhoods in northern factory cities. Because of their relative isolation and civic independence, these villages remained under the paternalistic control of the mill supervisor.

Compounding the problem, the villagers and mill workers were scorned by their farming or town neighbors, in part because the villages concentrated squalor and poverty in one noticeable place, and in part because of the southern antipathy toward nonfarm white manual labor. As will be seen in chapter 3, these antagonisms helped fuel community differences between mill, town, and farm residents; feelings that persist even today.

In many ways, the mill community of Hammondville serves as a perfect example. After working as a commercial agent for a South Carolina mill and then as a Confederate quartermaster during the Civil War, Colonel Donald Vance Hammond (pseudonym) planned his own company. In 1874 he laid the cornerstone for a mill in an unincorporated area on a site containing both water power and rail connections, surrounded by farms, within fifty miles of Greenville. The mill proved initially slow to get underway because northern capital doubted the success of southern textiles, and southern capital was difficult to secure. Within a decade, however, the Hammond Mill had become South Carolina's largest, and by the time of Hammond's death in 1891, Ralph Christian and Donna Roper noted, the company "had [become] one of the largest textile mills in the world."

Eventually other mills surpassed Hammond's, but his major accomplishments included the establishment of the industry in the postwar Carolinas and the laying of the foundation for numerous other mills in dozens of other Piedmont communities. Moreover, Hammond's mill trained thousands of superintendents and workers, who then took their skills and knowledge to other factories throughout the Piedmont.

Hammond's mill, however, was built in an unincorporated area in the middle of hilly farmland. Thus, from the beginning, his company needed to construct an entire town, literally from the ground up, as well as provide all essential services for his employees. Besides the mill buildings, historian Donna Roper wrote, management also constructed a house for the supervisor, a hotel for itinerant merchants and unmarried schoolteachers, and houses for workers. The mill also laid out streets and pathways, built a

Hammondville, South Carolina; village business district and surrounding mill houses from "Hotel Hill" (Photo by John M. Coggeshall)

school and paid the teachers, donated land for and constructed churches, and provided a library and two community buildings, segregated by gender. For the benefit of its workers, the mill also supported mens' and womens' sports teams, an annual Fourth of July celebration, and a mountain camp in North Carolina for worker vacations. From the 1870s through World War II, the Hammond mill and the Hammondville community were intimately interwoven, like the situation in virtually all Carolina Piedmont mill towns. The consequences of this relationship will be explored in chapter 4.

THE TEXTILE LABOR POOL

The textile industry was viewed by many southerners, from capitalists to academics to politicians, as the key to freeing hundreds of thousands of white tenant farmers and sharecroppers from the shackles of their debts. The industry drew labor from two primary sources, the South Carolina guidebook noted: "the workers came from neighboring farms that had been eroded into gullies, turned over for mortgages, or deserted because of lack of profit; and also from the mountainous sections of this State [South Carolina], North Carolina, Tennessee, and Georgia."

Descendants of the rugged Scots-Irish and German Up Country pioneers were expected to retain certain stereotypical traits. As sociologist John Gillin observed, the assumption was that this workforce differed from that in northern factory towns because the former "is practically one hundred percent 'Old American,' . . . it has had practically no experience with the metropolitan type of organization and culture, and it is closely allied traditionally with the southern Piedmont small-farm type of life and that of the mountain coves, which, in fact, many of its members still follow on a part-time basis." Melton McLaurin characterized this labor force as "simple, independent, poor, uneducated, and culturally homogeneous."

Unfortunately, WPA editor Mabel Montgomery argued, this "tradition of individualism developed by farm life and habits of mountain existence has helped delay the concentration of strength necessary to accomplish political and social reform." As will be seen, this characteristic (together with the very real fear of poverty) provided the mills with a steady and productive workforce but also prevented the consolidation of unionized labor and improved working conditions.

One of the two labor streams infusing the dusty cotton mills flowed from the sharecroppers and tenants of the Piedmont. As Tullos noted, these men and women had already been inured to long hours and hard labor by the daily and seasonal rounds of agricultural work, with the equal expectation of obtaining very little for their effort. Compelled by their stereotypical characteristics of self-sufficiency and evangelical Protestantism, Tullos continued, these mill hands "continued to work with all their might."

The reasons these farmers left one difficult occupation for another were interpreted differently by various constituencies, interpretations that influenced and reinforced stereotypes. For example, researchers like McLaurin believed that tenant farmers "willingly abandoned the land in droves to seek the more affluent life which the mills promised, and often delivered." Lois MacDonald quoted an older woman who greatly preferred mill life over that on the farm: " 'It's just grand. Bettern hoein' cotton; folks livin' right at you and you don't have to bother about the weather.' "

Other observers, though, felt that the farmers who surrendered to mill work represented the incompetents. These people had been weeded out from a lifestyle at which "they were failures," as a large landowner north of Kent told John Morland. Perhaps, Marjorie Potwin summarized, these slackers had spent too "much time . . . settin' and studyin'—day dreaming" instead of working; others were simply "parasites on the economic and social order . . . [who] begged the industry to make what it could of them."

Mill management frequently echoed this perception. For example, Thomas Parker, president of Monaghan Mills near Greenville, explained in a 1926 interview that his workers were " 'people who had not been able to make a success at farming, and when they arrived at the mill most of

them looked like sponges which had been completely squeezed out.' "
From this managerial attitude came in part the pattern of paternalism and
social class distinctions so characteristic of mill communities.

Most tenant farmers, though, while recognizing the benefits to life in
mill villages, nevertheless succumbed to this equally challenging life
through economic necessity rather than personal ineptness. For example,
Pauline Griffith's family had moved to one of the Greenville mill villages
about 1915 because "well, the crops were kind of failing at that time, and
they thought that it would be better to move. . . . They would have preferred to stay on the farm, but you've heard of famines in the Bible. It was
kind of like that. We could have survived but it wouldn't have been easy."
"I liked the farm fine when we were making money," Tallie Smith reported, "but, as things were, we couldn't get along atall."

To ease the transition from farm to mill village, many mill workers tried
to retain their rural background even when living in towns. For example,
some parents might stay on the home place, supplementing farm income
by sending younger family members to work in the mills. Others, like Tallie Smith, retained ties to both worlds: "I like it here in the Winnsboro
Mills [village]. I do get like sometimes shut in here. Then I get out on the
little place we rent and forget myself and the blues."

As a last resort, the farm could be brought to the mill village. Alexander
Batchelor discovered "a sympathetic touch with farm life" in the mill village he observed. In fact, many residents kept stock and raised gardens
until well after World War II. This "cultural baggage of the countryside,"
Hall wrote, influenced the value system in mill communities.

In order to bolster the regional labor stream, management turned to another significant body of impoverished, struggling farmers: those in the
nearby Blue Ridge Mountains. According to Jennings Rhyne, management
preferred this type of worker because of "his greater efficiency, his superior
capacity for hard work, and his rampant individualism." Labor scouts for
the mills often placed ads in local papers or directly solicited workers. For
example, Susie Simmons's family had been working in the coal mines of
southwestern Virginia when " 'a man come through there one time and
had a letter from the super' at Spartan Mills. He . . . said that we could get
a job in Spartanburg if we wanted to.' " James Edwards's father-in-law went
back up to Franklin, North Carolina, "and got ten other families and
brought them down here" to Hammondville. In fact, so many North Carolinians emigrated from the mountains to Hammondville that a street was
named after their home county.

Paternalistic mill management believed that mill work represented for
these mountaineers a significant improvement, Captain E. A. Smyth ex-
tolled: " 'It was interesting to watch the gradual development of the fami-

lies from the backwoods in North Carolina who brought everything they had in a one-horse wagon, everybody barefooted, and to see the gradual effect of living in a community surrounded by other people.' "

Many workers, too, recognized that life in a mill village might represent an improvement over an isolated mountain community. Robert Adams, in a 1979 interview in Greenville, elaborated: "Coming down from these mountains when some of the cabins didn't even have any wood floors in their houses, and could come into a nice mill village where you had nice wood floors and fireplaces to build fires—they thought it was great."

Not all tenants had the option of seeking economic salvation in the textile mills, however. The workforce remained "Old American" by virtue of racism: African Americans were forbidden by custom and by law from working directly alongside whites in the mills. What began as an outgrowth of white power resurgence after Reconstruction became, by the early twentieth century, de jure discrimination. According to Louise Jones DuBose, "the [South Carolina] General Assembly made it unlawful in 1932 for textile manufacturers to employ operatives of different races in the same room and offer them the same accommodations." In North Carolina, too, the state guidebook explained, "in furniture and textile plants they [blacks] do only sweeping, cleaning, and freight handling." This racist policy did not change until federally imposed desegregation swept the nation in the late 1960s.

In effect, African Americans had few available choices for economic advancement. Being excluded by law from equality in mill work, hundreds of thousands of blacks went north, seeking employment in newly emerging industries while simultaneously severing an extremely significant social link—the family. The white assumption of the day, shadowed by an oppressive cloud of stereotyped illusions, suggested that the "better" (more industrious) blacks fled, leaving only the shiftless, lazy ones in the South.

Those African Americans who did remain were forced by racism into a relatively narrow range of "acceptable" duties or were compelled to continue as sharecroppers and tenant farmers. While their impoverished white neighbors at least had the option of leaving the farm for the mill village, few blacks had the same escape route. Thus, eventually sharecropping and tenant farming became largely (although not exclusively) a black occupation, with land and house rents, crop seeds and prices, and personal and agricultural supplies all controlled by white merchants and landowners. The situation held great potential for exploitative possibilities, for in effect virtual slavery had returned to the Carolina Piedmont by the 1920s.

THE FALL OF KING COTTON

Within the space of one generation, the kingdom based on cotton collapsed. Few observers recognized the coming signs of disaster. With the benefit of hindsight, Louise Jones DuBose catalogued a few of the danger signals: "the tenant system . . . has resulted in appalling indifference toward preservation of land and the establishment of homes. With cotton as the principal crop, and its requirement of only part of a year's labor, there has been engendered a potent apathy to the raising of anything else. But the coming of the boll weevil . . . necessitated crop diversification."

The notorious boll weevil, a monstrous-looking beetle-sized creature with a long snout for boring holes into unripened cotton bolls, ravaged the monocrop landscape of the Cotton Piedmont (as well as the rest of the South). With profits already marginal, and with a well-entrenched debt load owing to a capital-draining mercantile class, tenant farmers were devastated. John Culberton reported that "some of my neighbors just gave up and moved away." Despite suggestions from the county extension agent, though, he refused to diversify because "my ears were filled with cotton."

Even landowners suffered. Ben Thomas lost his cotton crop to the boll weevil in 1922 and thus fell further in debt: " 'I had to buy and buy so much during 1923 that I spent every dollar I could get my hands on. All during the year, the . . . [tenants and sharecroppers] continued to ask for meat, meal, flour, sugar, coffee, hats, coats, pants [etc]. . . . When Christmas, 1923, came, I had nothing left that I could call my own. . . . There was nothing for me to do but put out the fire, call the dog, and call it quits.' "

For those who survived the onslaught of insects, another catastrophe loomed on the agricultural horizon: a major financial disaster struck the South. In 1929, the price of cotton fell from twenty cents a bale to twelve cents; after the huge harvest of 1931 the price had dropped to less than five cents per bale. "It was the conclusive disaster for the South," Cash wrote, for everyone: tenants, landowners, merchants, and bankers.

Because of increased bank foreclosures of the late 1920s and early 1930s, absentee landownership and thus tenant farming increased, Cash continued. Since owners needed a greater return on their investment, they either let land grow into scrub pines and thus collected subsidies or they opened it up as widely as possible for agricultural exploitation. Either way, more and more land emptied and more acres became exposed to potential erosion. Touring Union County, South Carolina, in 1943, sociologist Arthur Raper noticed the "decay of the old plantation economy with its resulting loss of soil fertility and human resources." He added: "Loss of hope is to man what a gully is to the land."

Soils in the Piedmont, being largely clay, typically permit poor drainage and rapid runoff. Drastically compounding this unfortunate natural characteristic, though, were improper terracing and plowing; the primary culprit, however, was the continued clearing of land for cotton. Thus, soil conservationist Brice Latham noted, Piedmont soils rapidly eroded, particularly "where we followed cotton after cotton here in this Piedmont section. So we were losing the life blood of our soil." "By 1940," Kovacik and Winberry concluded, "much Piedmont land was made useless for agriculture."

Recognizing the terrible destruction, the federal government established the Soil Conservation Service. So devastating was erosion in the Upstate that the first demonstration plot in the southeast was the basin of the South Tyger River in Spartanburg County. Government agents initiated widespread programs of improved terracing to prevent continued soil loss and filled gullies and stabilized banks to halt further damage. Unfortunately, one of the most distinctive floral features of the Piedmont (and the South in general) was introduced at this time: kudzu. Hailed as an efficient erosion-control salvation, the plant proved to be that and more.

Poverty, erosion, and Depression had ravaged the Piedmont by the mid-1930s. Carl Sauer had taken a train through Spartanburg to Washington, D.C., in early 1935; he wrote Howard Odum of what he had seen: "I must say that the cotton Piedmont is a lot farther gone than I had expected. The problem appears to me to be perfectly staggering. [The destruction] . . . is wellnigh incredible under the cotton economy, and the necessary breaking of that socio-economic pattern . . . is about as tough a task of regeneration as one can imagine."

Gradually, improvement for most arrived. Farmers diminished their overreliance on cotton by converting to other crops or by allowing fields to remain fallow (for reimbursement). The Soil Conservation Service stabilized the land while the WPA and other relief agencies stabilized the labor force. Several years later, the federal government employed thousands of other Piedmont Carolinians in order to construct and maintain public works projects. Eventually, even more escaped the poverty of the Depression by service in World War II.

The Cotton Piedmont after 1945

After 1945, the landscape of the Piedmont had changed drastically. Crop diversification entered its second decade and thousands of tenant farmers, both black and white, had found new careers or new (northern) residences. Textile mills modernized, decreasing paternalistic control of mill villages while diversifying in other directions. Postwar expansion introduced to the Piedmont additional industries as well, both domestic and foreign. Small cities became metropolises, and their suburbs engulfed former rural areas and mill towns. The addition of television broadened perspectives and eroded customs, as family activities shifted to accommodate new demands.

At the same time, however, these modifications did not always eradicate earlier traditions; they interwove, sometimes replacing and sometimes reinforcing themes from the past. Carolina Piedmont folklife persisted, but sometimes with new patterns.

AGRICULTURE

Agriculture in the Upstate today has changed drastically from the past century. The overthrow of King Cotton had begun a generation earlier; today the revolution has virtually been completed. Before World War II, William Vaughn recalled, "the constant topic of conversation . . . was the price of cotton and the fate of the crop." Today, James Edwards observed, "I do a little bit of driving around this area [and] I don't see anybody now around here with any cotton."

The white of ripening cotton has been replaced in some parts of the northern Piedmont with the gold of ripening peaches. During good years, South Carolina is second only to California in peach production, even surpassing the "peach state" of Georgia. Today, migrant workers sweeping north from Florida and Georgia harvest much of the crop; many live in poorly maintained camps reminiscent of the tenant farmers of past decades. Fields along both sides of South Carolina Highway 11 (at the edge of the Blue Ridge) are dotted with the distinctive shapes of peach trees. Motorists along Interstate 85 near Gaffney, South Carolina, not only see the orchards but also cannot miss the "Peachoid," a huge water tower shaped and painted like a peach, even including a green leaf. Signs along the highway warn sightseers not to pull off onto the shoulder but instead "to view peach, go to exit 92."

Perhaps the other highly visible "crop" on the former cotton fields of the contemporary Piedmont are pine trees, converted to pulp wood. Some of this land, removed from cotton production during the Depression, became part of Sumter National Forest; much of the rest then produced pines for profit. Today, for example, George Adams and his family have converted virtually all of their marginal farmland in the Hammondville area to the growing of pines for the timber industry. Charles Kovacik and John Winberry estimate that about 78 percent of the lower Piedmont lies covered with pine forests today.

INDUSTRIALIZATION

The region's textile industry persists with modifications. By the 1950s, the South in general, and Georgia and the Carolinas in particular, controlled about three-fourths of the nation's production. Industrial consolidation had placed about 30 percent of national production into three promi-

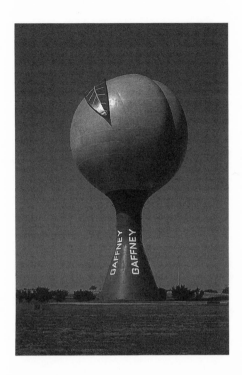

Gaffney Peachoid, near the
North Carolina state line
(Photo by John M.
Coggeshall)

nent Piedmont companies: J. P. Stevens, Milliken, and Springs Cotton Mills. Along with corporate conglomeration has come mechanization in order to improve competitiveness and cut costs. As one company purchasing manager explained: "machines don't typically get tired. . . . They don't take breaks and they don't get sick." These general industrial trends have meant the gradual decline of mill village paternalism and the increasing impersonalization of textile mill labor.

Textile mills no longer serve as the region's sole industrial labor provider, however. As John Edmunds indicated, "new industries are rapidly changing the lot of those who in past years were destined to spend their lives in the dusty, humid, blue-windowed cotton mills." As demographer Joseph Spengler argued, following World War II has been the "final emergence of a modern economy and the New South." This economic expansion has taken place in several principal areas and in several major industries.

One prime area of development in the Upper Piedmont today lies along the Interstate 85 corridor, stretching approximately from Charlotte through Spartanburg and Greenville to Anderson, South Carolina. Originally an area of textile mills along rail lines, the region today is served by road, rail, and air. The industrial base along this artery has diversified enormously because economic and cultural conditions have drastically improved. As economist Holley Ulbrich testified at a congressional hearing in the Upstate, the area is "becoming more affluent, gaining population and beginning to look more and more like the rest of the Nation."

Since the 1960s, numerous foreign and domestic corporations have located along this interstate corridor, including a significant number of engineering firms, Louis Foster noted. The industrial foundation here has evolved from cotton agriculture to cotton mills to synthetic fiber factories to the domestic and international firms that support the textile industry, Foster continued. According to the *Greenville News*, the area boasts one of the largest concentrations of foreign manufacturing companies in the United States, including BMW, Hoechst Celanese, and Michelin.

Another major region of nontextile industrial growth lies in North Carolina at the western fringe of the Cotton Belt. Drawing on resources similar to those of the textile industry (cheap labor, accessible supplies, local energy, and northern capital), the furniture industry developed during the late nineteenth and early twentieth centuries. According to historian Bob Korstad, these workers differed from their tobacco and cotton comrades because of the greater degree of freedom the former exhibited over their work. Furniture production became centered in places like High Point ("the Piedmont synonym for Grand Rapids," Rupert Vance wrote), Hickory, and Thomasville.

This expanding and diversifying economic base, however, has proven to be uneven; the rural areas and inner cities have remained on the fringes of development. As the region transforms, Representative Henry Gonzalez testified at a congressional hearing, once-thriving mill communities often disappear. For example, in the 1980s, J. P. Stevens closed its textile plant in Great Falls, South Carolina, the *Greenville News* reported, thereby eliminating 1,600 jobs in a town of 2,600 people. The article's writer continued: "And with the downturn has come an insistent message: The low-wage, low-skill businesses that built much of the modern South can no longer deliver prosperity in a world where the low-skill jobs once done in Great Falls can be done more cheaply in Taiwan or Mexico."

To protect vanishing jobs or to improve poor working conditions, one might have expected the area to have unionized in the past or to have organized in the present; however, that has not been the case. The Piedmont's staunch antiunion sentiment, Cash has argued, stems from several sources: a contradiction of the South's concept of individualism; another apparent (and unwelcome) Yankee invasion; and a challenge to the South's traditional concept of structured hierarchy, as expressed between black and white, tenant and landowner, and mill hand and operator. More realistically, however, mill workers threatening to strike faced eviction from their

Abandoned mill,
Hammondville, South
Carolina (Photo by
John M. Coggeshall)

(mill-owned) homes, ostracism from the community, and blackballing from other mill owners. The price for organizing was simply too high.

Thus, relatively few industries in the Piedmont operate today with organized labor. Not surprisingly, as Kovacik and Winberry note, the "absence of unions and employment legislation especially enticed manufacturers" and continues to do so. Open shop and a "probusiness" climate, an inexpensive labor pool drawn from dwindling older industries and agriculture, a well-established infrastructure of energy sources, highways, and airports, and general improvements in education and race relations, have all buttressed the region's strengthening industrialization. This process, in turn, has drastically transformed the Piedmont in the late twentieth century.

DEMOGRAPHIC AND CULTURAL CHANGES

Associated with the industrial expansion has been a concomitant explosion in suburban housing in both the Carolinas. As Dale Garroway commented: "we're becoming a retirement state. Anywhere there's water, and a few mountains, and four seasons, and pretty good weather, they come in here." Besides the weather, though, Rosemary Calder stated, a lot of outsiders have selected the region to live because "this area . . . puts you right in line with whatever you want to do. You're close enough to Atlanta, close enough to Charlotte, you're close enough to Greenville, yet still be out [in the country]. So we figure we got a good place to live."

In both the Carolinas, small towns and rural areas persist, but they are increasingly being consumed (physically, economically, and politically) by suburban sprawl and urban influence. The communities of Hammondville and Kent typify this transformation. Even into the 1950s, residents could shop in the small but thriving downtown stores of these communities while in outlying rural areas crossroads general stores provided convenient meeting places for traders and news seekers. Today, though, "just like all towns," Helen Quinnell commented, "it's [Hammondville's] sort of exploded from the center and gone on out to the satellite areas." "The land where we used to farm [now] has houses on it," James Edwards noted, and that subdivision blossomed only in the past decade. The commercial malls of Greenville and Charlotte are within an hour's drive of both towns, and empty storefronts may now be seen along their once-bustling main streets.

As the suburbs of metropolitan areas encroach directly on small towns like Hammondville and Kent, many people now live in the mill towns or the newly developed suburbs and commute daily to better jobs in the city. This transformation has changed the face and focus of communities like Hammondville, Helen Quinnell has noticed: "And now it's a bedroom community. . . . It's just not the same."

The out-migration of the younger generation has also transformed communities. "The young folks done left here, gone on off up the country and everywhere's else," Vernon Randle lamented. "We're becoming a town of old people," Geneva Patterson warned.

Ultimately for Hammondville, as in many other parts of the Piedmont, Rosemary Calder outlined the single greatest impact: "Well, when they sold the mill, I mean, when that went, everything else went. . . . Like our community stores and our grocery stores—everybody decided they're going [to shop] somewhere else now. Like us."

A dry goods store owner in downtown Kent noted the same trends: people tend to shop in the suburban Wal-Mart instead of his family-owned business. Newcomers increasingly draw their economic, social, and cultural interests not from the older mill towns but from larger urban centers like Greenville and Charlotte. Consequently, these outsiders have tended to further isolate both the rural communities and their long-term residents, who increasingly feel themselves to be strangers in their hometowns. That same store owner in Kent estimated that he used to recognize nine out of ten pedestrians walking by his store; today he recognizes only one in ten.

Because of outsiders moving in and locals moving away, regional values are transforming as well. One woman quipped: "You know, there's also a joke about the changes of the times—the Jewish people are now eating pork, the Catholics eat meat on Friday, and the Baptists are saying hello to each other going in and out of the liquor store!"

Better transportation has also reshuffled social groups in the Upstate, James Edwards believed: "Back then, if you were a farm kid you knew you were a farm kid, and you knew about where you stood. . . . You just kept your values for what they were worth. Whereas now, with the kids in the country, they got cars and everything else. So it doesn't make any difference, really, where you live now, because you've got ways and means of transportation, and you can intermingle with other kids."

Improved transportation has also, unfortunately, increased crime, as one man lamented for his formerly quiet neighborhood: "And that's one reason people don't visit, . . . things are so tense. It's almost now where it's dangerous for everybody to leave the house at the same time. If it's well-known that everybody's gone, you may come back and your house is burglarized." As he suggests, fear of crime has also decreased a traditional form of recreation—visiting between neighbors.

Mass media, especially television, have also been implicated in undermining elements of folklife. Ray and Maggie Nameth describe the transformation: "RN: For example . . . we have neighbors that we would like to go see, but I know some of them right now is watching soap operas—MN: And I mean—they like company, but we don't know when they would like it. . . . And that cuts down on, let's say, interaction in the community. . . . We probably raised a generation of people who are not going to know a lot of things that they learned down on the [mill] hill, or that their sisters learned with the ladies." James Edwards feared that television has destroyed family "devotion time," undermining traditional religious faith. Lucy Wallace worried that "the TV tray has replaced the dining room table in homes," thereby severing conversations that cemented generations. Linda Baker, a baby boomer, commented on the repercussions that television has had for her generation: "I can't think of anything we did that was influenced by living in the mill village, like a rhyme or a particular game. . . . We were already children of television. . . . When I was little, we were already getting our games and things from stuff like that a lot."

Conclusion

Because of a long-standing association between city and country, even the relatively large communities of the Carolinas retain certain rural values and behaviors, with ties stretching back at least to the nineteenth century. Despite the increasing trends toward urban growth and suburban expansion, Kovacik and Winberry concluded that South Carolina's "metropolitan areas and especially the suburbs retain certain manifestations that are distinctly peculiar to rural life-styles. . . . Rural traditions continue to play a major role in shaping South Carolina's [and North Carolina's] landscape and way of life."

CHAPTER 3

Contemporary Social Groups

Changes to the political economy of the Carolina Piedmont over the past century have had related repercussions on Upstate folk groups over that same period. As the region shifted to tenant farms interspersed with mill villages, town centers, and black neighborhoods, the groups inhabiting these places continued to interact with each other. Through this social interaction, group boundaries continued, maintained by stereotypical values and actions associated with each category. Then, as the area metamorphosed through the Depression and World War II, new groups such as northerners added their presence and perceptions to the intermingling of folk groups and beliefs. Today, these groups form part of the social background that supports and reinforces the traditional folklife of the Upstate.

African Americans

By the Depression, blacks in the Cotton Piedmont had endured a tremendous amount of economic disparity, political powerlessness, and social inequality. Many, as tenant farmers or sharecroppers, toiled long hours for very little annual yield. Others, ostracized from most mill jobs, served as "support staff" (for example, laundresses) for white villagers. Some worked as laborers in towns, while a few held professional positions as teachers, ministers, or merchants in black neighborhoods.

These tasks virtually assured that African Americans remained continually in contact with Anglo Americans, albeit on a less than equal footing. As an anonymous WPA writer explained, "the social life of the Negro is generally like that of the whites, though color lines are pretty strictly adhered to." In Kent in the late 1940s, a white informant offered John Morland this appraisal of blacks: " 'I have nothing against them. They are human beings, like we are. But I don't want to have to eat with them or associate with them socially.' " Another Kent informant granted that blacks should be allowed to vote and to acquire an education, " 'but they might as well realize right now that we will *never* permit them to mix socially with us. . . . We are just *not* going to accept them as social equals' " [emphasis in original]. The obvious consequence of this social segregation, as John Edmunds indicated, was that "the black found himself in a caste system where his very blackness was a badge of derision."

On the other hand, though, Louise Jones DuBose noted that in her era (the 1930s) "there are interracial loyalties and friendships that are characteristically southern in their nature," relationships that are "rarely understood except by Southerners." "We've always had real good relationships with the colored people that lived here," a landowner stated. One older woman succinctly expressed this traditional southern attitude of care tinted with condescension. When she was living in New York around World War II, she grew increasingly irritated with Yankees condemning her and all white southerners for their racism. She responded to one antagonist angrily: " 'Well, I'm going to tell you something. I been in this town a long time, and I never have yet seen anybody as black as my 'Uncle' Frank'. . . . We loved them a lot more than we did a lot of our relatives."

Consequently, from antebellum times to the present, blacks and whites have been engaged in a complex relationship of mutual avoidance coupled with mutual dependency. From this intricate pattern of symbiotic interaction and social exclusion has evolved an equally interwoven network of folklife.

The traditional interdependent relationship between blacks and whites began in childhood. For example, a WPA interviewer described the youth of Ben Thomas, a retired white farmer from Edgefield County, South Carolina: "He . . . went fishing occasionally in Turkey Creek with the Negro boys on the place. 'I played and fought with . . . [them], ate corn bread, drank buttermilk, and grew,' " Thomas observed.

A generation later, the same situation existed on tenant farms, James Edwards recalled: "When I was growing up I played with black kids, went to their house and they came to my house—course you never did stay all night with each other. But you still played together. You know, you accepted each other, especially the kids out in the countryside. You knew that they did the same thing you did. They picked cotton like you did." "I don't think there was an awful lot of difference after we came along," Martha Block agreed.

On the other hand, though, racial boundaries only permitted a certain amount of acceptable interaction, even for children. Poignantly expressive of this traditional segregation, Dale Garroway explained that, as a preschooler, he had an African-American best friend nicknamed "Hambone." After they started school, they separated. To this day, he was embarrassed to say, he never learned his friend's real name.

Young African Americans, accustomed to seeing their white playmates as virtual equals, eventually reached the invisible but very real boundary that determined appropriate social interaction for the rest of their lives. Velma Childers recalled this realization: "When you get growing up with children, it's just about the same. But when you get at least ten years old, then you came to yourself, you wake up and you say, 'Why, I think they are different. . . . Why are they riding the bus and I have to walk? Why did Miss Ellis have a washing machine and we had to rub our clothes like this?' . . . I wondered why it was so different, until I actually learned that. . . . And then you wonder why I can't have these same things, too. You could see . . . so much difference."

Into adulthood, the same pattern of social avoidance coupled with mutual interdependency persisted, as between Ben Robertson's landowning family and their black servants: "Our relationship with Mary and Jim, and theirs with us, were intimate and personal, and at the same time strict—on both sides they were strict, old-fashioned, and Southern. The standards of behavior for both sides were established and we knew it." A white urban aristocrat cited an "old aphorism" to summarize these feelings: " 'The Yankees love the blacks as a race and hate them as individuals; the southerners don't like them as a race and love them as individuals.' "

In effect, before desegregation, blacks had developed a complicated code that detailed how they were supposed to act in the presence of white people. Specifically, Ralph Patrick and John Morland explained, blacks felt that " 'white folks is white folks,' " implying that they can never be completely trusted. Black men must also completely avoid any contact or even suspicion of contact with white women; no speaking to them on the street, no entering their homes, and no driving around with them unless specifically hired to do so. Whites may also be needed as patrons to help one deal with the capricious and unpredictable imposition of the law. In these cases, prior acts of deference will have helped establish such paternalistic but essential ties. Thus, Patrick and Morland concluded, bitterness and resignation are common African-American attitudes because of the recognized but uncorrected legal inequities between blacks and whites.

African Americans traditionally had to know their place and to keep it. For example, in their study of Kent, Patrick and Morland observed that blacks generally deferred to whites in public but disdained them behind their backs. They also noticed that white racism prevented blacks from aggressively defending themselves as equals in any public confrontation.

Thus, African Americans could only attempt to manipulate situations to their advantage in subtle ways and defend themselves only obliquely. As an example, the researchers described a situation in which an African-American man sought to buy a used truck from an Anglo American. The black buyer believed the price to be too high, but he could not directly argue with a white man as if he were his social equal. But, with proper deference and a disarming smile, the buyer eventually achieved his price.

Several Greenville aristocrats described another situation in which a black errand runner for a local company (perhaps the husband of one teller's "help") found himself in an elevator with a few white men. They asked him if he were the company's "nigger," to which he replied, "Sir, I work for" them. He needed to maintain his dignity, the narrator explained, while simultaneously sustaining the racial inequities.

Whites, of course, expected these acts of deference; most likely, they would not have responded to anything else. For example, Ben Robertson's family's black cook described her employers as " 'my white folks.' " Another woman mentioned an old African-American tenant on her father's farm who referred to her and her sister as his "white children." These attitudes of black "ownership" of whites overtly expressed loyalty while covertly implying servitude; neither sentiment challenged the accepted system of rules. While most African-American domestics undoubtedly enjoyed the company of their white employers (and vice versa), they also thoroughly understood that subservient attitudes on their part engendered kinder and more generous bosses. Today, subservient attitudes by blacks toward whites are seen by both groups as old-fashioned, condescending, and even embarrassing.

African Americans also expect that social and legal desegregation has occurred. While officially it may have, traces of earlier times and older attitudes persist. For example, during fieldwork in an Upstate city, I noticed that there still existed a separate counter for black customers in a restaurant kitchen. While other African Americans ate at tables and at the counter in the front, the owner hinted that he preferred not to have to serve these customers.

As another example, a young professional woman described a situation in which one of her former coworkers had a young son, and "when he was about six or seven years old one of his best friends was a black child. And his mother, who worked with me, refused to invite the black child to his birthday party because he was black. . . . And she knew his father real well, and liked him and everything. And just because the little boy was black she wouldn't have him to the house for a birthday party. And that's just in the last ten years." While such blatant discriminatory occurrences in the Upstate are less frequent than in past generations, they are not rare.

Much more common today is the attitude of cultural segregation: that is, blacks associate socially with whites in schools, restaurants, and on the street, but both groups generally tend to ignore the other's existence. Margaret Bethea described this as an "unseen, but noticeable barrier between Blacks and whites." "Integration," John Edmunds continued, "stopped where the law stopped; the color barrier is uncrossable." For example, a white woman in Hammondville felt that the white church congregations in town would make an African-American worshiper feel uncomfortable should one ever attend a service. A community at the foot of the Blue Ridge is widely reported as deliberately excluding all blacks. At the annual Hammondville community festival, very few African-American adults came, although a few black children participated in school-sponsored events. Despite legal desegregation, whites and blacks rarely mix voluntarily during social events today.

On the other hand, blacks and whites have continued to adopt the folk traditions of each other, sometimes unconsciously and sometimes deliberately. As far back as 1939, WPA editor W. C. Hendricks recognized this interdependency, at least to an extent. While unwilling to acknowledge the obvious relationships between black and white beliefs, Hendricks admitted that divisions often blur. Helen Quinnell, in fact, believed that "lots of the whites went more toward the black ways than the blacks came to the white ways." Another woman remarked, "black people and poor white people have very similar traditions. It's just the mind-set that kept them from getting together." As will be seen in subsequent chapters, this mutual intertwining of folk traditions has created an enriched and colorful tapestry.

White Elites or the "Aristocracy"

The economic and political forces of Reconstruction, cotton farming, and the national Depression gradually reworked the Anglo-American portion of the Piedmont's population. Separated before the Civil War into landowners, small farmers, and the landless, a century later the social groupings had become even more rigidified. According to Dale Garroway, "before World War II you had your rural section and you had your city section—and your mill villagers." A woman from Kent, recalling her grade school days before World War II, ranked these groupings from lowest to highest: mill children; those from the country; those from the town; and those who were the offspring of the aristocrats. This last group Ralph Patrick termed the "old families" of cities such as Kent, who for several generations had had sufficient wealth to enjoy cultural advantages as well as to have avoided manual labor and perhaps even work of any kind. In fact,

Patrick discovered, the more distant historically the source of wealth, the more prestige there is for the family.

Gradually emerging because of the Piedmont's industrialization, though, was another group who lived alongside the older aristocrats in the expensive and exclusive city neighborhoods. Sometimes, as in Kent, the blue-blooded old money strenuously resisted any merging. On the other hand, William Brockington suggested that this new elite of textile managers blended well with the older group. Patrick and Morland observed that they also shared a general disdain for manual labor and for those engaged in it, with paternalistic consequences for other groups of whites and blacks so employed.

Despite the fact that, as William Jacobs argued, mill owner and worker share in common an ancestral heritage, the same "tongue," and the same religious beliefs, antebellum class differences had been strongly reinforced by the early twentieth century. In real life, both sides recognized the increasing gulf between the captains of industry and the foot soldiers. As Patrick and Morland observed in Kent, "even the [lower class] white people . . . 'know their place' and show deference to other white persons wearing the recognized badges of higher status. In a number of cases I have observed a person wearing work clothes show deference to a younger person who wears [a] well-pressed suit, white shirt and tie . . . by the form of address used in speaking to him. He is addressed as 'Mr.,' and remarks are prefixed or suffixed with 'Sir.' "

While significant class distinctions may have disappeared from the Upstate in more recent times, subtle ones persist. City residents and Yankees, for example, definitely see themselves as different from, and often better than, mill village residents and rural whites. The latter two both perceive themselves as morally superior to lower-class whites, who in turn feel that "at least we aren't black." African Americans generally vilify the prejudices of mill residents, rural whites, and those of lower-class whites. Internal and external stereotypical values and behaviors help to distinguish these Piedmont groups today.

Mill Villagers or "Lint Heads"

Most likely, those whites displaying deference to urban elites lived in one of two places: the countryside or the mill village. Even though price fluctuations, land erosion, insect infestation, and economic depression transformed more and more farmers into mill workers, these groups continued to see themselves as distinct entities in the Carolina Piedmont.

Stereotypes reinforced this geographical separation. Raised in a Greenville-area mill village, one man admitted that "of course, the mill people did not get the remarks and the discrimination that the blacks did, but they got plenty." "Cotton mill people," Everett Baker felt, "have gotten a bum rap over the years." John Morland wrote that town dwellers viewed the typical mill worker as "improvident, unambitious, poorly educated, unclean, and on a lower moral level than those who live in town." In fact, Ralph Patrick reported, Kent's aristocrats believed mill workers to be descended from the antebellum "poor white trash." "I would not walk through a mill village" during this era, Ray Andrews asserted; "I remember . . . getting close to Dunean Mill [near Greenville], turning around and hightailing it back to civilization."

A WPA researcher described the congregation of the First Church of God in Concord (northeast Charlotte) in the late 1930s: "Probably few of those present would be mistaken for 'town people.' The men are in shirt sleeves, many of them with collars open, the women are in their summer dresses and do not wear hats because the night is hot; however, it is not merely their clothes which make the people different, it is the way they sit, the expressions on their faces, the way they sing—and a certain indefinable quality."

Mill workers, as one might expect, keenly felt the boundaries created by these stereotypes. In earlier generations, mill workers recognized that town dwellers might be better educated but resented being called ignorant. Mill workers also believed themselves to be hard-working, honest, and sincere but town people to be "corrupt, haughty, and hypocritical." Because of these traits, mill residents felt that town merchants could not be trusted either.

In effect, a social wall developed between mill town residents and town dwellers. Because of this barrier, ministers in mill villages noted that their congregations "had a strong sense of inferiority" and were "suspicious of other people." "My mother grew up a lint head," Robert Chambers mentioned, "and [she] was very insecure because of that; because the mill kids were just really looked down on." "This sense of inferiority," Jennings Rhyne warned, "is directly transmitted as a kind of social heritage from generation to generation." John Morland added that teachers, upholding the standards of "proper" speech, personal cleanliness, and general knowledge, unwittingly increased this feeling.

The feeling of inferiority persisted by means of jokes, slurs, and social ostracism. Ralph Austin, recalling his childhood in a North Carolina mill town, remembered that outsiders "kind of slurred at them. . . . Sometimes it didn't make you feel good at all," he added. The most common epithet was "lint head," because the loose cotton fibers from the mill often became entangled in one's hair. "I remember one occasion," Tom Davis narrated, when this family in Hammondville "had the café and the meat market, together. Well, [their] . . . daughter worked up there in a dry goods store right above there. And she called somebody a lint head one time, and boy, that like to put them out of business. . . . Naturally, it'd make all the cotton mill people mad. And they almost quit trading with the café. . . . They fired her from the other store, for doing that."

While mill work has gradually disappeared in many places in more recent years, the earlier stereotypes toward mill communities and their residents persist. Robert Adams commented that, in the Greenville area in the late 1970s, "the people from the mill districts are always considered a little bit different from the people in the more developed part of the town." William Brockington satirized those who still live in these communities, the "lint heads" and "red-necks," as "earthy, conservative, bigoted, ill-educated, fundamentalist, provincial, small-town, [and] rural."

Facing these characterizations and stereotypes, it is no wonder that, as Pat Conroy wrote of Aiken, South Carolina: " 'The [Mill] Valley kids got an inferiority complex a mile wide. . . . They gotta fight against things that an Aiken kid never even dreamed of.' "

On the other hand, as mill work fades in importance, so do some of these stereotypes. Linda Baker, the daughter and granddaughter of mill workers, has heard "some comments that irritated me but weren't directed at me, over the years, [but] . . . I really can't remember anybody ever saying 'lint head' or 'mill hill' or any of that in a derogatory sense."

Rural Whites or "Rednecks"

Despite economic transformations to the Cotton Piedmont, a rural group has persisted in the Upstate. While subcategories and even overlaps exist (particularly between black and white), rural whites have long seen themselves as distinct from other groups in the region. As these farmers would trade in towns and sell produce in the mill communities, they perceived real and stereotypical distinctions between themselves and other groups. Through time, the occupation of "farmer" became much scarcer, but pride in a rural background has persisted. In a sense, the contemporary "redneck" continues the Upstate's deeply rooted tradition of independent, rural, and feisty Scots-Irish whites.

After the Civil War, as economic expansion transformed sleepy crossroads into developing cities and as merchants secured even greater control over farmers' assets, the social and cultural differences between rural and urban whites expanded, creating quite distinct social entities. James Edwards, raised on a farm, elaborated: "Kids from the city . . . seemed to be

more educated . . . than kids from the . . . countryside. . . . You could tell
the difference in their style of living or educational desires. . . . And most
of the kids from the city—they was the ones that were on the football teams
[because] . . . the football season, that was cotton-pickin' time, and your
dad would make you stay home and work on the farm. When you got out
of school—. . . if you got to go to school. Them kids that was in the city—
they had more leisure time . . . 'cause they didn't have to get out and work
on a cotton farm." When a child, Helen Quinnell had been asked by her
mill village teacher to indicate her father's profession: "I was ashamed to
put down that my daddy was a farmer. . . . Mill children didn't think
farming was quite up to them."

Likewise, farmers perceived differences between themselves and mill villagers, as Ben Robertson caricatured: "On Saturday afternoons, I would see
the cotton-mill people at the store. Their faces were pale in those days for
they worked in the winter from before daylight until after dark. . . . The
mill people at the store made me feel that they had been captured, that they
were imprisoned, that they had given up being free." Given these types
of impressions, one could understand why farmers might only reluctantly
surrender the freedom of their life for the prison of a mill.

The category of yeoman farmer has not faded from the Piedmont's social
landscape with the decline of agriculture, however. Today, historian Francis Boney argued, the group that has inherited that social position is the
redneck, a term that came into popular usage after the 1930s. Boney described rednecks as "any white southerner in the lower or working class,"
seen as being undereducated, racist, pugnacious, and sexist. Likely, Boney
added, typical rednecks enjoy athletics, country music, greasy foods, alcohol, and junked cars decorating their front yards.

More important, though, typical rednecks maintain a pride in personal
independence and a general disdain for elitist, urban(e) attitudes and people. As their Scots-Irish ancestors distinguished themselves from the
Charleston English aristocracy in the eighteenth century, so does this contemporary group see itself as different from others.

A good example of the contrast between aristocratic elitism and redneck
unpretentiousness happened during my fieldwork in Kent. At the corner
of two major highways in the center of town sits a granite marker detailing
famous southerners (Robert E. Lee, Jefferson Davis, and Revolutionary
War hero Thomas Sumter) who had passed through the area. After men-
tioning the tombstonelike monument to a gathering of locals in a restaurant, virtually all of whom claimed never to have seen it, a frustrated businessman became exasperated at their lack of interest in local elite history.
Finally a woman asked of her puzzled neighbors, "weren't you ever stopped
at the red light and just read it?"

From the point of view of Yankees and aristocrats, an extremely fine, perhaps even permeable, boundary exists between rednecks and poor whites (discussed below). For real rednecks, however, the boundary is both firm and unrelenting. Blue-collar employees, both male and female rednecks labor long and difficult hours to feed their families and pay for their modest houses and mobile homes. Pickup trucks provide transportation not only to work but also into the muddy fields for hunting and fishing trips, where hunting dogs and gun racks serve their purposes. Confederate battle flags (if present) represent to them a pride in the southern past, in which ancestors fought and died against an oppressive federal government. Because of limited income, recreations remain relatively simple: Sunday afternoon barbecues with family; weekends on the area's lakes; or an annual vacation to the beach. In their pride, their independence, their disdain for elitism, and their traditional religious faith, rednecks represent a contemporary transformation of their Scots-Irish ancestors.

Poor Whites or "White Trash"

As the large landowners and mill capitalists gradually merged into a general upper class and as the changing political economy drained economic independence from farmers, many sank even lower in the region's class system, particularly those working as sharecroppers or tenant farmers. Some merged into the rural whites ancestral to today's rednecks; others fled to the mills to form a separate but often overlapping group. With origins separate from antebellum yeoman farmers, historian J. W. Flynt observed, another rural group became increasingly distanced from the urbanizing lifestyle of the industrializing Upstate. These were the poor whites or "white trash," a group B. O. Williams characterized as "a very real and intricate part of the agriculture, industry and civilization of the Cotton South."

The poor whites, Williams continued, were defined not only by social class but also by generalities: "His person is unkempt, his morals lax, . . . his mind is dulled by inactivity, and he is unbelievably narrow in outlook and point of view. . . . Chewing-tobacco, fat back and pone-bread . . . are insufficient to give a balanced diet and consequently his large family of children are anaemic [sic]. . . . These 'poor whites' move about with the passing of every season . . . between cropper farming and the cotton mill. They are unstable, insecure, and indifferent."

Even contemporary African Americans recognized the social distinctions between "good" and "bad" whites. Ella Kelly, a former slave from

Winnsboro, South Carolina, recalled: " 'You know, boss, dese days dere is three kind of people. Lowest down is a layer of white folks, then in the middle is a layer of colored folks and on top is de cream, a layer of good white folks.' " Black women, Moses Lyles (another former slave) felt, recognized that " 'no white man would take a black wife, 'ceptin' it be a poor white trash man and then if they git one of them, him would beat her and work her harder than in slavery times.' "

An African-American woman in the Upstate narrated a tale from her youth describing the plight of a white woman who bore a mixed-race child out of wedlock. The young boy was teased by his black playmates, who suggested he " 'just go off somewhere where nobody don't know you, go into the white race.' He looked at them, said, 'Well, if I could go off and pass for a rich white man I would. But since I'm poor, I'd rather be [black] . . . than to be poor white man.' "

Poor whites resented and resisted these perceptions, both from other whites and from blacks, supposedly their social inferiors. This resentment often converted into enhanced prejudice against blacks, Louise Jones Du-Bose believed, in part because of the economic competition between the two groups. African Americans, one black woman noted, recognized the irony between poverty as an equalizer and race as a divider: "But we got along fine together. That's right—because we was all poor. And one couldn't say anything [bad] about the other one. . . . And black people would say, 'Why, those lower poor white children lick the 'lasses off your finger and then call you a nigger!' "

Poor whites resented any superior attitude from their racial equals as well. Fred Alexander, raised as a tenant farmer, recalled: "It hardened me to see some of the fellows at school having it so easy, while we had it so hard. I became surly with them and irritable. This got me into a great many school fights."

Today, poor whites create problems for any neighborhood, white or black. One man believed that as the better educated people abandoned the mill villages, "your less successful, lower-ability people stayed; . . . now today, that's the trash people." An elderly woman felt that a trailer park in her rural neighborhood contained an inordinate amount of white trash: "we've had murderers, we've had thieves, we've had people who abandon children—one of them is in prison now for molesting his own children. Just name it, we've got one up there." Poor white trash, stereotypically described as degenerate racists and drunken wife-beaters, are easily recognizable by other social groups in the Upstate, J. W. Flynt noted. All know one when they see one, but no one admits to being in the group.

"Yankees" or Northerners

While they may be a social and economic embarrassment to the Piedmont elite, at least the poor whites consist of indigenous elements who could trace their ancestry back to the early pioneers. The increasing industrialization and urbanization of the Piedmont, however, has brought another group to the Upstate; a group composed of outsiders. Especially despised after the war and Reconstruction, Yankees returned to the area in increasingly large numbers after World War II. Well-entrenched Upstate residents, though, have mixed feelings about this group.

Yankees participating in this second northern invasion seem to residents to be reconstructing the South a second time, smugly self-assured that they have the powers of civilization, logic, and righteousness on their side. This attitude has deep roots. In her WPA essay, Louise Jones DuBose warned that the typical South Carolinian "knows his faults, at least many of them. He will discuss them and propose remedies—but woe to the outsider who reminds him of them. The faults of his State are as personal to him as a wart on his nose."

"Foreign" ideas, delivered with characteristic Yankee arrogance, proved particularly unsettling for the southern value system. W. J. Cash noted that in the 1920s, southerners became increasingly irritated by new ideas emanating from northern-trained professors in the South's major universities. Theorists like Darwin, Freud, and Marx threatened the old order of fundamental southern values such as the primacy of Biblical authenticity, the supremacy of parental authority, and the legitimacy of political inequality.

Most threatening of all, however, northerners introduced the frightening concept of racial equality. Typical "Old South" patterns, Patrick and Morland reported from Kent, included "bitter resentment and aggression toward the 'Northerners' and 'Yankees' 'who don't understand our problems down here,' 'who don't know and understand the [blacks] . . . like we do,' and 'who don't realize the way we feel about it down here.' Resentment against publicity given in the North to 'the way we treat the [blacks].' . . . Assumptions of ill will toward the South as the motive for such publicity, because 'we don't hate [them] . . . we love them, as long as they stay in their place.' "

Even today, perceived Yankee smugness grates on most Piedmonters' nerves, still sensitive after General Sherman's and carpetbaggers' adjustments to southern living. One Hammondville woman described northerners as "arrogant; . . . they just feel sure of themselves." Many Yankee tourists have seen bumper stickers on southern cars that read: "We don't give a damn *how* you did it up North."

Another common complaint by southerners against outsiders, Helen Quinnell offered, is that "many times . . . people who have come from other sections of the country have talked and acted as if southerners are slow and dull and . . . don't know what's going on in the world. And that doesn't go over so swift."

Weary of Yankee arrogance, boastfulness, and self-righteousness, many Piedmont residents have adopted the attitude expressed by a young Upstate woman's joke: Why are Yankees like hemorrhoids? If they come down and go back up they're all right, and if they come down and stay down they're a pain in the rear!

Exhibiting an open-mindedness toward outsiders characteristic of the area in general, Elizabeth Block summarized: "I like foreigners, outsiders, all that kind of stuff. . . . You got good ones and bad ones wherever you are. So it's not that everybody's a 'damn Yankee' to me, 'cause I love some of those damn Yankees better than the ones right around here."

Conclusion

In the Upstate today, few informants recognized other ethnic minority populations as existing in the Piedmont. Most likely, whites and blacks in direct contact with Spanish-speaking migrant laborers, Hmong crafts-women, or Greek coworkers would acknowledge these groups as social components of the Upstate. However, when pressed to discuss regional eth-nic communities, nearly all whites offered blacks as the only such group in the area. From the perspective of most residents, the primary social groups are those discussed in detail above. These social groups, in turn, have shared and perpetuated various forms of folklife for the past century.

CHAPTER 4

General Social and Cultural Values
of Piedmont Folk

Despite the variations in real and perceived behaviors differentiating Up-state groups, the residents of the Carolina Piedmont share certain values and ideas. This common heritage is the result of the mixing of European and African traditions during centuries of change here in the United States. The Piedmont's general value system subsequently shapes and guides typical Upstate behaviors. The widespread popularity of family re-unions during the summer months, for example, can best be understood when viewed in the context of the deep-seated importance placed on the family. A discussion of these shared beliefs will help clarify and enlighten the subsequent discussion of traditional folklife.

General Characteristics

One of the classic characterizations of the "mind of the South" had been initially defined by W. J. Cash. In his book by the same name, Cash argued that, throughout the region, there exists a "complex of established relation-ships and habits of thought" common to most southern whites. Cash char-acterized the South as proud, courteous, violent, intolerant, exaggeratedly individualistic, attached to false values (including racial ones), and senti-mental. Howard Odum, another student of the mind of the South, believed that the region's rural nature, paralleling that of an earlier America, had consequently generated certain distinctive folkways. This explained, he continued, the region's emphasis on individualism, honor, and the family, which served as a religious and patriarchal refuge. Several years later, Odum added the common threads of "the Negro-white relationship," patri-otism, conservatism, the Protestant religion, and "loyalties to the past and to outmoded patterns." Ultimately, Odum concluded, these older ideas created in the South "a general inferiority complex." Contemporary writers echoed Cash's and Odum's observations.

To most northerners, the general image of the South was summarized by Carolyn Blue, the secretary of Arthur Raper, a professor from UNC-Chapel Hill. Miss Blue roomed for a time in a boardinghouse in Greensboro, Georgia. In 1940, she commented: "I am living in an environment which is straining to be the very atmosphere of the Old South, the Old South of magnolias, idle whites and overworked Negroes." Despite decades of transformations, described in chapter 2, the overall perception of contemporary observers is that these views of the South in general, and of the Piedmont in particular, persist.

HERITAGE

In his essay on South Carolina, Stephen Gardner captured one theme that pervades the value system of the South in general and the Piedmont in particular: an emphasis on "heritage." Louise Jones DuBose suggested that the typical South Carolinian is "proud of his past" because, as Ben Robertson explained: "the past that Southerners are forever talking about is not a dead past—it is a chapter from the legend that our kinfolks have told us, it is a living past, living for a reason. The past is a part of the present, it is a comfort, a guide, a lesson. . . . We are interested in our ancestors—they were us in another age."

CONSERVATISM

"Possibly the most pronounced characteristic of the South Carolinian is conservatism," Carl Epting proposed. This trait, directly related to the concept of heritage, marks North Carolinians as well; in fact, it characterizes the South in general. Kent served as a ready example. Ralph Patrick noted a tendency on the part of the town's elites to try to recapture a sense of the old southern aristocracy by modifying their Victorian-style homes to fit a more classical model. The blue bloods, Patrick added, denied access by the nouveau riche to this group, stifling community growth. He also observed that Kent in general deliberately resisted change by refusing to allow the Southern Railroad to pass through the town (thereby losing a significant commercial link) and by denying a request for a women's college (and its potentially liberal faculty) to relocate in the community. Both of these events are still cited by contemporary residents as evidence of the city's stubborn resistance to change.

Conservatism, however, need not be owing to unenlightenment, for it could be seen as a conscious choice, folklorist Michael Ann Williams noted. John Arnold, for example, accepted the fact that Lancaster, South Carolina, must modernize but also hoped that the city does not lose its heritage, "or at least the best of our heritage." "I still think we have a lot of conservatism," Lucy Wallace noted; "they're just not as conservative as they were—or in the same way as they were a number of years ago."

This powerful, selective, and ever-changing trend then becomes a pattern that explains and binds together other elements of Carolina folklife. While some current area residents ridicule their own or others' tendency to retain traditions, many others proudly acknowledge their debts to the past. Conservatism explains the persistence of many folklife practices in the contemporary Carolina Piedmont.

FAMILY AND RELATIVES

Another significant feature of Upstate values is an emphasis on kinship. "Family is important among Southerners," essayists W. Willimon and H. Cabell explained; "the most important information about a South Carolinian is 'who his people are.' " William Vaughn associated this trait with the Carolina's Scots-Irish ancestry: "they have always had, as part of that culture, . . . being very closely family knit and clan knit." James Edwards, comparing northerners and southerners based on his service experiences, believed that "family values, as far as cohesiveness of the family, was probably a lot higher" in the South.

Area residents stress their family heritage by conspicuously displaying connections to their revered ancestors. Kent's white elite, Patrick and Morland observed, proudly discussed their family lines and emphasized distinguished Confederate ancestors. Many times, associations are made through antique furniture or other objects. For example, WPA researcher Jack Delano photographed several African Americans from Greene County, Georgia, in the late 1930s who had posed proudly in their homes near portraits of relatives. Several prints, in fact, show individuals standing before dozens of family photos, almost as a montage of family history. These images carry a powerful symbolic meaning, as Maxine Williams, an African American, explained: "we didn't know to make history books; see, we kept history by old pictures."

Since family relationships determine so much of social interaction, it becomes crucial to establish these connections whenever one is introduced. "Our kinfolks on Pea Ridge are intermarried, webbed and woven like a rug, and in the old days the old folks could recite them all—who begat whom and where," Ben Robertson commented. Whenever asking about people in Kent, Ralph Patrick inevitably obtained detailed kinship information first. The social importance of these connections persists: "sometimes you place people by their relationships," Linda Baker explained. These essential associations then demonstrate "who fits with whom and that sort of thing," she added.

The placement of individuals into specific categories is critical, for family connections then determine, or at least influence, appropriate or inappropriate social interaction. Ralph Patrick, for example, noted that a distinctive element in the social life of Kent was "the inheritance of friendship and enmity through family lines." A new bride in Kent mentioned that her mother-in-law immediately sat her down and told her who her friends and enemies were permitted to be. However, since families did not immediately identify themselves as "good" or "bad," she explained, " 'I could never be sure when I passed a person on the street whether I was supposed to speak to her cordially or to ignore her completely.' "

A young Hammondville woman cautioned against gossiping in town, because everyone in town is related to everyone else (a situation true in virtually every small town). Even in larger cities such as Greenville, Patricia Vaughn cautioned, one needs to know "family connections and intermarriages and this kind of thing, because, [you] just have to be careful that you know something about the person you're criticizing, because it may be the first cousin of the person to whom you're speaking. . . . We just automatically think in these terms—family connections."

Over and over again, pervading the social interaction and folklife traditions of the Piedmont, the family interweaves its significance. "Heritage means a great deal to our people," Dale Garroway explained. Gladys Taylor suggested that this characteristic could also be seen through care of the elderly: "So many of my friends have real old parents, and they're looked after by their families as long as they can. . . . And then the idea that they like to get together, I think, is a family thing that's good. And they help each other. They're just there for you when you need them." From the stories that people tell, to the reunions where they are told, to the honor that the elderly storytellers are shown, families provide a crucial part of the Piedmont's folklife traditions.

RELIGION AND FAITH

The South's value of conservatism, when combined with the importance of religion, forms another extremely significant component of the mind of the South: fundamentalist Christianity. In a WPA essay entitled "Bible Belt and Quite Proud of It," Fronde Kennedy specifically linked these themes: "most Southerners know and love their Bibles. Many of their most sacred and hallowed traditions and customs are intertwined with it." These included, the North Carolina state guidebook continued: "the lack of liber-

A conservative religious faith reinforces many Piedmont values.
(Photo by John M. Coggeshall)

ality in the daily press, . . . the strictness of Sunday blue laws . . . various
church entertainments . . . [and] homecoming days that attract the old
attendants."

Cash, like Kennedy, argued that this element of the mind of the South
had been forged from the region's early history, perceived before the Civil
War as "the last great bulwark of Christianity." Reinforced by the isolation
of the war and Reconstruction, this attitude gained strength throughout
the late nineteenth century. When coupled with the area's relative scarcity
of immigration, a fundamentalist Christian heritage crystallized even more.
Marjorie Potwin's mill people, for example, firmly believed that "America
is for Americans, and they express that conviction in . . . scant intolerance
of any but the Protestant faith." " 'Here in the South,' " a woman in Kent
remarked to Ralph Patrick, " 'you will find the straight Gospel preached,
without any of this modernism that you find in the North.' "

Religion and biblically-based values underscore and justify a wide range
of contemporary Carolina Piedmont behaviors. Religious songs, for example, are frequently those mentioned by both black and white informants
as the most popular traditional ones. Church revivals and reunions play
significant roles in the rounds of community activities. Prayers begin family dinners after church services on Sunday afternoons, and these services

and suppers often provide the matrix for anchoring the area's traditional family solidarity. Even today, despite the eroding effects of popular culture and diverse groups, most Anglo- and African-American Piedmonters view religious faith as fundamental to their lives.

INDIVIDUALISM

To Carl Epting, the region's emphasis on religion supported another crucial component of the area's value system: individualism. This trait white Piedmonters in particular trace directly to their Scots-Irish past. "I remember many times at my grandmother's knee," one man reported, "hearing her lecture to me when I was too young to understand, 'Use it up, wear it out; Make it do, or do without.' And I'm afraid I've come to live by that principle the rest of my life." The area's informal history suggests that individual families carved the Upstate's small farms from the Cherokee and Catawba frontier and resisted as long as possible the collective plantation economy of the more culturally sophisticated Low Country aristocrats (see chapter 1).

One consequence of individualism suggests a conflict with more organized institutions. For example, Potwin described her mill villagers as "real Southerners, they stress the personal equation and hold individual sovereignty and the freedom of contract supreme. They have a fine independence. . . . They are sympathetic with each other in trouble; yet . . . 'every tub must set on its own bottom.' "

Casual attitudes toward labor reflected this quality of individual freedom, reinforced by the economic reality of shifting tenant and mill work opportunities. "They didn't want anybody telling them what to do," one current resident asserted. Ben Robertson elaborated: "Our time has always been our own time—we have gone fishing when we have chosen to, and if we have lost a few dollars by closing up the store we have just lost them." Vernon Randle, working for a white superintendent on a railroad construction project, had been ordered to do something he considered unreasonable. In response, he stormed, "The only thing I *got* to do is stay black and die!" "Even today," Allen Tullos concluded, " 'You don't have to work here' remains a familiar refrain in Piedmont factory towns." The emphasis on individualism (together with the very real political economy of mill villages) also mitigated against the formation of unions, and continues to do so today.

Individualism in folk traditions persists in the tendency toward the predominance of religious denominations that emphasize less formal rituals: for example, Southern Baptist, Methodist, and Pentecostal Holiness faiths. Despite laws (and values) to argue against them, practices such as moon-

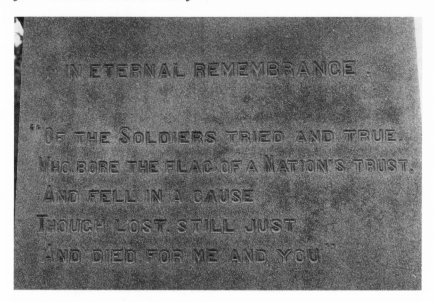

War memorial to the "Lost Cause" of the Confederacy
(Photo by John M. Coggeshall)

shining and cockfighting continue, defended as rights to do what one chooses. This self-assuredness also includes for many whites the justification to maintain and defend vigorously an anachronistic Confederate past as the preservation of an exalted regional heritage. Perhaps strongest of all, though, is the underlying accepted right to believe and to behave as one chooses, so long as no one else is affected; this is expressed through the maxim "My freedom to swing my fist ends where your nose begins."

THE "LOST CAUSE" OF THE CONFEDERACY

While Cash saw the South as generally patriotic (perhaps related to conservatism), for many whites patriotism intersects with the region's individualism and heritage; the synergistic result is a lack of respect for "centralized power," a term Epting used. To many white southerners in general, and to Piedmonters as well, antagonistic feelings toward centralized control leads to support of states' rights and the heritage of "The War." "I trust you understand what 'The War' is?" William Vaughn inquired.

W. Willimon and H. Cabell explain: "The Civil War is important. Most of our political sentiments are tied to our reverence for what we thought was the history of the 'Great War' and its aftermath. The myth of our lost cause was carefully nurtured in our state through a hundred years of . . .

Memorial Day speeches and barbecues. . . . Every little town has its Confederate soldier in the heart of its business district as a kind of shrine to what we think is the past."

That past draws meaning through the tinted glasses of selective, revisionist history. While any northern grade schooler could explain that the Civil War had been fought to preserve the Union and to free the slaves, few white southerners would agree. "On the contrary," Rosser Taylor maintained, "the South fought to protect the constitutional rights of the states. This was a cause so high and holy as to be treasured in memory."

It may strike northerners as unusual that the memory of the Civil War lives on so vigorously in the minds of white Upstaters (and southerners in general). However, the bitterness engendered in this region by the tribulations and transformations during Reconstruction explains the very real significance that this war still professes to area residents. The war, in fact, is still frequently termed the "War Between the States" (implying their equal right to decide their own fate) rather than "the Civil War" or "the War of the Rebellion" (suggesting revolution). "That was a real shocker," Lucy Wallace explained, when she discovered that the war had an entirely different name up North. Of course, white southerners also half-jokingly refer to the war as "The Late Unpleasantness" or "The War of Northern Aggression," which leaves no doubt about where their sympathies lie.

In local and family histories, the war still serves as a backdrop to reinforce contemporary values and stereotypes. For example, during a recent Hammondville community festival, Everett Baker narrated a story about "the last Civil War battle east of the Mississippi," which supposedly occurred about five miles outside of town. There, a group of Citadel cadets (a state-supported military school in Charleston) opposed a small band of Yankees and shot a northern officer off his horse. Some local ladies rescued him and nursed him back to health. After the war he returned to marry one of the women and to settle in the area. The Yankee officer bore the same name as a local person, Mr. Baker added, and the assumption was that a Hammondville resident thus had Yankee blood. The worried man humorously cautioned Mr. Baker: "Don't look no further [into his family tree]—I ain't no damn Yankee!" "Feelings still run deep," Mr. Baker concluded.

Symbolically, too, the war lives on in the Upstate. To honor the centennial of the firing on Fort Sumter and (surreptitiously) to resurrect the right of states to rebel against the federally mandated desegregation of the 1960s, the Confederate battle flag was placed atop the South Carolina statehouse; it remains there today. The capitol in Columbia, a city ravaged by Sherman's troops and/or by southern defenders, has never had repaired cannon marks in the stone of its side. These wounds are marked with bronze stars.

All over the Upstate today, on flagpoles, on T-shirts, on caps, and on bumper stickers, the Confederate battle flag proclaims the real or recreated heritage of many area residents.

RACISM

Confederate symbols do not express the same degree of pride for all Upstate residents. For African Americans, that portion of southern heritage recalls the bitter past of slavery and the injustice and ignominy of Jim Crow segregation that persisted for generations after Appomattox. As blacks (and many whites) acknowledge, another significant element of the values of the Carolina Piedmont is the pernicious attitude of racism that has long permeated social life and has considerably influenced social interaction.

Strong racial prejudice pervaded the Cotton Piedmont for centuries. Most whites frequently disparaged virtually all African Americans and their ways. Hartwell Ayer commented in 1895: "The Negro has been called the blot on the South. Whether he is or not it is not our purpose to discuss it. . . . He generally attends to his own business, when he has any, and if he has none and attempts to attend too much to other peoples' he lands in the place provided for those who attend too much to other peoples' affairs." Ralph Patrick reported that Kent whites expected blacks to be shiftless, lazy, childlike, and animalistic.

These stereotypes and attitudes might be softened by genuine or paternalistic concern. James Edwards, raised with black playmates, felt that racial hatred "really wasn't instilled in the kids." Well-intentioned adults inadvertently tainted apparent acceptance of blacks with paternalism. For example, the editor of Hammondville's town paper wrote in a September 1923 obituary of a local African American: "While [he] bore the color of one typical of his race, yet we believe his soul was as pure and white as the driven snow." Ralph Patrick described the general attitude in Kent as: " 'we love . . . [blacks], as long as they stay in their place.' "

A Hammondville African American who lived through desegregation noted with irony the contrast between the past and present: "Well, being a black person, I like it integrated better than I do the separate societies that we had. I mean, there's just so many things you couldn't do, that you can do now. So many places you couldn't go. . . . That's one of the reasons most black people not that crazy about 'the good old days,' you know? They wasn't really all that good in a lot of respects." Jason Lambert concurred: "If we'd had justice way back, we'd been better off. But we come up on the rough side of the mountain."

Today, many traditionally raised whites struggle with the concept of racial equality. A younger woman noted: "My parents have never taught me to . . . think I was wonderful just because I was white, but you get a lot of that around home. And the further back you go with the older people, the more you get that. . . . The older people . . . invariably call black people [names] . . . and think they're not as good as white people. . . . That no matter how well you educated them or brought them up or whatever, they still wouldn't be equal to white people. . . . And everything else they might think about—that you shouldn't get this job or they aren't worthy to go to school with your kids or something like that, all proceeds from having that basic attitude."

Sometimes, one woman cautioned, this racist attitude lies beneath a surface of friendly compliance. As an example, she stated that she had heard local white officials discuss African Americans in very positive terms in their company but use very negative epithets when only whites were present. She also described a situation in which an official of a state beauty pageant had publicly expressed his satisfaction that, several years ago, a black "Miss America" had been chosen. But in private this same official stated that "he didn't think that black women should be in the 'Miss South Carolina' pageant. And that the black people had their separate 'Miss Black America' pageant and we may as well have our separate 'Miss White America' pageant. . . . I was absolutely appalled."

On the other hand, as William Brockington pointed out, attitudes about integration and racial differences are improving. Whites more accustomed to blacks as social equals, and whites raised in less traditional households, help the area adjust to modern legal and social rules.

Contemporary African Americans, though, still witness racial antagonism in the Upstate. One African American responded: "It's still that-a-way. I mean, some peoples, they don't never get out of it. It's born in them through generations; it's going to follow them to their grave. But the only thing they do, they try to go along with the program, 'cause there's nothing they can do about it now." Leon Berry concluded: "That's what our trouble is today—equality—it ain't got here. . . . And before the end of the time it's going to be here. . . . As the Bible say, 'Before the end of the time,' he say, 'the first going to be last and the last is going to be first.' "

Racism and racial stereotypes are not exclusive to the Piedmont or even to the South; racism pervades American culture. For the Piedmont, however, this attitude justifies and underlies certain types of contemporary social interaction and expectations. Cultural exclusion explains the continuation of racially based neighborhoods and the discomfort felt by African Americans at certain community activities. Deeply rooted stereotypes support racist jokes and stories as well. Despite the widespread recognition of interwoven traditions, despite the growing acceptance of racial equality, and despite the disintegration of official segregation, racism still forms a significant component of the Upstate's value system today.

PATERNALISM

Another fundamental feature of the stereotypical southern value system is paternalism. A widespread pattern of deference, both in behavior and address, toward those in authority may be traced to the region's plantation heritage. Cash supports this argument, noting that "it was an essential part of southern paternalistic tradition that it was the duty of the upper classes to look after the moral welfare" of everyone else.

Traditionally, one could observe this attitude through the patronizing (or genuine) concern of white landowners for black tenants, for example. An Anderson County woman elaborated: "I grew up on a farm. . . . And any road you went down there was a tenant house where a black family lived. And my father took care of those people. If they were sick and needed a doctor, they got a doctor. If they ran out of money before they gathered the next crop, he supplied the basics that they needed. . . . They would come, and you could write down in a book who got what." As will be seen in chapter 12, this indebtedness created the potential for the devastating exploitation of sharecroppers and tenants, whatever good intentions their patrons may have had.

In cities, too, white patrons protected their black clients from the uncertainty of the differential application of the law. Patricia Vaughn provided two examples where members of her family assisted relatives of their black maids by paying their bail or by vouching for their character. "They needed them," she believed; "to be protected from all sorts of misfortunes," her husband added.

Mill owners, likewise, virtually controlled the lives of their employees until after World War II because they also owned the land and buildings in which their workers labored, lived, shopped, worshiped, played, and vacationed. This paternalistic benevolence is reflected in the community newspaper of Hammondville, in which the editor wrote that the Hammond Manufacturing Company "has always realized that it has some responsibility for the moral conditions of the town. This is not an incorporated city, a large number of employees, young in life, must be safeguarded from evil associates and immoral conditions." Because of this concern over their welfare, researcher Eugene Shaffer felt, mill workers "rendered a feudal loyalty" to the owners, who in turn "devoted a generous portion of their profits" to "their people."

Paternalism might also be heard, Helen Quinnell noted: "I think there was a lot more respect—an affectionate respect is as good as I can come to describing it—for people in authority. . . . I don't think there's much affectionate respect any more."

This attitude of paternalistic (perhaps patronizing) concern for others deemed less important may be seen today in the customary expectation of political patronage through party-sponsored rallies and barbecues, the general devaluation placed upon manual labor and workers, and most definitely in the persistent class distinctions and racial divisions already discussed.

SOUTHERN HOSPITALITY

Apparently contradicting the area's racism and antagonism toward outsiders is another significant regional value: the stereotypical southern hospitality. The North Carolina state guidebook credited this quality to "a spirit of delightful informality, or from just plain 'southern don't-care.'" Typical South Carolinians, too, their guidebook offered, commonly exhibited "a neighborly spirit, derived from years when everyone was poor, from living in small communities, and from a native love of hospitality." Exemplifying this attitude, Tallie and Mattie Smith told their WPA interviewer, "'You'll always find that our latchstring hangs on the outside of the door.'"

To Ralph Patrick's Kent aristocrats, southern hospitality meant that "men are expected to be 'gracious hosts'; women are expected to be 'charming hostesses' who know how to manage their households and their servants and who know how to entertain lavishly, but 'graciously' and in 'good taste.' The Blue Blood female is expected to 'give wonderful parties with delicious refreshments,' to be a good conversationalist who knows what to do with her guests." As Lucy Wallace served refreshments to several of us on her family's antique silver service and china, Patricia Vaughn noted: "I want you to know that you are experiencing at this moment the height of southern hospitality. In this house, and the good things that Lucy has just served you—this is the best."

This characteristic feature of the value system of Carolina Piedmonters may also be seen today in many expressions of folklife. Food contributions to mourners during wakes, family generosity during reunions, labor exchanges between farmers, and even the porch visiting between neighbors all demonstrate typical southern hospitality. In fact, one could even argue that the overwhelming support of this Yankee researcher by residents of the Piedmont perfectly exemplifies this value.

SOUTHERN CHIVALRY

A connection between the values of heritage and conservatism, flavored by a paternalistic concern for others, is the concept of southern chivalry.

The cult of chivalry, Patrick noted, included a concern with honor, with virtue, and with a sense of obligation to inferiors. Ben Robertson described this trait in general: "Like almost all Southerners, white and black, we were born with manners—with the genuine grace that floods outward from the heart." From the perspective of the aristocracy, Patrick concluded, "the desirable male personality is modeled on the 'cultured' and 'chivalrous' Planters of the *ante bellum* period, while that of the female is modeled on the 'gracious' mistress of the Old South plantation."

Quite often, chivalry was expressed by a stereotypical, traditional honoring of women. In Kent's black community, Patrick and Morland noted, mothers and grandmothers occupied a "genuinely high place" in society. Most of the time, though, true chivalry was reserved for elite white women. At first, Helen Quinnell quipped that an aggressive southern woman is a contradiction in terms (borrowing a line from *Fried Green Tomatoes*). But then she added: "But I think there's always been that southern woman who was—*Steel Magnolias?* . . . The driving force, really, but she let her husband be the—whatever he was going to be. . . . But I think basically in those days southern women tried to make you think that they were not in charge and not the ruling force, but they were." In Arthur Raper's collection of papers on southern lynchings, he included a series of articles about Coleman Blease, a candidate for U.S. senator from South Carolina in the 1930 election. In a speech at Union, Blease stormed: "Whenever the Constitution comes between me and the virtue of the white women of South Carolina, . . . I say, 'To Hell with the Constitution.' "

Today, vestiges of southern chivalry may still be seen, a visiting professor at Clemson University in South Carolina observed, because the restroom is labeled "Ladies" rather than "Women." Patricia Vaughn, on a trip back from New York, drove through a little town "and I saw a boy carrying the groceries for a customer out to the car. I *knew* we were back South! This was *never* done in northern regions. And it's still done here." Ray Andrews believed that "being a southern lady" for most women today might be a bit anachronistic. Still, male concern for the "purity" of women continues to influence the appropriate context of certain male behaviors such as off-color jokes.

SLOWER PACE OF LIFE

Southern hospitality, when blended with chivalric heritage and a touch of paternalism and individualism, yields another stereotypical southern trait: the slow, deliberate pace of life. Patricia Vaughn succinctly linked the traits: "There's a quality there . . . to the life in a southern city that you really do not find elsewhere. . . . Well, it's just softer, I guess, more relaxed, more considerate of people." Of course, like all stereotypes, insiders and outsiders would view the same quality from differing perspectives; what seems normal to southerners might seem extremely slow to Yankees.

The difference, however, has been noted for decades. For example, blacks who moved up North often returned, James Johnson explained in his WPA interview, because " 'when he goes up North he has to step 'round fas', 'cause if he don't he gits in de way of they Yankees dat move 'bout quick.' " Carl Epting believed that the typical South Carolinian, in contrast, takes life a little slower, napping in the afternoon and spending time talking with friends. Ben Robertson, too, became lulled by the slower pace of life on his family's farm: "there is a quiet timelessness to *time* here," he wrote. This trait, Epting hypothesized, makes the South Carolinian "person-minded, considerate, of others, at least, when those others are like himself. . . . There is no hurry in his life and he has time to devote to others. He goes to his church on Sunday, and remains long after the services merely to be with his friends."

This tendency toward sociability, however, potentially could lead to apathy, despite the energy of the pioneering spirit, Louise Jones DuBose cautioned. Ralph Patrick argued that Kent's relaxed lifestyle directly conflicted with the area's Protestant work ethic. Cash perceived this trait expressed through the South's resistance to workplace modernization and unionization. Ray Andrews joked that if the owner of a hardware store placed a sign in his window one afternoon announcing, "Gone Fishing," his competitor across the street would do exactly the same thing.

Change, though, may be coming. Dale Garroway compared the recent industrialization of the Upstate to the primarily rural Low Country and concluded that this economic transformation has introduced a faster pace of life. Patricia Vaughn has a friend working for a Greenville engineering firm, which has adopted a new workplace pace, antithetical to older southern values: "It's not cost efficient to spend fifteen minutes of your hour just talking about family. . . . Every minute has to be productive." "Everybody seems to be on the go a bit more than they used to," Arthur Masters concluded.

The stereotypical "slow and easy way of life, the way of the South . . . still survives. And prospers nicely," Stephen Gardner wrote. Moreover, it may be seen in numerous expressions of folklife: conversations after church and during business transactions, the initial establishment of kinship connections between strangers, and the delight in storytelling, for example. Even the length of stories and the drawl in which they are told, to many northern ears, display a southern lack of concern for speed. From a southern point of view, however, the pace of life in the Piedmont is perfectly adequate: "We don't want to be faster, thank you," Linda Baker summarized.

Conclusion

Whether one is Yankee or southerner, tenant or aristocrat, black or white, these values form part of the background of Carolina folklife. Formed through history, these traits in turn explain and reinforce the traditions of the Upstate. Beliefs weave through social groups, shaped by them and simultaneously supporting them. In turn, distinctive behavioral patterns derive their meanings from these values. Older patterns influence more recent ones, and they change with the arrival or departure of other groups.

CHAPTER 5

Folk Speech

A discussion of the varieties of folklife expressed in the Carolina Piedmont might begin anywhere, from the organization of space to social life to worldview. But perhaps it might make the most sense to introduce Upstate folklife by the sounds specifically associated with it: the "southern accent" itself. While distinguishable regional, ethnic, and gender variations exist, the interaction of daily life takes place in a distinctive voice, immediately noticeable by outsiders. For Upstate residents, whether black or white, rural or urban, wealthy or poor, the sounds of their voices identify them as southerners.

Southern Speech

The region's noticeable speech pattern, like other expressions of human activity, may be interpreted differently by various groups. In other words, the "southern accent" only becomes so when contrasted with speech patterns of outsiders. To many nonsoutherners, for example, a drawl often sounds excruciatingly slow, especially when associated with the stereotypical southern slow pace of life. The editor of the North Carolina state guidebook, in fact, described "the speech of the southerner" as appearing "to ignore effort in its slow, carelessly articulated syllables." Southerners, of course, appreciate the fine quality of their carefully crafted speech.

Another frequently articulated outsider misconception of southern speech is that it makes the user appear to be ignorant and uninformed. In her southern accent, Linda Baker explained: "I think the media's had a lot to do with that perception. And there are people that think that. . . . They think if you speak with a southern accent that you must live with the

Dukes of Hazzard and have an IQ of 25 and play a banjo and all these stereotypes."

Southerners, of course, defend their speech as vigorously as they defend their values against outside interference. Recently, Greenville Technical College instituted an English course designed to help southerners control their accent and thus better integrate into the business world. From Charleston, that Low Country center of haughtiness and heritage, the newspaper fired a retaliatory salvo over this linguistic Fort Sumter. In an editorial entitled "Talking Southern is OK," the writer replied: " 'Can ya'll stand it? The truth is that the Southern way of speaking is among the loveliest sounds in America. It has character and resonance that sets it apart from the unaccented, homogenized speech that afflicts most of the nation.' "

Regional Variations

NORTHERN AND SOUTHERN SPEECH

In the South, southerners themselves facetiously recognize that, as Schaefer Kendrick wrote in a *Greenville News* editorial, "English English is a foreign language." Thus, southerners are presented with "bilingual" situations whenever surrounded by Yankees or other foreigners. James Edwards, for example, discovered humorous difficulties when completing his military service: "By the time I got up to Wisconsin I'd . . . been in service long enough and tried to speak halfway right. I never had any problem with anybody understanding me. . . . I've had times where people would, you know, they'd say, 'I enjoy the way you talk.' "

In fact, Mr. Edwards was often singled out as being a curiosity. In his night-school English class, "I was the only southern boy . . . we had. And the teacher, . . . when we studied . . . different types of speech that people used in different parts of the country, she thought it was the greatest thing in the world that I could read the slang language, you know: /yawl eech yit/ and /yawl kum/. You was picked out as being a different breed of person than they were. But I guess the same thing would happen if the shoe was in reverse and there'd be someone from . . . [Wisconsin] down here, you know."

In the context of everyday speech in the Piedmont, though, a southern accent does not sound distinctive to native speakers. When asked to characterize her pronunciation, Linda Baker had some difficulty: "It's not an example to me. It's just the way everybody says it." One illustration she offered was the typical pronunciation of "fire" as /fahr/. She continued:

"Well, one of our favorite jokes around here. . . . Did you know the three wise men were firemen? . . . Do you know why? It says in the Bible they came from afar!" Both Ms. Baker and Vernon Randle (an African American) also pronounced "mire" as /mahr/, and John Morland identified similar pronunciations for "where" (whar) and "there" (thar) among Kent's mill residents, but not those from the town.

To southerners, "you might as well speak a foreign language if you 'talk like a Yankee,' " Margaret Bethea wrote. Arthur Masters commented: "Yes, the accent's definitely different; . . . the accent as well as the words are different." On several occasions during fieldwork, in fact, my northern ears failed to comprehend the plain English of my southern hosts. I once mistook the word oil [/awl/] for "up," and another time thought I heard "wall stove" instead of "oil stove." My most embarrassing moment occurred, however, when I misunderstood David Hawkins's pronunciation of "Irish" (/eye-sh/) (that is, white) potato as "ice" potato. After correcting my mistake, he looked extremely concerned about my inability to comprehend basic English.

Surrounded by native speakers in potentially "hostile" territory, Yankees with attitudes of superiority, expressed in a haughty voice, are often targeted. Linda Baker explained: "And of course you have stereotypical perceptions on both sides. Because you may have a shrill New York City accent (lady I'm talking about), or something, then the southern women are probably going to immediately be antagonistic toward you because you sound that way."

On the other hand, accent differences, while still demarcating regional distinctions, might not necessarily lead to ethnocentrism. For example, in her college classes, Linda Baker recalled, there were "lots of Yankees, and we would laugh at each other. We used to get one of my friends from New York City to say 'chocolate' 'cause we loved to hear him say chocolate. I can't say it like he said it. And they'd get us to say stuff too. So it wasn't just the Yankees getting us to talk; we got them to talk too."

LOW COUNTRY, UPSTATE, AND MOUNTAIN VARIATIONS

Enhancing the geographical, cultural, and historical distinctions among the coastal, Piedmont, and Blue Ridge regions are different accents, nearly as distinct as Yankee and southerner. "There is a certain flatness of tone that is common to the [Piedmont] region," Patrick and Morland wrote, while Louise Jones DuBose argued that Up Country speech "has not the distinction of the Low Country in either content or idiom, but Elizabethan archaisms survive in the more remote places." In pronunciation, too, the

Low Country resident "speaks in a special intonation," the South Carolina state guidebook offered. "Why, you can't hardly half understand some of them people down there," James Edwards added.

The greatest contrast, the South Carolina state guidebook argued, existed "between the coastal Gullah and the talk of the mountaineers." The former dialect, with direct ties to West African languages, contrasts markedly with the dialect of the Scots-Irish descendants of the Uplands. Dale Garroway, for example, recently overheard the speech of African-American women weaving traditional baskets in the Charleston market: "Now there were some words I picked [out], but I mean a lot of that I couldn't even understand what they were saying. They'd holler back and forth at one another. And they were just rattling, and, you know, I didn't know what they're saying."

This centuries-old Gullah influence on the speech of Low Country whites explains the dialectical distinctions still perceived today. Ray Nameth noted: "Now there's a lot of difference (course there is in the whites, too) . . . in the lower state than there are in the upper state. You've heard old [U.S. Senator Ernest] Hollings talk on television. . . . He has a Low Country drawl, or whatever you call it. And we have some nephews that was raised in Charleston. . . . The speech is different."

Even Upstate African Americans find Gullah virtually impossible to understand. Patrick and Morland observed that "the speech of the upcountry Negro is quite different in cadence and tone from the speech of the low country Negro." Jason Lambert assented; his friend, Ron Kellogg, added: "definitely a difference in the talk. . . . Way they sound, too, is different from the way we sound."

While not quite as significant as the gulf between Gullah and the Upstate, the contrast between the Piedmont dialect and that of the mountain area to the west is also recognized by area residents. Dale Garroway, for example, feels that there exists a "big difference in the verbage in the mountain people and the people right here—in words that they would use." Specifically, he suggested, "the way you can tell the ones from the mountains is they don't say 'y'all' they say 'you-uns.' " Tom Davis, whose grandparents had come from the North Carolina mountains to work in the Hammondville mill, often introduced participles with the article "a," creating words like "a-going," commonly heard in Upland speech. Pronunciation also differs slightly. For example, he pronounced the word /help/ as /hep/, again very similar to that in other southern mountainous areas. The distinction, although slight, does help to differentiate places of origin.

INTRAREGIONAL VARIATION

In addition to recognized regional distinctions in speech patterns, intraregional differences also exist. Linda Baker explained: "I was amazed, when I started thinking about it, where that there's not just a distinct difference between the Low Country and the Up Country patterns of speech but there's a completely different sound (it's different to my ears) in little pockets right around here."

For example, she continues, the family of her friend (who grew up in a nearby mill community) "don't sound like we do to me. . . . They have a kind of a flat, country-sounding voice that's hard to explain exactly." Specifically, Ms. Baker offered, her family has always pronounced "mire" as /mahr/, as in "mire up in the mud." Her former college roommate, raised within ten or so miles of Hammondville, pronounced the same word as /mayur/.

Another possible regional variation in speech exists between blacks and whites, although evidence for this is ambiguous. In the past, this difference may have been great, owing largely to the enormous gulf between the educational opportunities available to each group. On the other hand, because of the continued interaction between Anglo and African Americans, these distinctions may not have been as substantial as one might guess. For example, the interviewer of farmer Ben Thomas (the latter having been raised with "the Negro boys on the place") noted that "his writing is very poor, and he makes use of slang words and Negro dialect very freely in expressing himself."

One traditional distinction, though, between African- and Anglo-American speech existed in the forms of address for themselves and for each other. In times past, these terms indicated crucial social hierarchies, even after the disappearance of slavery. For example, well into the twentieth century, whites continued to use the appellations of "uncle" or "aunt" to describe older African Americans. The pseudo-kin terms ostensibly created a closer, more respectful relationship. Whites also often used the first names of African Americans when addressing them, reserving the more formal surnames for themselves, Patrick noted. Again, this practice created an artificial sense of familiarity between social unequals, perhaps soothing white consciences.

Most blacks, though, considered this custom to be condescending. However, prevented by racism from retaliating directly, African Americans retained their dignity through the subtle manipulation of personal titles. Patrick and Morland had noticed that in Kent, "it is a definite pattern for 'respectable' Negroes in the South to use initials instead of first names for public documents and on public occasions; this prevents the use of the first name by whites."

The ethnic labels used by whites to describe their black neighbors continue to differentiate groups today. In many interviews, whites struggled to modify their terms, sometimes consciously and sometimes accidently.

An African-American tombstone donated by white patrons (Photo by John M. Coggeshall)

Many, raised in earlier generations where "colored" and "boy" were commonplace terms, have gradually transformed; others have only grudgingly accommodated to changing times. For example, one retired Hammondville mill supervisor displayed this struggle over appropriate terminology while narrating a story of mill desegregation: "Just like this boy come to work up there. He was supervisor and he was staying with me training, you know? And I says now, 'If I call you a nigger,' I says, 'don't think nothing about it.' I says, 'I've called them that all my life.' I says, 'I'm going to *try* not to. But if you get mad [at that], I'm going to ask you how you feel about being called 'burr head.' But he laughed it off, you know, and we never did have any trouble. And I liked the old boy and he liked me too." Such labels, where they exist, indicate and reinforce social segregation and racial antagonism in the region today.

A final area of intraregional variation, more in speech habits than in actual dialect, involves the difference in appropriate speech behavior between genders. Southern ladies typically were removed from the company of indecorous remarks by chivalrous southern gentlemen. In earlier times, in situations of male storytelling such as at general stores, James Edwards did not recall "even the men standing around, doing a lot of talking of things where it wouldn't be presentable to women. You didn't have, I don't think, the profanities used back then that they do now." Maggie Nameth agreed: "You know, I can't remember hearing a woman use profanity when I was growing up. And I remember hearing very few men use profanity. And some of those same men could turn the air blue when they were talking to men. But in front of children or women, they did not use it."

This practice has been modified in more recent times, as Linda Baker suggested: "People my age [late thirties] pretty much talk about anything in anybody's company, it seems like. And my friends do. We feel comfortable talking about a lot of things that my mother and father, and especially back to my grandparents, wouldn't speak of things."

On the other hand, traditional values still influence appropriate and inappropriate speech patterns between males and females today. For example, a workman at Linda Baker's place of business used a mild expletive in front of her female coworker. As Ms. Baker explained, the workman's supervisor "fussed at him and told him he didn't talk that way in front of a lady. And he didn't really say all, I think, that much. You still get that a lot around here. . . . That's still going on, generation to generation."

One other continuity from earlier generations involves the appropriate use of titles when addressing women, particularly older ones, out of traditional southern deference to authority as well as gentility. Ralph Patrick noted that in Kent in the late 1940s, the salutation "Miss" and a person's given name was often used as a sign of respect and familiarity when talking to older ladies. The title "Mister" indicated the same quality but was used much less often. Northern faculty at Piedmont colleges and universities, though, enjoy the "sir" and "ma'am" attached to student questions and responses. Related to the ideal of southern chivalry, the practice of indicating status through speech still appears in the Piedmont, but with less frequency than generations ago.

General Conversation Patterns

The folk speech of the Upstate sounds different to the ears of outsiders not only because of the accent but also because of the timing and direction of conversations. The stereotypical slower pace of life in the Piedmont (and the South) leaves much time for talking. The pattern of southern conversations, then, follows what John Morland had discovered in Kent: people typically begin conversations about an unrelated topic and only gradually get to the main point. To northerners, Upstaters appear to wander from the topic, and thus Yankees try to retrieve what seems to them to be a wayward conversation. Southerners, of course, interpret Yankee interruptions as due to their typical abruptness, impatience, and arrogance.

The slower pace of life also affects visiting and socializing in commercial places of business, particularly those that are privately owned. A restaurant owner, for example, terminated his interview because he needed to return to work; then he noticed another friend sitting at a nearby table and spent the next ten minutes talking to him. In downtown Kent, a storekeeper (now deceased) in a general merchandise store had a formalized arrangement of furniture to enhance his ability to visit with his customers. In the front of his store, his desk faced the window fronting on the main street, allowing him to tilt back in his chair and watch the parade of humanity pass by. Next to his desk was a comfortable easy chair and couch for customers who wanted to lounge and socialize. One woman, initially inquiring about repairing a plumbing problem, then sat and talked for about ten minutes more.

This custom of prolonging conversations during commercial transactions continually confuses outsiders. Accustomed to brief business contacts between merchant and customer, northerners cannot understand the southern penchant for transforming a normal commercial transaction into a genealogical or medical review. The southerner wants to know about the state of health of the customer's kin and, if a newcomer, from where and from whom did the stranger come. Simply desiring to complete business and move on, the delayed Yankee is perceived by the friendly southerner as cold and pushy. The northerner, on the other hand, views the southerner as long-winded and rambling. Thus, stereotypes persist.

Perhaps one of the most frequent initial topics of conversation relates directly to other basic southern values: family and heritage. Louise Jones DuBose noted of South Carolina: "With the small area of the state and with families living here over a period of years, there is a community spirit which is somewhat amusing to outsiders. 'Who was your father?' . . . is one of the first questions one South Carolinian asks another. And in most cases it develops that the speakers, though strangers themselves, have many friends or relatives in common. This accounts for a great deal of the informal friendliness which exists. Almost everyone is traditionally acquainted or distantly related."

Discussions of family relations between conversants create wider webs of connections, because relatives of friends inevitably become friends as well. For example, Linda Baker discussed the closeness of mill families and disclosed how her grandmother frequently told mill coworkers about her, "and every so often we'll be out at a restaurant or shopping at the K-Mart or something like that, and run into somebody, an elderly lady or something. And my grandmother'll say, 'This is my oldest grandbaby!' And the lady will just be so happy to see me, even though she's never seen me before in her life; she might even hug me or something just because I'm [name's] grandbaby. But you get that more with my grandmother's generation and some with my mother's."

"Wayward" southern conversations, enhanced by the earnest attempt to establish links between speakers, create another characteristic conversational pattern: "They'll tell you more than you wanted!" Patricia Vaughn warned. Ray Andrews added: "Don't ask a question unless you expect an answer!" To illustrate, Mr. Andrews related a description of southern conversation he had read in the *New York Times* book review section. The author wrote, "If you are in Connecticut and you call up and you say, 'Is Joe there?' 'No, Joe's not here.' Now, if you did that in Greenville, say, 'Is Joe there?' 'Well, Joe's not here right this minute; he's gone down to the drugstore. He won't be gone too long 'cause it looks like rain and he didn't take his umbrella.' " "That's absolutely true!" Lucy Wallace asserted.

Characteristic Words or Expressions

In addition to a distinctive accent and the seeking of conversational connections, Piedmont residents also intermix characteristic words or expressions with their speech. These are not unique to the area, for many are commonly found in other southern regions as well. To the ears of outsiders, these expressions, together with the southern accent, create a regional distinctiveness. Locals, too, recognize these verbalizations as quite different from those of outsiders. These words, then, help to maintain the regional identity of the Piedmont.

Perhaps one of the most widely recognized "southernisms" in the area, Louise Jones DuBose wrote, is the correct plural of "you": " 'You all,' when included in a question, is never answered except in the plural, which is hard for a great many unknowning [sic] people to understand." James Edwards recognized that this expression, quite familiar to him and his friends, might also be incorrect when addressing nonlocals. When recently some outsiders entered his place of business, "I caught myself out there the other day, some lady and her husband came in. . . . And I said, 'How y'all doin' today?' It's something you grow up with, you never get it out of your system. . . . You still have your ol' slang sayings."

Other "slang sayings" frequently heard in the Piedmont (with connections to other regions of the nation) include "I reckon" for "I suppose," and "right" as an intensifier, as in "I done a right smart amount of work." Someone at the Hammondville community festival remarked, "I'm fixing to go" when preparing to leave, and several informants have used the verb "holler at" to mean telephone or talk. One also often hears the use of "country" or "section" to describe a general area, and Geneva Patterson used the verb "to move off" instead of "move away," a form that conveys images of tenants moving off a landowner's property. Several older residents described items that had faded as having "played out," an expression conjuring images of agricultural fields. Linda Baker joked that Yankees "used to say that they liked to hear us give directions, where 'something was pert-near to over-yonder.'" "To lay by" and "lay-by time," originating from cotton farming, today have lost their agricultural meaning; however, many Upstate residents still recognize the terms. Many informants describe the past as Don Underwood did: "They got some old-timey ways down there." These expressions subtly convey the long-standing rural nature of the Piedmont.

Mill work, like other occupations, spun its own set of folk terms. Everett Baker recalled that, while all machines had names for replaceable parts, the loom had the most. The parts were named after their shapes: "You had a frog, and a gizzard, and a snake, and a toe, and a finger—all kind of names. When you looked at the part, that's what it looked like. . . . The people that lived around here were farmers. . . . It was those people, as they got acquainted with a piece of machinery, they didn't have a lot of reading education, they needed that part, and they said, 'that toe' or 'that finger' or 'that frog.' It just evolved that way, I guess. . . . In fact, they still call them that. We had them on our computer [inventory] records, before when we took those looms out. We still had them on there."

Other connections between Piedmont and southern vocabulary may be seen in kin terms. Very commonly throughout the South, as Tom Davis explained, children call their fathers "daddy. . . . My son called me daddy; well, my daughter does too." This practice extends throughout one's life, so that it is quite common today to hear middle-aged adults, both males and females, describing their elderly parents as "momma" and "daddy."

Foods and food traditions provide another category of unusual or varied expressions. In "Grandma's Vocabulary," Mary Collum and Frances Burnet described such foods as "ish-taters" for white or "Irish" potatoes, "pinder" for peanut, and "sweet brad" for cookies. "Crackers," according to WPA writer Lucie Platt, might also refer to store-purchased cookies, while "nabs" refer to snack crackers. A scalloped dish might be termed a "pie"—for example, "macaroni pie" for macaroni and cheese. "Butter beans" specifies "lima" beans, while "hoppin' John" (various spellings) describes a mixture of rice and "cowpeas" (black-eyed peas) often served on New Year's Day.

In earlier times, Rosemary Calder relates, meal terms and times were "breakfast, dinner, and supper. Dinner got in the middle of the day. We don't call it that now—we call it lunch." However, "Sunday dinner," held in the early afternoon after morning church services, retains the term and the social significance from earlier generations.

Certain nouns periodically invade the speech of Upstate residents, sounding unusual to northerners. Numerous Piedmonters call grocery shopping carts "buggies" and license plates "tags." Older men occasionally refer to their suspenders as "galluses," while many of both genders label the burners on stove tops as "eyes." Both in speech and in advertisements, "pine straw" denotes pine needles packed into rectangular bundles and used for mulch. Ethel Harmon used "wash hut" to describe a laundromat, recalling earlier generations who boiled laundry outdoors. Vernon Randle termed the tongs that he formerly used to grip railroad ties as "tie dogs," and some informants describe fireplace andirons as "fire dogs" (see "sun dogs" in chapter 7).

Characteristic verbs also sprinkle Upstate speech. Older adults might encourage grandchildren to "give some sugar" as they hug others. In the Upstate, one "mashes" (rather than presses) a button, and electrical appliances are "cut off" (not turned off). The verb "tote" may be used by older informants (perhaps blacks more than whites) to mean "carry." Instead of Upstaters "being able to" do something, they "might could" (or "might not could") perform a task. Upstaters never "grow," either up or old; instead, they "get up some size" or "get some age" on them.

Place Names as Folk Speech

In the Piedmont as elsewhere in the United States, folk groups sometimes have the luxury of designing the eponymous landscape to reflect their own interests. Many times, of course, place names reveal the point of origin of the founding (white) settlers, indicating pride in heritage. For example, Kovacik and Winberry argued that Upstate names like York, Lancaster, and Chester suggest southeastern Pennsylvania as the area of original emigration. Indeed, many Piedmont Anglo-American pioneers emigrated from there.

Vernacular place names might also be less illustrious than those from the British Isles or pioneer America, but they still strongly designate a place. In the Piedmont today lie hundreds of unincorporated settlements, some the remnants of clusters of tenant houses on old estates, others the locations of extended family residences, and still others piecemeal developments conveniently located near rural crossroads. Each of these places, while not formally marked on the map, has a name, which often reveals much about the history or humor of the area.

Some place names developed from old family estates. The region just outside Hammondville, for example, consists of small commercial developments, some modern homes, a few still-inhabited former tenant houses, and some others now vacant. Nearby lives a descendant of the former landowner, and the neighborhood still bears the family name. On another side of town, the unincorporated area has taken its name from an earlier train stop, itself named for a prominent local family. "It's sort of an undefined area," Gladys Taylor commented, "sort of like Possum Kingdom."

This eponym requires folk etymology to explain, provided by Ms. Taylor: "Well, down this-a-way . . . they call it 'Possum Kingdom.' But you can never find anybody that says they're from Possum Kingdom. You'd say, 'I'm just above Possum Kingdom' or 'I'm just below Possum Kingdom.' . . . And I don't know why they call it that, unless they have a lot of possums there, maybe." James Edwards, however, admitted to being from Possum Kingdom: "But the old saying is, if you go down there, somewhere within four or five miles of that settlement, and you asked them how to get to Possum Kingdom, they'd tell you it's two miles down the road. But if you go two miles down the road, they'll tell you it's two miles back up!"

As Gladys Taylor observed, "And that's the way it used to be [with] 'Dark Corner.' Nobody, around the edges—'You from Dark Corner?' 'No, no, I'm below' or 'I'm above.' Nobody would be from Dark Corner." This mysterious place, Ms. Taylor mentioned earlier in our conversation, was familiar to many: "I grew up in the upper part of Greenville County, above Travelers Rest. Some people would mistakenly call it Dark Corner—it's not quite up to Dark Corner, though. . . . It was called Dark Corner because, back in the early days when times were so hard, men made whiskey—you know, they had stills. I remember when I was a child, the men called revenue officers. And they'd come and cut the stills up and sometimes people would get killed . . . during the time when they were making whiskey. . . . Most everybody from around up that way were Scotch-Irish. That's a pure strain up there. . . . And they only made whiskey for a living because the land was harsh."

Other place names derive from local industries. The small crossroads of "Slabtown," marked today by a general store, a small sewing center, a Baptist church, and scattered mobile homes, has been named after a sawmill that once operated in the area. The general store, although of modern construction, is fronted with large, flat slabs of wood, and the nearby church has an identifying sign made with the same material. The store's proprietor had done this deliberately, in order to preserve the place name of her family's settlement.

Conclusion

Folk speech, whether preserved in place names or expressed through the explanations for them, helps to demarcate groups and thus serves as a significant indicator of regional identity. While the southern accent appears generally similar throughout Dixie, especially to untrained Yankee ears, Piedmonters recognize the distinct and subtle variations that exist in Carolina cotton country. The Charleston and Gullah dialects certainly differ from the accent of residents from the Blue Ridge, and Upstaters utilize these linguistic boundaries to help maintain cultural ones. In a sense, the accent(s) of the Carolina Piedmont represent the sounds by which the area's folklife is created, modified, and maintained.

CHAPTER 6

Storytelling and Verbal Artistry

One of the stronger genres winding continuously through Carolina Piedmont folklife is that of storytelling and other verbal artistry. From the general stores and quilting parties of earlier generations to the family reunions and fast-food restaurants of the present, Piedmonters have long enjoyed the pleasure of telling tales. Politicians and other public characters sometimes form the center of these stories, while more private ones circulate about family members. Traditional folktales continue, as do stories about supernatural phenomena, some believed and some questioned. Practical jokes and humorous anecdotes have an equally long history in the Upstate, and persist just as strongly today. Told in the characteristically southern style described in the previous chapter, stories of all types enliven social gatherings in the Carolina Piedmont.

The Social Context of Storytelling

Despite stereotypes of straw-hatted men dozing on park benches in the blistering August heat or blue-haired matrons rocking on spacious verandas in the cool evening shade, Piedmonters do not spend all waking hours telling stories in casual social situations. Undeniably, however, the arts of spinning tales and timing jokes are well-respected and frequently enjoyed in the Upstate, and have been for generations.

James Edwards, recalling his youth, describes one of these earlier storytelling contexts: "Well, usually out in the outlying areas they had . . . a little country store where, maybe in the early part of the evening . . . men would gather. . . . And they would have their checkerboards . . . and they'd stand around and do a little talking or swapping knives or swapping

Contemporary general store in an outlying rural area
(Photo by John M. Coggeshall)

dogs. . . . Most all the stores, between the building and the gas pump, would
have a little shed over the top of it. . . . And sometimes they'd sit up under
that shed. Or, most all of them had pot-bellied stoves inside in the wintertime . . . and they'd stand around the stove."

Those trapped in the mills could not gather at the crossroads stores, and
yet these workers enjoyed storytelling just as much as their country relatives. John Morland noted that long, leisurely, informal conversations form
"an important part of the recreational life of the mill worker." After work
or on breaks, mill operatives would gather at popular spots like the fence
along the riverbank near the Hammondville plant, Everett Baker recalled.
"Here the fellows . . . would sit on the cement wall in pretty weather and
swap stories and tell fish tales, while drinking a Coke or coffee." Topics,
Mr. Baker continued, included "just current events, you know, back then
no TV. . . . So-and-so got a new car, or so-and-so got married, so-and-so
had a baby; it was just general . . . talk that you'd hear at the grocery store,
or the filling station, wherever you lived . . . local stuff." While women
might contribute, Mary Gattis added, many other times they sought the
privacy of the ladies' rest room for their joke-telling sessions, mindful of
gender-based decorum rules. Segregated at the mill, African-American
work crews from the yard and warehouse congregated outside the black

canteen during lunch hour, where some of the older men played checkers, Arthur Masters recalled.

In the towns and cities, Ray Nameth observed, folks used to tell stories in places like barbershops, "or if they'd gotten a haircut they'd stay there for hours, you know, just listening. You'd hear a lot of stuff at the barbershop. Women didn't frequent the barbershop too much. Yeah, there'd be some rough stuff told at the barbershop." On city streets, too, men would gather, Mr. Nameth continued: "You'd hear somebody up the street just laughing—you know somebody done told a dirty joke."

Urban African Americans, generally segregated from white company, formed their own storytelling sessions outside black-operated stores or other neighborhood settings. Patrick and Morland, in Kent, described such a setting: "I heard 'Hambone' hold forth one afternoon for about four hours to a group that averaged about 8 men; most of the men could verify or had participated in one or more of the escapades that he recounted to the tune of prolonged guffaws. For example, there were stories of crap shooting groups and whiskey carrying expeditions that were broken up by the cops."

Vernon Randle portrayed a neighborhood hangout with which he had been familiar: "Sit around telling lies and talking and juding [?] one another. Talking all kind of old talk and saying everything. . . . Just something to keep up the devil—laughing, carrying on, fun, and all kind of foolishness."

Any convenient location would enable such informal gatherings of friends to congregate. Mr. Randle added: "Used to have a old bridge over there, had a cement terrace on each side of it. We used to sit there on that bridge till twelve, one o'clock at night. Just lived up there on the bridge, sitting there talking . . . telling lies, and talking and going on. . . . One'd tell a big lie on the other one just to get something started, you know, get to arguing and laughing about such stuff." As if to illustrate, during one afternoon of a scheduled interview Mr. Randle, Don Underwood, and two other neighbors held an hourlong recollection session behind Mr. Randle's home. The participants sat on makeshift chairs or benches with well-worn seats and cushions, indicating that such discussions were common occurrences.

Country stores and mill streams have virtually all been replaced by Wal-Marts and employee cafeterias, but storytelling remains a popular pastime; the activity has simply shifted locations. Folklorist Anne Kimzey offers one example from her field notes: "Met Betsy Dillbeck, editor of the McCormick [South Carolina] *Messenger,* for breakfast at the B-Mart. This is the traditional spot where the local gossips (white men) hang out every morning for coffee. . . . Betsy goes to keep up with what's going on in the community."

The Hardees restaurant in Hammondville, open to both genders, serves the same social importance, particularly for the retired white mill workers. Some of them journey each morning to the Community Center (the former Hammondville Men's Building) for walking in the gymnasium; afterwards they congregate for breakfast, coffee, and conversation. Several informants mentioned that Hardees biscuits most closely resemble those their mothers (or wives) used to make, thus making the store an even more popular dining area. By about 9:30 A.M. the crowd begins to dwindle, perhaps to meet again for lunch in one of the town's mom-and-pop restaurants. Not unique to Hammondville, the popularity of sharing breakfast and conversation with friends at Hardees is well known in the Upstate.

About Piedmonters, Ben Robertson observed: "It is about people that we talk; it is not about things. A thing is worth discussing only when it illustrates the character of a human being. . . . We will seldom discuss an issue as such—we consider an issue, but we prefer to tell about a symbol that stands for the issue or we will tell you a story about some person involved in such an issue. We are story-tellers in the South."

Stories from the Piedmont

As with many other aspects of Piedmont folklife, the categorization of stories into specific genres is an artificial way of classifying them; local raconteurs do not pigeonhole their repertoires into these categories. Moreover, the distinction made here between stories of local characters and those about politicians becomes impossible to perceive in the heat of a storytelling session; of course, it makes no difference to teller or listener. These categories simply sort the Upstate's stories into recognizable genres.

LOCAL CHARACTER STORIES

These vignettes, usually relatively short, highlight real people from local communities. Because of prevailing racism, stories told by whites in earlier generations often featured African Americans as fools. W. F. Barbee, of High Point, North Carolina, remembered an episode involving a renderer who suspected that a Negro was selling him some mule bones, stealing them, and then reselling them to him. In order to outsmart him, the renderer wrote his name ("Exum") on the inside of a skull, which the man offered for sale several days later. The buyer pointed out the name to the Negro and asked him how he might account for that. "The negro scratched his head for a moment and said, 'Fore Gawd, boss I remember now; that was the old mule's name.' "

Sometimes, though, the black "fool" becomes the clever respondent, as in this contemporary example told by David Hawkins: "We had an old colored gentleman we called, his name was Uncle Perry. . . . And it was his job to go around and clean these things [outhouses] out. And there's a lot of stories been told about Uncle Perry. The kids always kidded him, you know. . . . One kid hollered at him, said, 'Hey, Uncle Perry, you got a load?' He said, 'Yeah, all but one so-and-so. Hop on.' "

African Americans also teased each other. Vernon Randle, self-described rascal in his youth, admitted to having been incarcerated numerous times for drunkenness in his wilder days until he realized that he was "paying out of jail like I was paying rent on it." During this time, he remembered tormenting a fellow railroad worker: "Yeah, I used to work with some tough fellas. . . . A good man couldn't work out there, 'cause too much devilment going on. . . . One old fella—said he was a preacher. . . . Boy, we used to make that man *so* mad! Say all kind of old thing before him and all around him, ask him all kind of old crazy questions, and *keep* him mad. He finally quit!"

Other stories involve eccentric neighbors. Helen Quinnell described a local character called "Uncle Mose" who was: "a law unto himself—did what he wanted to do. . . . They'd say, 'Well, I believe it's stopped raining.' And he'd say, 'Naw, it's just gone back after another load.' " David Hawkins told about "one old gentleman here who was . . . a very straight, back-stiff, very precise gentleman. And you'd walk by and say you'd see him this morning, you'd say, 'Good morning, Mr. Abernathy.' He'd speak to you: 'Good morning.' You'd see him in the afternoon and speak to him again, he'd say, 'I spoke to you one time already.' And that's all he'd say."

Some stories recall humorous incidents in the close-knit neighborhoods of mill communities. Linda Baker told a story about her father, who used to skinny-dip with his childhood friends in the river that ran through Hammondville. One of the village streets ran steeply down a hill toward the riverbank, and on that hill perched the home of an old couple who loved to sit on their porch in the evenings. Practicing southern chivalry, however, the gentleman also knew that the nude boys would offend his wife. So, after supper, the old man would stand on his porch and tell them, "Boys, y'all have to come in now; me and the missus is going to sit out on the porch."

Mischievous youngsters sometimes encountered even more clever adults. Maggie Nameth offered an example: "We had one boy in school there . . . who would do anything, tell you anything, to get out of school. . . . [And so] he told the first principal that he needed to go home, that he just had a tooth that was just killing him, just couldn't stand it. And he had to go to the dentist. So the assistant principal said, 'I'll just take him to the dentist.' . . . After they got inside the waiting room the boy said, 'I can't have this tooth pulled.' Said, 'I haven't got any money.' So the assistant principal says, 'That's all right, I'll pay for it!' I know they pulled a perfectly good tooth."

Maggie Nameth contributed another story about her hometown doctor:

> During the First World War, a man that had been overseas fighting came home. . . . And he'd been home two or three days and his wife had a baby. . . . The morning after the baby was born the man came to Doctor [name]'s house. . . . And he said, . . . "You know I've been gone a year and a half, my wife just had a baby." And said, "Now she told me that this is my baby. And that the only reason that she was this long in having it, she wanted to wait for me to be back home to have it. Now, . . . I want you to tell me the truth." Says, "Can a woman wait a year and a half to have a baby?" And said, Doctor [name] said, "Well now, son, I'll tell you something." Said, "When a woman makes up her mind to do it, she can do what damn thing she wants to!"

Fables and foibles of small-town political figures also provided numerous characters for stories. For example, a lawyer originally from Kent remembered a local sheriff whom he described as "Barney Fife" (after Don Knotts's character on the *Andy Griffith Show*). Like Barney, this sheriff enforced the law to the letter. One time, the lawyer swore, the sheriff arrested his aunt for "indecent exposure"; she was wearing a sundress with a low-cut back.

Tales of political informality reflected the rural atmosphere of the Piedmont. For example, an informant once served as a local magistrate in a small Upstate mill village. One time, his wife remembered, "we had a spate of teenagers driving fast through the community. . . . People were complaining about it. . . . I remember [my husband] . . . saying that he could put a dog on trial for speeding and get a jury . . . and they'd have convicted him, everybody was so anxious to do something to somebody!" A current resident of Kent, describing how political factions had torn apart the town some years ago, joked that both sides finally compromised over a neutral candidate; a stranger "came to town for a co-cola and got elected mayor!"

The political power differential between blacks and whites readily surfaced during the unequal enforcement of the law. As African Americans knew and most whites quietly acknowledged, disenfranchised Upstate blacks often lived at the mercy of their white neighbors. For African Americans like Lucindy Brown, the inequality frightened her entire community: "Well, I'll tell you. They had very little say-so. A man once pulled a ear of corn out of a white man's cornfield and he got ten years. . . . They had no justice. They just did what they wanted to do to you—" "—knowing nothing wasn't going to be said," Vernon Randle added. As social scientists recognize, the arbitrary enforcement of regulations against a powerless group effectively maintains that control, thus reinforcing segregation.

A few stories had even more sinister overtones. Given southern racism, tragedies were bound to occur. One Upstate white resident speculated about a local incident: "Up there where the mill's at there's a cornfield. Bunch of them [wealthy local elites] hunting and drinking. He shot a little . . . boy up there one time. He said he thought it was a rabbit, but if the truth was known . . . , he done that for a laugh. That's the kind of feller he was. They [his family] had so much influence and power, the feller didn't even try him."

FAMILY STORIES

As described in chapter 4, one's family heritage forms a significant value for Piedmonters. Told on the front porches of old houses or at the picnic tables of family reunions, tales and anecdotes of family members, living and deceased, form oral libraries of family history.

Many of these tales involve older generations having difficulty adjusting to modern conveniences or contrivances. A merchant in downtown Kent described an adventure he had had when living with his brother in Washington, D.C., many decades ago. Trapped in a traffic circle in the days before stoplights, he had driven around and around four times. Eventually he swooped too close to a traffic cop standing on a pedestal in the middle; the policeman whistled him to stop, which he did. The officer yelled: "What do you think you're doing?" "I'm going home." "Where are you from?" "South Carolina." "Well, then, go on—you don't know any damn better!"

James Edwards told another about his independent-minded grandfather-in-law, a seventy-year-old man in the 1950s: "The highway patrolman stopped him . . . asked him for his driving license. He told him he didn't have any. Patrolman told him, said, 'Well, you got to have a driving license.' Said, 'Now, I've been driving since before you was born. I didn't have to have a driver's license . . . then and I don't have to have one now.' And he just drove off. Said the patrolman just shook his head."

At the Quinnell family reunion outside of Hammondville, I listened for over an hour while a small cluster of male relatives regaled their spouses and other guests with stories about "Uncle Pete." His son (now an old man himself) told me, "He was opposed to labor—his labor!" Everyone who entered his house, from repairmen to relatives, had to carry in an armload of stove wood. One time he fell asleep while smoking but was so drunk that when he started to feel "warm," he simply moved to another bed; meanwhile, the other bed burned up. Another time he came home drunk and tried to climb up the back stairs, but "Grandma" kept hitting him with a broom and knocking him back down. "Took him half-hour to get up!" a grandnephew laughed.

At a church revival one summer, a former mill worker (now a preacher) held his three-year-old grandson on his shoulder while a group of adults talked after an evening service. The boy whispered in his grandfather's ear to tell a favorite story; he laughed and then offered a tale originally told by *his* grandfather, also a mill worker. It seems that his grandfather, while working in the mill, had lost a finger joint in an industrial accident. When the storyteller was a young boy, he picked his nose, and to get him to stop, his grandfather held up his mangled finger (which the grandson imitated by tucking his own finger down) and warned him that: "You know how I lost that finger? Booger bit it off!" Both grandfather and grandson then laughed, and the latter added that he personally did not believe it could happen. In fact, he admitted, he still picks his nose.

RHYMES

A relatively rare component of verbal art, rhymes represent both traditional and self-composed types. An example of the former is the well-documented folk rhyme encapsulating the tribulations of African-American sharecroppers. As described in chapter 12, black "croppers," frequently illiterate, thus had to depend completely on their white bosses for computing accurately their share of the annual crop. As might be expected, the African Americans were often cheated. Prohibited by custom and by law from direct retaliation, blacks then resorted to humor and sarcasm, as the following rhyme indicates: "Naught's a naught/And a figger is a figger;/All for the white man,/None for the nigger."

Vernon Randle enjoyed reminiscing about the "old junk" he and his friends still occasionally joke about. For example, he recalled this rhyme:

> I done got old and feeble, yes sir;
> My pilot light done gone out;
> And what used to be my sex, you see,
> Is now my water spout.

> Used to get up in the morning and take a shave,
> Standing there, looking me right in the face;
> Get up in the morning, tie my shoes,
> Got a hung-down head and the aching blues!

"That's going to happen when you get old," he teased.

Vernon Randle's poetic skill did not end with such aging witticisms. Like several other older informants, Mr. Randle had an enchanting lilt to his voice as he described personal experiences, transforming some narratives at times almost into song. In the following example, he secondarily accented the verbs and primarily accented the adjectives, in effect creating a dactylic intonation: "had some good years and had some bad years; went through some rough time and through some easy time." When speech becomes poetry, the effect upon an audience increases dramatically.

Adults are not the only repositories of folk rhymes; children, too, possess them. Linda Baker recalled the context and the tradition of a rhyme from her childhood:

> Do you know that little chant that Mother and her brothers and sisters used to say it at night? And my age did too, when we were little. . . . If the kids were out playing, and it would be twilight and about dark and they'd start to scatter to go home. And it's sort of like whistling in the dark . . . whistling while you're nervous as you were walking home. You'd skip down the street together, going home in the dark, and you would sing out, "Ain't no Boogers out tonight/Daddy killed 'em all last night!" And that was something you did to keep from being scared going home in the dark from your friend's house. And we did that when I was little, and Mother did it, too. And we got it from our parents.

One other example of a contemporary children's rhyme was overheard at a community festival in Travelers Rest, South Carolina. During an evening performance of a "womanless beauty pageant," several grade-school boys sat in front of me, squirming impatiently at the ceremony. As one contestant lip-synched Billy Ray Cyrus's "Achy Breaky Heart," the boys smiled slyly at each other and sang: "You can smell my fart, my achy breaky fart." They laughed at their cleverness and wrestled with each other until an exasperated mother sat between them, effectively ending the episode.

An interesting expression of folk thought in the Piedmont occurs through rhymed poems to deceased loved ones, published as memorials in local and regional newspapers. Often accompanied by photographs, the poems appear on significant personal holidays, such as the anniversary of a birth or death or on Mother's or Father's Days. Known in other regions of the South as well, these memorials reflect the deeply rooted Upstate value placed on family and conservative religious faith.

Some of the poems contain flowery and sentimental lines either copied from other sources or written in that style. Other published poems contain very personal, almost intimate, recollections:

> The love for a son is very strong
> It grows and grows from the day he's born. . . .
> You watch him mature and bring much joy

> And you're proud to say, "That's my boy!"
> Then off to the store he goes one day
> Never returning to love and play.
> Yes, the Lord blessed me the day you were given
> And I long for the day you're in my arms in heaven.
>   Love, Mom

Or this memorial, equally personal and personalized:

> My little brother, special and kind
> Day and night you're on my mind.
> To lots of people I sit and speak
> Of the many ways you were unique.
> From your weird haircut and your big blue eyes,
> To your big ol' gut and fat pudgy thighs. . . .
> The days ahead will be sad and blue,
> I know it's because I'm missing you.
>   Love your brother

FOLKTALES

Folktales differ from family stories in that they contain elements, or entire plots, that may be traced back to Old World antecedents or that have become so widespread in contemporary American culture that they have lost their known origin point. Often assumed to be the victim of modern conveniences like television or video games, folktales do seem to play less of a role in the daily lives of contemporary Upstate residents than in former times. Traditionally, a good storyteller would entertain "any time he found somebody with two ears," Maggie Nameth asserted. Today, professional storytellers, frequently appearing at community festivals, have continued the tradition but in a more polished manner, perhaps gradually superseding the more personal raconteurs of families. Since storytelling remains popular in the Upstate, though, authentic folktales have not completely disappeared.

Adults remembered with fondness earlier tale-telling sessions. For example, a Greenville-area resident described such a setting from her childhood: "And every Sunday afternoon he [her grandfather] would sit under that big shade tree out there (I can go to the spot right now) and get all of us children around him, and read the Bible to us. And then he liked to tell us these old-time stories, too, about the fox with the rabbit. . . . He'd entertain us that way, don't you know. And we just loved them." Unfortunately, the interviewer did not ask for an elaboration about the story.

Linda Baker recalled a well-known story from her childhood: " 'Bloody

Bones' is what they used to scare all the children with—both Mother's generation and mine. . . . And, I don't know—it's kind of murky. It wasn't real specific. It was like somebody murdered, there was nothing left but like the skeleton with blood all over it? It was a creature called 'Bloody Bones.' And they would get you at night, you know, and this kind of stuff. And there was some little story about hearing a rattly noise over here. And you're going along the road at night and he speaks to you—'What's that noise?' 'It's Bloody Bones!' you know, and all this kind of stuff. And you'd get chased by Bloody Bones. That was a standard story."

A hint of a traditional folktale from adult informants may be found in John Morland's field notes. He described the story of a man trying to decide which of two women to marry so he offered each a challenge: a badly tangled ball of string to be unwound in twenty-four hours. The next night he went back to visit each woman and found that the first had gotten discouraged and quit but the other had untangled it and rewound it neatly. That was the woman he married—the one who showed the greater patience and skill.

An elderly African-American woman from Belton, Ida Johnson, provided another. A grandfather takes his two grandsons out to the woods to show them all the trees, including the oak. The boys each saved an acorn; one threw his into the yard and the other kept his in a drawer, where it eventually molded and turned to dust. "That night there came a thunderstorm" and washed dirt over the acorn. It sprouted, but "it had a hard time living, too." People would walk over it, wagons would drive over it, "but it kept trying to live." Finally, "great trees from little acorns did grow," offering shade to weary travelers or sick people and a place for children to play. Thus the moral of the story is that everyone should try to help others.

Several informants supplied versions of a folktale that draws special meaning from the social inequality between landowners and sharecroppers, often compounded by racial injustice—conditions common in the cotton Piedmont. Vernon Randle provided a succinct variant: "One old man, they said he picked his cotton and everything, and he had a bale he had never had ginned. The old man, the landowner, he settling up with him: 'Well, you made it good this time, you just got out of debt. You don't owe nothing now, you don't owe nothing—nary penny.' He told him, 'Well, I got another bale of cotton to be ginned.' Say he said, 'Whoa, whoa! Let's go back over these figures again!' "

TALL TALES

A well-told tall tale strings the listener along, as possible truth becomes buried by increasingly outrageous statements, until the teller arrives at a virtually impossible statement, at which time the entire audience explodes in laughter.

Ray Nameth remembered a character in town who "wouldn't let you outdo him. . . . I was telling him about being up out of Hendersonville [North Carolina]. . . . I was just making this up. And a fella told me that he gathered forty-two bushels of apples off of one limb of a tree. And Mr. [name] said, 'I can take you and show you the tree—my granddaddy set it out!' " Another time the man found himself trapped on a railroad trestle with a train bearing down on him: "Well, he didn't know hardly what to do; he had on an overcoat. And so he just grabbed the tail of his overcoat on each side. And jumped off that trestle. And glided down, wind holding him up . . . he landed on his feet!"

Two African-American informants also provided tall tales, the first of which appeared initially to be simply an episode in George Jackson's life. While walking through a field behind his house, we stumbled across a small turtle, which prompted him to tell about another "terrapin," as big as the lid on an oil drum: "I run and jumped up on his back, shu . . . he kept going like I wasn't up on there. . . . I jumped off him, got my stick, and I went back there and I . . . whupped him pretty bad. But boy, he was in a hurry to get back to that pond; he got over in that pond he was safe. . . . And I tried to catch that rascal, he got back to that pond, shucks, he just walking away from me. I jumped up on his back, shucks, he was walking with me like I wasn't up on his back."

The other tale began as what appeared to be a legitimate question. During an interview in the home of Richard Sanders, his neighbor, Don Underwood, had asked me if I believed humans had actually been to the moon. Mr. Sanders quietly smiled while Mr. Underwood continued: "You think they been to the moon? . . . I'm going to ask you one question. How many space men got sent up before they put blacks in it? . . . First man went up was John Glenn, wasn't it? I don't know who that next one went up. But that third one, I think a black person was thinking of flying with them. . . . But, they didn't make it—that thing, guess what? Blowed up, didn't it? Killed those people in it. All right. You think about this here, now. Wonder why it was blowed up? [At this point Sanders began laughing quietly.] They know them black peoples get back here they going to tell the truth, what happened. . . . 'Cause they know when *we* get back, we's going to let the cat out of the sack!"

The context of this tale probably explains the content. I was interviewing Richard Sanders, an African American, when his neighbor, Don Underwood (also an African American) stopped by to visit. Mr. Underwood told this story within the first several minutes of our meeting. I believe it was done as a test, to measure (in a humorous, nonthreatening way) my degree of racial sensitivity and willingness to tolerate stories about white injustices. Such stories then immediately followed.

STORIES OF SUPERNATURAL PHENOMENA

While some folktales (like "Bloody Bones") also deal with ghosts and supernatural hauntings and while some stories of local apparitions contain elements also found in traditional tales, ghost stories for most Upstaters form a separate category in oral tradition. Such stories involve the hauntings of particular places, such as homes and cemeteries, and are frequently told as if true, based on eyewitness accounts. Most Upstate residents, though, do not believe in such phenomena but enjoy the tingling sensation from well-told stories.

Like many other themes in Carolina Piedmont folklife, however, some of those involving the supernatural become difficult to trace to their origin. Stories of "haints" have long been associated with African Americans, and such ideas logically could be connected ultimately to African origins. On the other hand, though, folklorists Newbell Puckett and Charles Joyner note that many whites have traditionally attributed a stereotypical belief in the supernatural to the "superstitious" or "primitive" nature of blacks.

However, both Puckett and Joyner argue that many (although certainly not all) of the stories of ghosts and haunts from black informants stem ultimately from European tradition, entering African-American culture first from owner to slave. For example, Isaac Johnson, born into slavery in North Carolina in 1855, remembered in his WPA interview that "Master would tell the children about Raw Head and Bloody Bones and other things to scare us."

Blacks, interpreting and modifying these stories through a filter of African oral tradition, then passed these tales back to their white employers or their children as they worked as cooks or babysitters in white households. Eula Durham, an Anglo American from Bynum, North Carolina, recalled: "This old colored woman that used to live up there above us—she'd come down there at night and stay with us some times when mamma and papa was workin'. She'd tell us some of the awfullest tales you ever did, and just scare us to death. I was too scared to even go to bed. 'Bout 'Raw Head and Bloody Bones,' you know, and things like that, just scare us to death." Through time, the disparate traditions became interwoven so tightly that it has become virtually impossible to separate strands today. The resulting composite then becomes even more enchanting because of its richness.

Some ghost stories involve the haunting of specific homes. Arthur Masters recalled a story his father had told: "Him and his mother lived together, and they moved in a man's house that he built for his son (this was a white man). . . . But his son somehow died before he even got to stay in the house. And he said something was wrong about *that* house. He said because, there'd be times at night, you were on this side of the house, sound like you could hear a little knocking on the other side. And if you went back there, the sound would be up here. And he said, if one person stayed up here and the other went back there, this person thought the sound was coming from back that way, and that person would swear the sound was coming from *this* way."

Linda Baker offered a current tale with a similar theme: "There's a haunted house . . . not far from me, and it's had some disturbances. . . . And the people that lived there had somebody supposedly psychic come and listen to the aura of the house. And they said that the house is on, somewhere where some Indians were killed or something, back before it was settled. And that it's Indians that are haunting the house and not locals."

Vernon Randle described another ghostly phenomenon: "People used to tell me there's a (I was young then) something called 'Jacoby ladder.' And I said, 'What would it do to you?' 'Well, it won't do nothing.' Just like you off at night, you think you inside of your house you see a light. You take that light in your house, you follow that light, just follow that light. Next thing you know you don't know where you at."

Other ghost stories involve the reappearance of deceased loved ones as visitors, a well-known motif in folk literature. Vernon Randle provided an example: "I was going up the road one night . . . I heard something coming behind me. . . . I just looked around there, a white goat—billy goat. . . . And I said, 'What in the world that goat doing here?' And I got to thinking and I said, 'Ain't nobody around here got no goat!' I says, 'What in the world was that?' But I didn't think no more about it. My granddaddy died about two days after that. Now that must have been something or other that told me, that showed me that he was going to die."

Wilma Masters also had an eerie premonition: "I saw my oldest brother's death. I was in the bed and it woke me up. What happened—I dreamt it was, somebody comes to my job and told me he was dead. Said they find him dead in the field. And you see, that next day [my husband] come to my job and told me he was dead." Mrs. Masters had also presaged the death of her baby sister: "A lot of people say that is a token, that God is showing you something going to happen."

Cemeteries, not surprisingly, frequently harbor haunts. On the edge of Hammondville's black community sits an abandoned black cemetery, which Linda Baker's mother had told her used to be haunted. Arthur Masters knew the place well: "But I've heard people say that there was a place on that road out there that seemed to be something different, I don't know. . . . Summer nights, people used to walk back and forth out there to church a lot. Say you'd be walking, coming out not far from the graveyard, right along there, cool like the nights would be, and all of a sudden you walk out of coolness and you walk into a warm spot of air. And then . . . you'd be back in the cool air again."

Sometimes, though, fright created confusion, which led to embarrassment, as Don Underwood admitted in this autobiographical episode from his childhood:

> My momma always wanted me to be in by eleven o'clock. I done got through playing ball. . . . [I had on] brand-new overalls. . . . That night I walked back from a little old juke joint near home. I got even with the Bush Hill. . . . A lot of people had wrecked on there, got killed. 'Fore I got to the Bush Hill I hear a hot thing run across the front of me—just a hot flash, you know. And I look back and something goes, "Scrunch!" I says, "Wonder what the God did that scrunching?" Jump on up a little bit further . . . "Oh—again! This thing's getting closer to me," I says. And I turn myself around, hear "Scrunch" again, it looked like something ready to grab me; man, I took off running! And I didn't stop until I got on my momma's front porch. . . . I fixed my [supper] plate and I'm sitting down at the table; when I sit down my overalls said, "Scrunch!"

Today, belief in ghosts and haunts varies among individuals. Richard Sanders expressed complete disbelief: "I ain't never seen one, and I been out all time at night, I slept in a cemetery, and all that stuff. I never seen them—I don't believe in it." Arthur Masters had another explanation: "Well, I've heard that sometimes, things like that happen. Then I've heard that maybe it'll only happen every other generation can pick it up. I've heard it that way, too. If that's the case then, see, my dad could do it and I guess it skips over me." As both he and his wife acknowledged, though, their children have never seen ghosts, which Mrs. Masters attributed to a nonfolk cause: "All they hear is the music. They can't hear it too good, 'cause they have it played up so loud it's just drowning their ears off!" Still, as many informants have stated, local apparitions haunt the Piedmont, and Upstate residents enjoy the feelings of horror and humor engendered by their presence.

JOKES AND PRANKS

In addition to the various types of tales and stories, Upstaters also relish the impromptu practical joke or the brief, humorous anecdote. As with the other categories discussed earlier, the boundary between joke and story is an arbitrary one, but (as in general American culture) the length of the episode generally determines the category. Jokes, as expressions of folk thought, reveal the hopes and fears of those telling them. Likewise, jokes reflect the characters or social settings of the time, and so represent a tiny window on the past. Most important, though, jokes are fun to tell and hear.

As part of their study of Kent, the researchers recorded not only jokes but the context in which they occurred. Ralph Patrick described a party at a family's "river cottage" for the college crowd. While the women fixed supper inside, the men sat on the porch and told jokes. For example, a carpenter was being followed everywhere on his job by a pesky little boy who exclaimed "my daddy's got two of those" every time the carpenter used a tool. Finally the exasperated carpenter pulled out his penis and asked the boy if his father had two of those. "Yep" the youngster replied, "one this long for when he pees, and one *this* long for when he chases the cook around the kitchen!" The story reveals the fear and humor of miscegenation (the cook most likely would have been black) and the context in which it was told reveals the desire to prevent "proper" ladies from hearing such crude humor.

In a revealing sign of the times, Jimmy Elgin (a retired cotton mill worker) told a story about "the fellow that . . . dreamed he died and went to heaven. There was a beautiful cotton mill there, and so he asked St. Peter why they weren't running that mill. St. Peter looked at him right funny, said, 'Well, you're the only fellow that has ever come up here knows what it was.'" The joke not only humorously disparages cotton mill laborers but also hints at the declining work in, and thus knowledge about, a formerly prominent Upstate way of life.

Ray and Maggie Nameth delighted in describing a local character who had devised a particularly crafty and complex prank. He took a rubber ball, attached a squirrel's tail to it, and placed it inside a cage-like box on a spring contraption that he could release at will. Maggie Nameth continued: "And he would go, say, to the barbershop, and he'd tell them that he had a mongoose in there. And you could just see the tail of it, out of the box. [Said later in conversation:] (You know, he'd warn them ahead of time, 'Now, be careful. Don't get too close—they're pretty vicious animals!') They'd be getting down over it, looking at it, and then he would flip the switch, and that rubber ball that had the tail attached to it would fly out—"

"Go bouncing across the floor and see that old tail going that way!" Ray Nameth laughed.

"He had the people say some choice things, too, after they calmed down a little bit!" Maggie Nameth chuckled.

Women, too, might tell and enjoy risque humor, but rarely in public. After a long joke-telling session by her husband, Mary Elrod contributed one about an old-time doctor. To help his son learn the trade, the doctor took him along on house calls. At the first house, the doctor told the bed-ridden patient that she ate too much candy and needed to cut back. The puzzled son could not see anything wrong, but later his father told him that he had noticed the candy wrappers under the bed. At the second house, the bedridden patient was told that she did too much reading, because (the son discovered afterwards) of all the magazines under the bed. At the third house, the exhausted patient was warned: "Too much religion." At this, the son was greatly perplexed. " 'Well, daddy, I understand the candy, and I understand the magazines, but how in the world did you figure that she had too much religion?' " He replied, " 'Well, son, didn't you see the preacher under the bed?' "

Jokes from the African-American community reflect the same decorum shown to ladies and preachers; off-color jokes are for male company only. For example, Patrick and Morland overheard this joke at a men's club meeting after the preacher had left: it seems that an elderly couple had decided to get married but found themselves in bed together before the wedding. The old man asked the woman to fondle him a little first in order to help him get started. She replied that she had been using a hand crank for twenty-five years, and now wanted a self-starter!

Sometimes joke-tellers played on the southern value of chivalry toward ladies. Velma Childers offered an example from her childhood: "One time he [a class clown] said, 'You can't say anything in front of [name]; you can't stand to say "bureau" in front of her.' Somebody say, 'Why you can't say "bureau" in front of [name]?' ' 'Cause it has "drawers" in it!' "

In addition to the general southern value of preserving the dignity of women, however, jokes from the African-American community also reveal more group-specific ideas as well, particularly those involving race rela-tions. For example, Patrick and Morland offered, a Catholic priest stopped overnight in South Carolina and then needed a place to say Mass Sunday morning. He assumed that anyone out on the street early on Sunday must be Catholic, so he asked the first person he met, a black man, if he were Catholic. " 'Naw suh, Boss,' the man replied; 'ain't it bad enough to be a nigger?' " Besides the self-deprecating but ironic humor about being black in the segregated South, the joke also illustrates the prevailing theological orientations of most Piedmonters.

Wit may also produce spontaneous quips, which the bystander must catch or risk being overwhelmed, perhaps by additional statements that could evolve into tall tales. One man in Kent, for example, mentioned that he was pleased to have lived as long as he had but "I still check the obituar-ies every day to see if I'm still alive." Elizabeth Block told me she once owned a mixed-breed dog: "I called him a 'poinsetta' because he was part setter and part pointer." Ray Nameth once asked a neighbor how he was feeling, and the man replied "Tolerable—you know what that means, don't you? . . . It means that you're able to eat, not able to work!" Folklorist Laurel Horton, conducting fieldwork in the Hammondville area in 1987, asked an informant if he had lived here all his life; he replied, "No, not quite all my life; I ain't dead yet, you know."

MILL PRANKS

A significant subcategory of Upstate humor involves practical jokes associated with mill work. As described in chapter 2, mill employment reshaped the political economy and social structures of the Cotton Piedmont. Most area residents were affected either directly or indirectly by this economic force, and so some faced, or many heard about, pranks in the mill.

Not all were victims, as Everett Baker explained: "As long as you was naive enough and looked like a victim, you could expect it. If you wised up, . . . went on about your business, . . . never did bother you again. But the next new guy that come in, they'd try to get them another one." Arthur Masters felt that a "pretty serious-type person" such as himself would be ignored.

Many practical jokes involved sending the dupe for an imaginary piece of equipment. Mr. Baker remembered initiates being sent for "cloth-stretchers" after veteran workers feigned concern about the shortness of a bolt. Another employee might pretend to experience a mechanical breakdown on his machine and a novice might be told to fetch a left-handed hammer or monkey wrench. Other times, as both Tom Davis and Jimmy Elgin remembered, young employees might have to locate nonexistent elevator keys or "red blueing," perhaps racing zealously from floor to floor until someone intervened or they caught on.

Other jokes involved physical humor. Mary Gattis, for example, described a situation in which her fiancé had come to the mill to court another woman. All dressed up, the suitor stood beneath a window, and some men from an upstairs work area then dumped a bucket of dirty water on him. Everett Baker told of several instances where men would seize fellow employees and pour machine oil down their pants, glue their hats to shelves, or nail their shoes to the floor. Sometimes, he noted, those engaging in the joke became victims themselves shortly thereafter.

Cross-gender jokes apparently were less common, perhaps because of the inappropriateness of male humor (from a woman's perspective) or perhaps because genders remained somewhat segregated during many leisure activities. Still, instances occurred. A young woman Mr. Baker knew had just started work in the mill and had heard about "set marks" on cloth but had no idea that they were caused by errors in the weaving process, thus creating "seconds" (imperfections). Early one morning, as workers lolled around on these seconds waiting for the shift change, one of the senior men said, " 'Get up off that cloth. Don't you know you're making set marks?' 'Oh,' she jumped off, 'Oh, I'm sorry. I didn't know I was doing it.' "

Some people at the plant still pull practical jokes, Arthur Masters stated, "but management don't really like too much practical jokes or horseplay or stuff. . . . Sometime it could turn into something real serious, you know—a practical joke that don't go over too well, somebody'd get angry and it could turn into something ugly." Thus the increasing impersonalization of mill work due to corporate ownership after 1945, together with the associated intensification of labor, caused the gradual decline of these practical jokes.

Such humor also declined because, in effect, the nature of social relations on the job had changed. In his analysis of mill pranks, folklorist Doug DeNatale argued that this type of humor served several important functions. At a time when workers saw themselves "like a family," pranks served as an initiation to that group. Schaefer Kendrick discovered this when he, as a young college student, worked for a summer in a Greenville mill to earn money for his next year. First sent for a "seam stretcher," he eventually caught on when sent for "a bucket of steam." DeNatale added that such pranks also served to level out social class rankings. Kendrick, of a higher social class than his fellow employees, had been teased about his diligence on the job by workers in the plant: "It was their way of telling a young college student not to get too big for his britches." Kendrick's industriousness, though, reflected a deeper reason for workplace teasing, as DeNatale noted; those who work harder throw others behind and make ostensible equals look unequal in the eyes of supervisors. Thus, DeNatale concluded, industrial pranks helped workers balance their individualism with their interdependence.

Conclusion

The art and skill of weaving a story or telling a joke has long formed a significant part of the social lives of Piedmont residents. Family reunions, gatherings of old friends, or breaks at work offer Upstate residents times to entertain and enlighten audiences. While popular media have influenced both the frequency and content of such stories, the varied traditions of verbal artistry in the Upstate remain widespread and popular. Folktales, supernatural stories, and ordinary jokes represent well-worn elements in Piedmont folklife; some of these have been replaced by newer ones while others retain their original flavor. Either way, the humor reinforces other aspects of Upstate traditions.

CHAPTER 7

Customary Beliefs

Interwoven with ideas based on modern scientific thought are those rooted more firmly in folk tradition. While contemporary Piedmont residents have a knowledge of general science and have access to professional medical care, customary beliefs about natural phenomena and supernatural healing persist. Despite individual variation in acceptance, characteristic of the folklife of the Piedmont (as well as other parts of the nation) are acknowledgment of the power of celestial bodies to influence terrestrial events and the (sometimes mystical) efficacy of certain plants and practices to heal the body and mind. In effect, these older traditions parallel modern ones, sometimes meshing with and other times replacing them. Despite change, these strands retain the warmth of tradition and the strength of persistence.

Natural Phenomena

WEATHER PROGNOSTICATION

As might be expected within an agricultural economy, a major portion of the folk belief system of the Piedmont formerly included means by which individuals could predict the weather. For example, Nora Wood's "daddy" used to say that "if corn has thick shucks on it, it's going to be a cold winter." Birds huddling together, like the flock of robins outside Helen Quinnell's house, reminded her of her grandfather's belief that this indicated oncoming bad weather. As she pointed out during our next interview, "we *did* have bad weather, didn't we?" Ray Nameth once asked an arthritic friend if he could tell when a front would pass through; he replied: "I can tell you when they're going to have a front in Texas!"

Other beliefs more specifically targeted rain. For example, Vernon Randle described the well-known idea, reported by his great-grandfather, that the dip of the crescent moon indicated whether it was holding or spilling water; thus rain might be absent or imminent. A moon with a ring around it, both David Hawkins and Jason Lambert felt, could predict rain by the number of stars (equal to days) within the ring; "and that's a *true* sign," Mr. Lambert asserted. Both Helen Quinnell and Elizabeth Block utilized clouds called "mare's tails" (thin cirrus clouds) to prognosticate oncoming rain. Ms. Block, like many other Upstate residents, speculated that the old signs sometimes no longer hold, perhaps due to the climate-altering construction of artificial lakes in the Piedmont today.

The simultaneous occurrence of rain coupled with sunshine creates a puzzling natural phenomenon, one that has been marked with a particular folk saying. Several years ago, while walking across my college campus during a sunny rain shower, I passed a stranger going the opposite direction. He remarked, "Well, the devil is beating his wife!" Puzzled, I asked him what he meant, and he replied that people used to say that whenever it rained and the sun shone at the same time. The idea still exists in the Piedmont.

Another curious natural phenomenon occurs at sunset and could also be used to predict rain. Vernon Randle's grandfather taught him: " 'Shine yonder sun dog.' I'm looking for a dog on the ground; I didn't know what he was talking about! He showed it to me. It looked something about like a rainbow, a pretty good-sized thing, about no piece off from the sun. . . . 'It's going to rain.' . . . I'd just laugh at him. . . . But it would rain; yes, it would."

While some of these weather beliefs persist, they are more frequently recalled by older residents as reminiscences from their grandparents' or parents' generations. Today, customary beliefs about the weather are intermingled with the complete acceptance of modern meteorological forecasting. For example, while both Nora and Albert Wood provided their interviewer with several traditional forecasting beliefs, Mrs. Wood added: "We watch the TV for the weather, and the newspapers." Most elements of the folk knowledge system in the Piedmont reflect this blend of modern practicality and traditional retention.

SOLAR AND LUNAR INFLUENCES ON NATURAL PHENOMENA

More widely held, though, are ideas linking the phases of the moon and the relative position of the sun in the sky with natural and human activities. The belief that astronomical phenomena have a direct influence on terrestrial events is deeply rooted in European tradition and quite well known in the Piedmont today. In any contemporary almanac one may locate the "signs," the position of the rising sun in the constellations of the zodiac, which changes every day or so. Each sign, furthermore, is associated with particular human body parts, so that operations affecting those parts should be avoided when the "sign" is said to be "in" that part (and that constellation). The phases of the moon are also believed to influence natural phenomena; as the moon increases, for example, so do earthly objects. Firm believers in the signs, therefore, consult almanacs to obtain essential information about the position of the sun and the phase of the moon before undertaking certain specific activities.

Generally, a WPA author reported, the belief is that root vegetables are to be planted in the dark of the moon (waning or new) and aboveground crops in the light of the moon (waxing or full). For example, Albert Wood suggested that corn should be planted on or as near to the full moon as possible to guarantee a full ear. A person doing this, Don Underwood asserted, "would have some great corn too." Otherwise, the stalks would be too long. Ron Kellogg (a county extension agent), although disbelieving, thought he remembered that one should plant Irish potatoes on dark nights. Jason Lambert faced disaster with his okra crop one year because he did not consult the almanac. The next year he planted in the correct sign "and I made okra."

Besides planting specific vegetables by moon signs, one also should plant the entire garden by Good Friday, David Hawkins stated, "because on Good Friday you could figure that your frost was just about over." During a recent spring, a hairdresser in Clemson, South Carolina, mentioned that her mother had admonished her for not getting her garden in by then.

Just as the moon is said to influence garden plants, it could also affect timber. Thus, Ron Kellogg stated, people used to believe that wood would "keep better" if cut during "the full moon in March," Jason Lambert interrupted. Mr. Lambert then explained that this would "make it be light and burn good. See, the sap won't be in it. Let the sap get in it, dark nights, and the wood would be black and soggylike." "You know, the moon controls a lot of things," Albert Wood concluded.

Just as in the past, acceptance of these beliefs varies as much as the position of the sun in the sky. Tom Davis reported: "Now a fella told me the other day he didn't believe in any signs. . . . I says, 'Well, the Bible speaks of signs; "Time to plant, time to pluck." ' And I says, 'I believe in signs.' God give some people that gift, to know these things."

On the other hand, as Vernon Randle jeered, "By the moon? Tah—don't think about no moon. People would tell the old man [his grandfather], 'Why don't you wait, set that thing a certain time of the moon?' He'd tell them he wasn't planting in no moon; he's planting in the ground! The moon wasn't going to grow nothing for him. He didn't think about nothing like that."

Nora Wood, like many other contemporary residents, recognized a generational difference today: "The young people, they don't pay any attention to it, but the older people does." Ron Kellogg agreed that some people still plant by the signs today. In effect, many younger Upstaters respect their elders' wisdom and accept, at least tentatively, these ideas.

BELIEFS ABOUT HUMAN ACTIVITIES

Both sun and moon signs also affect human activities. As described earlier, the association of the sun's signs with particular body parts thus means that operations affecting that part should not be done when the sun is in that sign. Maggie Nameth provided one example: "My father was in the Veteran's Hospital one time in Columbia. And they was going to do some thyroid surgery on him (which at that time . . . the surgeons didn't know a lot about). And I remember he called my mother two or three days before the surgery and told her to check the almanac and see where the sign was." Her husband, Ray, continued: "I know a fella that wanted to have his teeth pulled. And he searched for a dentist that would do it when the signs are right." Disbelievers like Helen Quinnell's father, though, used this belief to their advantage: "So he would wait until the sign was in the wrong place, then he'd get up early in the morning and go to the dentist 'cause there wouldn't be many people down there."

Signs even influence the growth and thus the cutting of human hair. A hairdresser in Clemson, born and raised in the Piedmont, mentioned that two of her present customers, both white women, schedule their appointments around moon phases.

Besides the growth of hair, moon phases might also affect the timing of human births. Maggie Nameth explained: "Now most people (and it still holds true today) most people will tell you that babies are born by the moon. . . . And a lot of nurses that work on maternity floors will swear to you that that's true. Now, not all of them. But during a full moon, I believe, that the maternity floors will be full. . . . And they say it happens so frequently that they have to believe that there might be something to it."

Folk methods to predict the gender of a developing fetus are widely known in many parts of the United States, including the Piedmont. John Morland cited a local Kent woman who said that "some people think that you can tell the sex of a baby before it is born by whether the woman gets bigger in the back than in the front. If she gets bigger in the back it means a boy and if she is bigger in the front a girl." Maggie Nameth noted that the position in which the mother carries the fetus also indicates gender. "If it was up high it was a boy, if it was down low it was a girl," her husband said.

"Uncle Zeke" [pseudonym], a retired farmer in the Anderson area, has the power to predict the birth dates and genders of babies, according to his neighbor, a hairdresser in Clemson. Women from the neighborhood used to consult him before ultrasound, the hairdresser asserted, and Uncle Zeke had accurately predicted both the gender and arrival dates of all her mother's and her sister's babies. During her own pregnancy, then, the hairdresser agreed to consult Uncle Zeke, mostly to humor her mother. He examined her from the front and from the side, rubbed her belly, and predicted (accurately, it turned out) the baby's gender. Then Uncle Zeke consulted a calendar with all the moon's phases on it, and asked the baby's conception date. He then predicted (within two days) the date of birth. Like many other Upstate residents, this woman enjoyed testing such traditional methods but ultimately put much more faith in ultrasound.

Folk Healing and Medicines

TRADITIONAL HEALERS

Beyond the realm of professional medicine and yet linked with it lie the experienced skills, psychological sensitivity, and mystical spirituality of traditional healers. These practitioners include root doctors and religious faith healers; paramedical remedies include various foods and beverages, herbal potions, prayers, protective amulets, and magical spells. Acceptance of the efficacy of such items relates closely to elements in the worldviews of some Upstaters, particularly a belief in the power of evil supernatural forces.

One of the most familiar terms associated with African-American devil beliefs is the "Booger Man." George Jackson explained: "That means when you do wrong or something like that, somebody say the Booger Man going to get you. That was just bad folks, you know. . . . Used to tell little children, 'That's all right—the Booger Man going to get you if you doing something wrong and you shouldn't do.' . . . That'd be the devil, you know." As Linda Baker added, though, the concept was also familiar to whites: "Do you know what boogers are? . . . Boogers are supernatural things that are going to get you. A booger—a haint—a haunt—a booger."

Belief in these evil spirits also necessitated protection from them, and some Upstate residents traditionally have conducted a number of practices to safeguard themselves. Stiles Scruggs, in his WPA interview with Abner

Dinkins of Columbia, mentioned that the black laborer possessed "what he said was a fetish. It looked to me to be little more than a charm or amulet." Likewise, George Burris, an African-American servant in Charlotte, told his WPA interviewer: "This is something I'm wearing around my neck to keep the witches from riding me. I can' tell you what is in it 'cause if I did it wouldn't do me no good."

Another common protective measure for African Americans, W. N. Harriss explained in a WPA article, is "to ward off disease, or bring good luck: Take a ten cent piece [at that time silver], drop it in a quart of water and boil down to a pint. Remove the coin, and while hot bore a hole in it and insert a string. Three days befor [sic] the new moon tie the coin around your ankle—and watch the charm work."

Wilma Masters, to the amazement and amusement of her husband, knew about this charm as well. After obtaining a dime from a stranger, she stated, the believer should "go straight home, take them a rusty nail, and put a hole in it, and let that dime sit in turpentine overnight. . . . I had an aunt do it once. . . . [She] got up next morning, took a cloth that was pretty and white, and patted it dry. She never wiped it, she just patted it. And she took that dime, took two or three strings of white thread, and put it around her leg. [The purpose?] . . . Somebody want to put some kind of spell on you, just block it." Both she and her husband had seen these charms around the necks, arms, and legs of people they knew.

While some illnesses might be owing to punishments from God and thus resolved through faith healing, and while others might be physiological problems cured by means of general folk knowledge or professional medical care, a few might be owing to devilment or bewitchment. These supernatural ailments thus would require the "root doctor," an individual with knowledge of and contact with supernatural forces. "One day you go to a doctor," Wilma Masters cautioned, "and the doctor can't get it off you; you're going to have to find some woman to tell you what was wrong." While malevolent spirits have long antecedents in European folk tradition, similar beings also appear in West African cultures. As with so many other Piedmont beliefs, these two worldviews have generally meshed and blurred borders.

Since, as Mary Gattis observed, professional doctors lived in only a few fortunate communities in earlier generations, most Upstaters were compelled at one time or another to utilize folk medicine and healers for at least some ailments. Richard Sanders explained: "Back in them days they'd know what to do for it, you know? See . . . they go to each other's houses and find out what you're supposed to use for this, and if you know something is good then you try that. That's how they kept their children healthy."

Drawing their powers from opposite-gender transmission (that is, males can only tell females and vice versa), these healers were well known in their communities. Anthropologist Holly Mathews described such practitioners as very similar to psychologists. They would listen to their patients' problems, hear them suggest their own solutions, verify these solutions with the voice of traditional authority, and then prescribe some herbs or charms. "The old black root doctor was the poor man's psychiatrist," an Upstate man confided.

As with virtually all folk knowledge, Leon Berry admitted that "some folks believe in it [root doctors] and some don't." Arthur Masters discussed his general disbelief in root doctors: "A lot of people go to these—" "—root doctors," his wife interjected. "What they call voodoo. They think somebody can sprinkle something across your doorstep or something, and you'll have bad luck and all this stuff. I never did believe in that. There's people believes in it—a lot of the older people. But I don't remember my parents believing in that too much. And I've heard that a lot of people say, somebody's cast a spell on them, and they need to go to somebody to get it off." Wilma Masters felt that "there's still some of them kind of people around now that claim that they can bring you good luck."

With the gradual availability and acceptance of modern medicine, one might have expected the healers and the beliefs that sustain them to have faded. However, belief persists, Holly Mathews professed, owing not to ignorance but to design. As anthropologist Carole Hill argued, people often combine both traditional and modern medicine as "strategies for survival," utilizing whichever method works at the time. Folklorist Karen Baldwin added that folk cures also continue because their artistic, symbolic, and cultural contexts persist as well, including an emphasis placed on the elderly as important sources of information. Mathews, though, concluded that faith in rootwork also stemmed from desperate people searching for some sign of emotional support in a desolate world of poverty. Vernon Randle offered: "You never see no white folks hunting no herbs and roots and things like that. I guess if they had money they'd go to the doctor. But black ain't had no money; they had to go get something. . . . I guess that's where the black learnt all kind of stuff like that."

As with many other aspects of Piedmont folklife, acceptance of the efficacy of traditional healers and medicines integrates several strands of folk traditions. From Africa came the beliefs in root doctors, warding off bewitchment with magical charms and potions. Anglo Americans contributed the Elizabethan concept of humoral balance, while German Americans (and other traditions) may have added hands-on healing. Native Americans passed to both African- and Euro-American groups a well-established ethnobotanical knowledge of medicinal plants. As Holly Mathews added, the common bond of Christianity provided the syncretic blend of all these traditions with a unifying theological explanation and justification. Today, both African and Anglo Americans share many beliefs and practices involving folk healing, but they appear to be more prominent among the former group.

TRADITIONAL CURING PRACTICES

Folk healing today incorporates a complex web of varied traditions and practices. For some, cures may be accomplished by root doctors utilizing African-derived concepts about bewitchment. Other Upstate residents, relegating those ideas to "superstition," firmly believe in the God-given powers of certain individuals to stop blood or to heal burns. Still other residents relegate all folk cures to superstition but fervently accept healing during religious ceremonies, done by God through the medium of humans. Virtually all Upstaters simultaneously utilize, to varying degrees, the Western, technologically based health care system. Folk cures have not been excised by modern medicine; they operate alongside it as parallel beliefs.

To stop bleeding, some Upstate residents rely on a well-known American folk method known from both African- and Anglo-American tradition. The WPA writer Mary Hicks, for example, recorded this cure from North Carolina blacks: "To stop a deep wound from bleeding or a hemmorrhage read the Lord's prayer, or Ezekiel [16:6] which goes: 'And when I passed by thee and saw thee poluted [sic] in thine own blood, I said unto thee, live.'" However, Tom Davis, an Anglo American, was also quite familiar with the remedy: "And my daddy could stop blood, too. . . . This Miss Hall was a neighbor of ours. And I remember my nose bleeding one time; it just kept a-bleeding and a-bleeding and a-bleeding. . . . I got weak, and they had to call Miss Hall. And she stopped that blood. . . . She was saying whatever she said to herself. And the blood stopped."

Closely related to the mystical ability to stop blood is the power to "talk out fire," that is, the ability to take the pain out of a burn. The belief has been widely reported from folk groups in the United States, including in the Southeast and the Piedmont. According to a WPA writer, a German-American healer from Lexington County, South Carolina, cured burns on a patient's hands "by brushing the hands three times and repeating the words: 'I saw three angles [sic] coming from the West, two had fire and one had frost; go out fire, and come in frost.'" Mary Hicks reported the same cure with a different prayer from "Negroes" in her WPA paper: "'Bread, eat not, water, drink not. In the name of Jesus Christ.' The fire will leave at once."

Many contemporary Upstate residents are familiar with the practice.

During one interview, Arthur Masters claimed to know little of such healing; his wife, though, had actually been cured in this way. She still had a reddish-purple spot on her arm, otherwise unscarred, which she displayed. As a child, Wilma Masters continued, she had been badly burned "down to the bone." Her aunt, who had "a gift from God," immediately brought her mouth down to the area and mumbled some inaudible words three times over the burn—once at the side, once in the middle, and once on the other side. Almost immediately, Mrs. Masters stated, the pain left. "She had to talk it out twice a day to get that to heal back up," which it eventually did, she continued. "It don't give me no trouble now," she observed.

Vernon Randle, like many other Piedmont residents, maintained his doubts about this ability. Robert Chambers, however, weighed his modern skepticism and religious faith against his traditional beliefs: "To this day, I know white people right today that can talk out, or speak out fires, for a burn . . . and take off warts. . . . It's connected with certain pieces of Scripture in the Bible. . . . And these are not people that are fringe . . . this is people that are well based. . . . There is a thin line—it works sometimes, it's connected with Scripture, and yet it has the ring of black magic."

TRADITIONAL HEALING MATERIALS

In addition to scientific pharmaceuticals, traditional Upstate folk medicine cabinets contained two additional resources: wild plants and manufactured items. The latter materials included patent medicines, alcohol (such as whiskey), and commercial products. These materials are (or were) then frequently combined with wild resources such as "ginseng and snake-root," which M. F. Maury listed as marketable forest products in the late nineteenth century. Typifying this traditional amalgamation of natural and manufactured substances is Rosa Kanipe's description of a well-stocked medicine cabinet from her childhood in North Carolina: "In this cabinet was castor oil, salts, liniment, a bottle of good whiskey for snake bites, cough medicine made from cherry bark and whiskey and sugar, [and] a tonic made from Sampson's snake root."

As Ethel Harmon told Anne Kimzey, " 'Our drugstore back then was in the backyard.' " An elderly man once told Ralph Patrick and John Morland, "There's something in the woods good for everything that ails you." Vernon Randle, knowledgeable about many natural cures, elaborated: "The old folks used to take us out in the woods, . . . hunting them [plants]. . . . My great-granddaddy—now he knowed every bush and every thing that could be mentioned of. . . . I learned it. I learnt what black snake root was, ratvein, . . . physic grass, and all that. . . . Them old folks back then, shoo—didn't go to no doctor. Go somewhere in the woods, hunting some kind of old weed or old bush or something or other to get something off it. . . . Course it would help them, though—yeah, it would help."

Folk medicines, whether from store or forest, drew upon the interwoven traditions of blacks, whites, and Native Americans and utilized a wide range of botanical materials. Plants provided leaves, roots, bark, and berries for teas, purgatives, and various other types of medicines but often required processing methods that incorporated physical as well as mystical cleansing. Today this knowledge is largely restricted to elderly or rural residents, but some Piedmonters still collect the traditional plants and produce the medicines. A few utilize them.

Teas were probably the most common form of folk medicines. Anna Pearsall, in her WPA interview, remembered "many of the old people used to use root herbs, barks, and leaves for making hot teas to cure certain ailments." Periodically, young Upstaters recalled receiving certain types of tonics, particularly in the spring, to assist in digestion or to "purify the blood." Eula Durham remembered such an instance with distaste: "Lord, my daddy used to, every spring he'd make every one of us take a big dose of black drop[sic]. . . . It's a yellow powdered medicine. Then you put it in water and drank it, said it purified your blood. . . . One day he'd give us, and I took mine, I told him, 'I've got to get outdoors to drink mine.' And I poured mine out, you know. And he caught me. So he made me take a double dose—like to kill me."

Another tea, also a purgative, came from a substance called "physic grass." Arthur Masters's father prepared it: "And you could pull that up and boil it in water . . . and they would drink it. . . . When he boiled it, I think he put a little sugar in it. . . . Served the same purpose as a laxative." Vernon Randle concurred: "That stuff—that's made to work you. And instead of taking oil, or salts, or something or other, make you some physic grass tea. Boy, you'd have to hurry up and go, too! Whew! I never did like all such stuff as that, but I had to take it."

Other teas included the much better tasting sassafras tea, reported by Ethel Hilliard as well as Jason Lambert. In fact, Mr. Lambert continued, a friend brought him some sassafras tea this spring, and sometimes "you can find it in the store." Tom Davis remembered: "If you had kidney trouble or something, they'd make a tea with that ratsvein. . . . It was a little green, notchylike plant, it just growed real low to the ground. And it had . . . a little, like a purple reddish-like marking in the leaves." Vernon Randle's "daddy-in-law" utilized this plant extensively: "That all he studied about—ratvein. He'd go out in the woods and here he come with a armload of that old stuff. . . . Lay that stuff up and let it dry, boil it and make him a tea out of it. And drink that old stuff. Tell me, 'Don't you want some of this?' 'Man, ain't nothing matter with my kidneys!' "

Another very frequently mentioned resource was black snake root. Nora Wood described its use: "I can remember my grandmother used to dig what she called black snake root and yellow root out of the woods. And she'd put that on [the stove] with a certain amount of water and cook it, you know, get the juice out of it . . . and make a salve out of it. And when she got it done it would look like just clear petroleum jelly—Vaseline." Vernon Randle created different medicines from the same plant: "Black snake root—they say that was good for the fever. Now that stuff was bitter—great goodness! But [if] you'd get sick you had to take it." Black snake root also made a tea, Mr. Randle recalled.

The material called "yellow root," Wilma Masters stated, "look like a little old hickory, but the root is yellow." Mr. Randle added: "Take them, put them in water. It turn the water yellow. You drink off of it, they say it's good for your kidneys. . . . I don't know if it is or not now, but that what *they* said. But we had to drink it." Earlier in our conversation, Mr. Randle offered other uses for yellow root: "They make out like it's good for high blood, and rheumatism, and I don't know. . . . They crazy about that yellow root though." Yellow root, Wilma Masters informed me, may still be purchased at the Anderson Jockey Lot; I have seen some vendors selling it.

Several informants also mentioned a plant material they called "boar hog root." Vernon Randle described it as "just little old long, stringy roots; they say you chew that." A friend of his who had purchased some at the Anderson Jockey Lot told Mr. Randle that it would "make you want women." "I don't know whether that's true or not," Mr. Randle concluded. "I never did fool around with nothing like that."

MIDWIVES

Another extremely valuable source of traditional medical care came from community midwives, who were often (but not always) African Americans. As described by Holly Mathews, a woman would "engage" a midwife early in her pregnancy; the midwife would then instruct her in all aspects of prenatal care. At the birth, the midwife would either assist the doctor or deliver the baby herself and would then remain with the new mother for a period of time to help with its care or to maintain the household. Midwives drew their calling from spiritual authority and an association with an older female relative or respected community leader, coupled with a lengthy period of tightly regulated apprenticeship. For these reasons, both whites and blacks deeply respected the personal, professional, and spiritual commitment of these women.

Midwives represent another example of the intricate interconnections between African- and Anglo-American traditions and peoples. Unwelcome to eat at white tables as social equals, black midwives nevertheless directly assisted in the birth of numerous white infants, generation after generation. Maxine Williams's aunt, a midwife, was active in the upper Piedmont into the 1940s: "And she delivered . . . more babies than the doctors did, back then, because people didn't go to hospitals. They delivered rich and poor, black and white. . . . [Today, she's] got babies scattered all over Oconee County." Alice Gassoway's aunt learned midwifery by "doing it every day along with the doctor." Ida Johnson worked as a midwife after having received some medical training as a nurse. Often assisting doctors, she commented, "I'd do the work, and he'd get the pay."

All of Albertha Gilchrist's children had been born with midwife assistance, but she added that these women have largely disappeared today. Mathews offered several reasons. Owing largely to the prejudices, greed, and elitist attitudes of professional obstetricians and gynecologists, midwifery began to fade from the Carolinas after World War II. Concomitantly, the rising cost of prenatal and postnatal care increasingly excluded many in the lower classes from essential medical services—precisely those who had most often been helped in the past by midwives. Infant mortality has consequently risen drastically in the Carolinas. As professional medicine now seeks more cost-efficient means to increase care and decrease mortality rates, Mathews warned that restoring midwives "will be difficult because the tradition has been broken."

Conclusion

Folk medicines, weather prognostications, and bewitchment have a long history in the Piedmont. Like many other aspects of Carolina folklife, this knowledge consists of varied elements of black, white, and Native American traditions, blended together and reinforced further with the authority of Christianity. Grandparents passed their knowledge on to their descendants, who in more recent generations have developed a balance between modern and traditional ideas. While some older strands of traditional knowledge may have faded, others persist.

CHAPTER 8

Social Gatherings and Activities

African- and Anglo-American traditions would remain separate if not for social interaction, for it links beliefs and provides a context for their use and understanding. Social activities like holiday celebrations and family reunions offer appropriate contexts for the reinforcement of cultural values. Other practices, like neighborly visiting and Sunday dinners, connect generations to traditional values and integrate regional groups. As with other aspects of Piedmont folklife, these social activities have changed through time, but they continue to offer public and private situations in which Upstate values and beliefs are reinforced or redefined.

Informal Celebrations

SUNDAY DINNER

The foundation of all other family-related activities is Sunday afternoon dinner at an older relative's home. "You looked forward to Sunday dinner more than you did any other day of the week," Patricia Vaughn recalled. Willimon and Cabell explained why: "Sunday dinner in the South . . . was an institution, a weekly family reunion with a traditional politesse equal to that of a summit meeting. It never occurred to you not to go to your grandmother's if you lived within riding, walking, or shouting distance. Nobody told you where to sit at dinner; the order was predestined long ago and you followed it. . . . Everyone finally assembled after dinner on the wrap-around front porch. . . . Sunday dinner established the rules when you'd passed from childhood to adulthood, passed on family stories, entertained you, and introduced you to unbelievable culinary delights."

As if to emphasize further the vital link between food and family, John Morland observed that in Kent, neighbors rarely invited each other over for meals, but relatives always did. This allowed families to intensify their history as it was shared and reinforced, Maggie Nameth related: "You'd hear a lot of family stories when you were sitting around talking. . . . And you learned a lot about your family, good and bad, that never was printed but was just passed along, by word of mouth."

These Sunday visits followed a well-established protocol dictating the social relationships between genders and age categories. As befitting proper southern attitudes toward ladies, the genders never mixed during these visits, as Helen Quinnell noted: "Oh, Lord, no! . . . Weather permitting, the men sat out on the porch and the women sat in the living room." Typically, children could eat only after all the other adults; this often created acute food shortages, as Arthur Masters remembered: "The best part would be picked over when they got to eat." His wife added, "They'd get the chicken neck and feet!" With the arrival of special guests such as the preacher, this meant more appropriate table manners and less available food. We children "always had to stay back till he got through eating," an African-American woman grumbled. At times it "looked like he was going to eat up everything!"

Several informants felt that Sunday dinners no longer had the ceremonial importance that they once held because change had come imperceptibly. Gladys Taylor knew of a neighbor lady who used to have almost twenty family members over for Sunday dinner; when her daughter died, the tradition transformed: "All of a sudden we realized that they were going out to eat on Sunday. . . . Those things are just past, and you don't realize what's happening. All of a sudden you don't do it any more."

On the other hand, many area residents still try to gather with relatives several times a month. After Sunday services, many Upstate families return home to a meal with a smaller and more easily managed circle of relatives than in previous generations. Other families, still dressed from church, might eat out in local restaurants, bustling with after-church crowds on Sunday afternoons. Robert Chambers and his family "go out for chicken, either Kentucky Fried or Hardees, once in a while, on Sunday afternoons."

Sunday dinners simultaneously connect several fundamental Upstate traditions and behaviors. These gatherings allow the passing on of family stories as well as the regular consolidation of kin, thus reinforcing the southern value of family solidarity. Foods and food preparation strengthen earlier practices while providing a comfortable forum for experimentation to create new ones. Finally, such dinners, often sandwiched between morning and evening church services, tie generations of family members to religious values as well.

FAMILY REUNIONS

Besides the informal and relatively frequent Sunday dinners, families in the Upstate also congregate on more formal occasions as well. Family reunions, held in past generations during "lay-by time" in midsummer, often drew as many as two hundred people. Reflecting the social significance of the event, the family reunion traditionally followed a precise script.

The location and date of the reunion remained annually consistent. "Generally, the host is the member of the family still living in the old ancestral home. The house, itself, more rigidly speaking, is host," Louise Jones DuBose wrote. Sometimes, James Edwards added, the family church might be the customary location, but the timing of the event remained the same from year to year. Each family established a certain weekend for the event and then never wavered.

The sequence of events never varied either. On picnic tables (often improvised from pine boards and saw horses) under shade trees, James Edwards explained, "the women usually always get the food together and everything, and they'd line it up on the tables so that the vegetables'd be in a certain place." "Even houses where you could have eaten on the inside, for some reason at family reunions you put that food on the outside, eat it out there," Maggie Nameth noticed. Meanwhile, James Edwards continued, "most of the men just stand around talking" while the children "start a ball game or a horseshoe game, or they'd shoot marbles." "Usually it would last from maybe one o'clock to about five o'clock; some of them may be all-day affairs," Mr. Edwards concluded. As sated feasters nodded off in the late afternoon, Louise Jones DuBose rhapsodized in her WPA essay, "there is a feeling of peace and plenty, of security in tradition."

The sharing of recipes and the annual reappearance of special food items also served to maintain family ties, Mr. Edwards continued: "I remember, you know, if you went through and you got a certain thing that you thought it was awful good, a lot of times you'd just try to find out who made it. . . . There was a lot of comparisons through the years. People have different recipes. People in the family knew about them and they'd always look forward to it." Maggie Nameth added that women took pride in the fact that family members savored their devotion to tradition: "Each woman would have certain foods that she would bring every time—certain things that she cooked well, or somebody said, 'That's real good.' "

As Gladys Taylor observed, people still serve many traditional foods at family reunions " 'cause we've got enough of our older people who require that kind of food." Her sister, for example, always makes "macaroni pie." "So they're in touch with their past enough to know what good food is and how to fix it and everything," Ms. Taylor continued, "so they still do that."

A typical family reunion (Photo by John M. Coggeshall)

In fact, she noted proudly, the generation behind her also maintains the tradition: "They are determined that it won't fail."

The connection between generations persists in the Upstate, in many ways unchanged. Regional newspapers carry announcements of family reunions throughout the summer and early fall, always including the location, a telephone number to call for more information, and the request to bring a "covered dish to share." One such announcement advertised the annual Quinnell Family Reunion.

The gathering was held at the home of a relative on several hundred acres, part of the ancestral "home place" on the outskirts of Hammondville. In the backyard, under the shade of large oak trees and an awning were placed seven picnic tables, a long row of food tables, and dozens of folding aluminum chairs. The crowd only numbered about fifty, partly because this was the branch of the family that drank, one member explained, although this seems to be a typical crowd size for Upstate reunions.

The celebration began about one in the afternoon, and shortly afterwards everyone lined up to fill their plates with barbecued meats and other typical foods (see chapter 11). Several adult relatives had begun cooking on a homemade grill the evening before. One of the cooks mentioned that in recent times fewer children attended because family size had decreased since his youth. Also, he added, kids today eat first, followed by the adults; the opposite of what he remembered when he was young.

After eating their fill, the adults congregated in the chairs or around the tables to talk in small groups while most of the children went swimming in an aboveground pool. Young adults drifted away first, after paying their respects to the hostess and the older members of the family. Guests eventually formed a tight cluster around an old man telling stories about his eccentric father. The man's nephews supplemented his tales with additional anecdotes. Spouses and children listened and laughed for over an hour in the mid-June afternoon. By about 5:30 the exhausted hostess began cleaning up in earnest, and the remaining feasters reluctantly dispersed.

Family reunions remain popular and powerful because these ceremonies continue to reinforce significant aspects of Upstate value systems. The location of the reunion, whether country church or "home place," provides a symbolic center to which families are pulled, reinforcing and renewing kin ties. The setting also offers a place for families to reenact stories that in fact may have originally occurred at the "home place" stage. Recipes form another tie to the past, filling the senses with sights, smells, and tastes of earlier times. Simultaneously, though, food traditions offer the possibility of change, allowing for the ongoing and necessary envelopment into the family of younger generations and in-laws. During family reunions, old values are solidified and new traditions become established; the strength of the family as a Piedmont institution is renewed.

INFORMAL VISITING

Besides the socializing among families on Sunday afternoons, friends and family often visit informally to enjoy the ensuing conversations. This traditional form of entertainment relates directly to the perceived slower pace of life in the Upstate, where neighbors and friends (as well as family) have more time to stop and talk, renewing old friendships and creating new ones. Farm journals from the nineteenth century record numerous examples of visiting and overnight stays between families. Butchering and food processing activities, Ron Kellogg noted, also drew crowds: "It became a kind of a community affair, 'cause several people come to help you. People used to visit each other a whole lot more because, no telephones, you know. You'd get together at somebody's house, sit back and talk."

In mill towns, too, David Hawkins recalled that families formerly took the time to visit, often creating "a community, a togetherness feeling, much more than it is now. Everybody knew each other. People gathered up after people got off of work at night, sit in straight cane-back chairs . . . and talk, and just had a good time." In her WPA interview in 1938, Colie Craft, a mill worker in Columbia, mentioned that her mother was teased quite a bit for spending all her time visiting neighbors; her mother replied: "I tell 'em I've worked in the field since I knowed how to get out there, and I think I ought to have some rest now."

Information passed easily throughout the villages. Ray Nameth recalled that groups of men and boys would gather down by the river to talk over important events while the women would "be gossiping about something" somewhere else. His wife then interjected: "As if that wasn't gossip they were doing down there!" The consequence of this community intimacy, David Hawkins joked, was that "this family could just about tell you what that next family next door ate every day or something like that."

"Everybody knew everybody on this street," Laura Kirkpatrick remembered about her black neighborhood in Charlotte. Arthur Masters elaborated: "We'd have little local gatherings in the area. . . . In fact, back then, occasionally you'd go out to a relative's house and eat there. . . . And they would put on a big spread, you know, cook a lot of food. . . . Just talk . . . mainly that was it. The grown people would do that. The kids would just get out and run around and play. . . . Most of the time, when the grownups would stay in a big conversation, then the children was not to be there in with that conversation. They'd tell you to go out and play or something."

In the towns, farmers congregated on Saturday afternoons, mingling with townspeople and mill workers according to precise but unwritten social rules that maintained appropriate divisions between rich and poor, mill and town, male and female, and black and white. Women and children frequented the shops and movie theaters, congregating to discuss the week's events. Meanwhile, men typically visited other stores or gathered in the shade of trees to talk politics or crops.

After church on Sunday or after club meetings, Ralph Patrick related, Kent's elites did not disperse immediately. Instead, all were expected to "stand around and talk for awhile." Otherwise they would be considered unfriendly. Such gatherings helped dispense vital commercial and political information; these conversations spread town gossip as well, which helped maintain community ties and community standards of etiquette. Those listening and commenting quickly learned what the "blue bloods" considered to be appropriate and inappropriate behaviors.

The sum of all these visitations, informants agreed, functioned to solidify neighbors and families and to reinforce social ties. Mary Gattis explained: "You know, I really think . . . families were much happier then [before World War II] than they are now. I do. You have everything in the world . . . but people were closer together then because they didn't have all these worldly things. . . . You didn't have much, but you had a lot of love. And you had time to give it." James Edwards concurred: "You know, you worked in the fields together, you come home together, you eat together. During winter times you sit around the fireplace or around the stove same time. You had a lot more, I guess, family cohesiveness than you have now." As several informants have noted, the leisure to visit began to disappear in part because of the emergence of new forms of recreation in American culture. One of these forces was television, which steadfastly eroded the "quality time" families had formerly spent telling stories or playing music. Increasingly, as families focused more on the television and less on the porch or hearth for entertainment, family closeness and neighborly friendliness dissolved into a national cultural homogeneity.

Another trend dissolving the strong ties binding neighbors through visiting was the greater distance people lived from each other, coupled with the improvements in roads and automobile transportation. School consolidation brought in children from outlying rural districts and subsequently required parents to struggle to sustain their children's social networks. The increased distance between homes (when compared to those between mill houses) also has mitigated against close, neighborly ties.

Another erosional force on visiting, Arthur Masters believed, has been the increasing pace of life: "Seems like you just stay busier now. There's always something to do, or it's dark, you take a bath, watch TV, time to go to bed, time to go to work. . . . Life's probably just a little faster now than it used to be. I think back in the olden days, everybody moved at maybe a slower pace or something." "People used to call on their neighbors," Lucy Wallace sighed. "Now they're not there for you to call on."

Despite the apparently overwhelming forces of television, transportation, and time, John Edmunds wrote, "social affinity [still] plays a large and important role in the life of people of all strata" even today. Families and friends still gather in homes, Roy Elrod explained: "A bunch of people . . . come here and pile up here about fifteen or twenty at a time, talk and tell jokes, and tales—just have a huge time around here." In fact, he continued, neighbors usually stay until ten o'clock at night, nearly every day. In Kent's black community one evening, I noticed many African-American families strolling through the neighborhood while others called to them from their porches. Ethel Harmon admitted to Anne Kimzey that she still gets her news from "the barbershop and the beautyshop." In one Hammondville restaurant, the owner described the daily gatherings of locals as "just like a family."

INFORMAL SOCIAL ASSISTANCE

An additional outcome of all this visiting was the strengthening of the web of social obligations that bound neighbor to neighbor during times of personal crises, reflecting the deeply rooted values of southern hospitality as well as family closeness. Among the black families of Lancaster, "people felt an obligation to help each other," John Arnold observed. In Laura Kirkpatrick's community, too, neighbors would take food to the sick or clean their house. The same was true in white communities, Tom Davis added: "Neighbors was good back then, about sharing with one another. . . . If there was sickness in the house, there's always somebody ready to help. And if the breadwinner was sick, the neighbors seen to it that they got food."

Mutual cooperation was to be expected in mill villages, Maggie Nameth noted: "In fact, in a lot of serious illness, you depended on other women from the general neighborhood to help out—and they did. . . . I mean, there was a kind of a close-knit feeling that, they didn't let anybody go lacking in something like that." Mrs. Nameth even described a situation where a newcomer to Hammondville had died; since no one in town knew the man, no one could serve as pallbearers. The school principal was asked to send six teenagers home to change into their Sunday clothes so they could serve.

Among farmers, Vernon Randle recalled, one found the same spirit of neighborly assistance: "Somebody'd be . . . getting behind in the farm, we'd go there and work two or three days, you know, to help them out of it. . . . And wouldn't charge nothing! Just helping one another. . . . And if they got in trouble . . . with the land, you know, grassy or something or other, they'd help one another. . . . Yeah, they good about helping one another."

Area residents differ as to whether this tradition holds today. Laura Kirkpatrick and Wilma Masters, for example, believed that this neighborly assistance had declined, while others acknowledged that they still do much the same type of exchanges with their neighbors as done in the past. Tom Davis and his wife trade extra vegetables from their garden, while Rosemary Calder, a single woman, appreciates her neighbors' concern about her health: "Neighbors would come in if you were sick, help out; they still do. Those that live around, and they know you're sick, come see if they can help you out." "People still take food," Patricia Vaughn observed, "but it's not prepared in their kitchen." Today, she noted, most well-wishers buy ready-made food trays from supermarket delis.

WAKES AND FUNERALS

Death, whenever and wherever it occurs, requires strong bonds of neighborly and familial assistance for the bereaved. In earlier generations, wakes and funerals fulfilled several significant social functions for both whites

and blacks: they strengthened neighborhood ties; they linked families together and reinforced kin networks; and they intensified fundamental Upstate values. Funeral customs also demonstrated the complex interweaving
of folk traditions between African and Anglo Americans. While both
groups recognized practices unique to each, they also perceived numerous
overlaps as well. Not surprisingly, these common bonds reflect the shared
values of the folk groups of the Piedmont.

Prior to professionalization, funeral preparation would often be done at
home. The body would be cleaned and dressed by the deceased's relatives,
and then, Tom Davis continued, the body would be laid out "on what they
called a 'cooling board' "—a long, narrow wooden board—in order "to let
their body cool off." Around the deceased would gather neighbors and
friends and family, Mr. Davis recalled, to "set up" with the departed. As
informants confessed, wakes were also good chances to socialize.

Among the elites of Kent, Ralph Patrick observed, "It is customary for
the neighbors to send food to the bereaved home, and to come over and
take the burden of household duties off the family. . . . But an alternate
pattern that is followed by some of the well-to-do is the sending of the
[black] maid to do the work that would have been performed by the woman
herself."

In Kent's mill village, John Morland described an all-night wake for a
resident who had died. As the larger kin network gathered, they segregated
into same-gender and same-age groups. The men discussed farming and
mill work and wondered how many relatives would appear. The women
talked about various operations and passed around their infants. As with
Kent elites, the families had all brought food. After eating and socializing,
the families left the next morning for the church funeral service.

The lack of embalming created some special challenges. Maxine Williams explained that the weather dictated the length of the wake: in cold
weather "you could keep them out pretty good; [otherwise] . . . you had to
bury them hurriedly." Other problems were more serious. Ron Kellogg
had heard "some powerful stories" about individuals awakening from a
"trance" on their way to the cemetery, pounding desperately against the
sides of the casket to let the funeral party know that they were still alive.

As Mary Gattis and Helen Howard noted, these ostensibly solemn occasions were also potential times for ribald humor and practical jokes. Ms.
Gattis recalled a wake she had attended as a younger woman. Everyone was
sitting out on the spacious front porch when a relative snuck off somewhere
and got a white sheet. Suddenly this specter appeared around the side of
the house, "and I wish you'd a-seen people jumping off that porch!" she
laughed.

While African-American funerals and wakes closely paralleled Anglo-

American ceremonies, both white and black observers detected some variations as well. John M. Vlach argued that African Americans traditionally took elaborate care in the planning and preparation of a funeral because of the old African attitude that the deceased "can continue to affect the lives of their families and friends."

Two particular funerary customs existed in the Upstate, reported by both Anglo and African Americans. Lucy Cobb cited them in her WPA essay: "When a rural Negro dies . . . all clocks and watches are stopped and mirrors are draped." The origin of these traditions, however, remains questionable. While many white informants believed these ideas stemmed from black traditions, few contemporary African Americans knew of the beliefs. Newbell Puckett, in his study of African-American folklore in the South, ultimately concluded that both beliefs arose from English origins.

Today, professional embalming has replaced cooling boards attended by relatives and kin; and undertakers and clergy now prepare the deceased and conduct the ceremonies of interment. Social lives have also changed, as Helen Quinnell noted: "People don't go to funerals like they used to. And I think basically, it was, they didn't have anything else to do. . . . Whether we admitted it or not, it was a gathering. Nowadays people just don't have to do that to see other people, or don't have time to do that. . . . So it's not as big a social deal as it used to be."

Still, older traditions persist among both whites and blacks. For example, Minnie Dunn criticized the recent burial of a white friend in Charlotte as having occurred too soon after the death; not enough of her extensive network of friends and relatives had been notified because of the ceremony's rapidity. Especially in small towns, Tom Davis observed, churches and neighbors still provide food and company for the relatives of the deceased, "in typically Southern fashion," the *Greenville News* reported. Another woman explained: "We still do that *all* the time—and this is the black community as well as the white. When somebody dies, you feel obligated to take something over to the family. When we lost our daddy, we had stuff that lasted us six months, so much was brought over by nice neighbors, up and down the street. . . . It's such a nice tradition."

PARTIES AND FOLK MUSICIANS

In previous times, informal social gatherings proved to be extremely popular for both young and old, often providing rural communities with their primary source of entertainment. Reflecting on the joys of the past, Gladys Taylor remarked, "I can't imagine, thinking about it now, how simple those times were. You'd just get together, and anybody who wanted to could dance. And we always had somebody who could play the piano and

somebody who could sing. And that's all it took to entertain people. . . .
We were just as happy as we could be to get all of us gather together at a
friend's house and just talk. . . . It didn't take a whole lot to entertain us in
those days."

Musicians had a different attitude toward performing, James Putnam
explained: "Most of the guitar players back then, they didn't play like the
people play now, you know. All the guitar players back then, they would
mostly go out and play for fish frys and things like that. And when they'd
play for fish frys, they done it for fun, to see who could outdo each other."

Various musical instruments provided the accompaniment for these parties, depending upon the interests of the crowd and the skills of the neighborhood. Like so many other elements of Piedmont folklife, the origins of
musical instruments and the styles of performing may be traced to different
continents. Musicologist William Barlow, for example, argued that both
the banjo and the "kora playing style" arose among the Wolof and Man-
dingo groups in West Africa. This style, of picking the melody high on the
neck while strumming with the thumb, later influenced the region's blues
guitarists.

Instruments changed through time, as groups exchanged ideas and copied popular performers. Robert Chambers described the process as a
"blending, rolling over." Back in the time of slavery, Leon Berry noted,
guitars were unknown to the slaves; only banjos and fiddles. Skilled performers, Berry continued, "could play them things so it would make your
hair rise on your head." James Putnam, too, remembered that five-string
banjos were more popular in his youth. Guitars appeared more frequently
by the 1930s. One well-known local band included a cowbell and wash-
board as well as a guitar. "We even learned how to take an old comb, a
straight comb that what you'd comb your head with, like this here, and put
paper around it and make music," James Putnam recalled. For her home
entertainment, one Anglo American preferred "string music" or "country
music," which included the mandolin as well as some of the other instruments described above.

Musicians learned their skills from various sources. For example, Roy
Elrod commented that "my daddy learnt me how to play when I was about
thirteen years old, behind him, with a fiddle. . . . And I been playing ever
since, I guess." Like many other folk musicians, he learned his repertoire
by listening to the radio and from hearing others sing the songs.

The musicians created parties, and parties encouraged musicians, James
Putnam continued: "And some would bring their violins, and some would
bring five-string banjos, and some would bring whatever they could play.
If they could dance, or if they could play a guitar, or juice harp, or whatever
it might be, they'd bring that. And join in with the rest of them playing."

FOLK DANCING

While both blacks and whites enjoyed these impromptu parties, they tended to differ somewhat in their traditional dances and steps. Whites usually preferred square dances, in part because "round" dances by couples were forbidden to some, as Longstreet Gantt noted in his WPA interview. Some blacks, though, learned how to call these steps. As James Putnam explained, a subtle interchange of styles ensued: "Most of the people back then, you know, there wasn't too many Black people knowed about how to call a set. . . . But where they learned it from, they learned it from . . . the White people." Leon Berry even knew someone who could "call figures . . . just like a preacher standing up in a pulpit."

At other times, in rural areas, neighbors simply enjoyed each others' company, as Martha Block related: "We used to have square dances around in the community, at everybody's house. Well, somebody'd just decide, 'Let's have a dance tonight.' Then ask somebody, 'Is it all right to come to your house to dance?' . . . And we had two young boys—one could pick a guitar and one picked a banjo. And then we had another fella in the community that picked a banjo. . . . So we had a good band. . . . I started square dancing when I was about nine years old. . . . We always went with daddy to the square dances."

Square dancing displayed a great deal of variability in its performance, as described by Mary Hicks: "Some callers rhyme the figures, some sing them chanting continually, others call occasionally and give only simple directions. A band of three or four pieces, usually consisting of a guitar, banjo, violin and harmonica, furnishes the music. Songs include such old favorites as 'Turkey in the Straw,' 'Old Joe Clark,' and 'Seeing Nellie Home' as well as modern tunes. . . . A resourceful caller adds steps to the figures which will make them longer and often makes a new figure."

While improvisation and informality may have infiltrated traditional forms of Anglo-American dancing, these features characterized various forms of African-American dance. For example, James Putnam described the social context where black dancing would usually occur: "A bunch of people would be sitting around . . . and somebody'd say, 'I'll bet you I can beat you buckin'.' Somebody says, 'Oh, no you can't.' 'Get out there now.' And somebody had to pat, you know, and they could find somebody that could pat real good, and they'd choose that person, you know, to pat." In a photograph from Greene County, Georgia in the early 1940s, Jack Delano depicted a group of chain gang prisoners, all black, dressed in broad striped clothes, lounging around their barracks at night. In the photo, one inmate dances out some clogging-like steps while two others rest on the edge of a bed, one playing a guitar and the other clapping. "And when you do some kind of buck dance to go along with the music, you called every bit of it together; it's called, 'Hoosey Hot Shot,' they called it," James Putnam explained.

Putnam listed the "Charleston, and slow drag, and buck dance, and . . . tap dance" as popular among African Americans. In addition to these, Mr. Putnam included "trucking," with its own music, "slow drag" dances, and the "rubber leg" and "camel walk." For these latter two, one's legs did the dances; the rhythm of the music assisted the dancer. For the "Frog Dance" and "Rabbit Dance," the stances became more complicated; one crouches on all fours and dances. For the "Frog Dance," "you turn around the other way." Each dance "had a certain kind of music to do it with," Mr. Putnam added.

On tape, James Putnam tapped out the rhythm of another dance: "Now there's another way . . . we used to call, back then they called it 'hambone': Hambone, hambone, where ye been?/Been around the bone and I'm going again./Hambone, hambone, what ye taste like?" (Barely audible, the interviewer asked him to "keep going," but unfortunately he did not continue.)

FOLK MUSIC

Enlivening the parties and dances throughout the Upstate would be both popular tunes as well as folk songs. As many informants have suggested, the elements of folklife that constitute the Piedmont's musical heritage are as interwoven as many other aspects. Charles Joyner argued that black South Carolinians tended to retain the style of African music while adopting the forms of European traditions. Whites, on the other hand, tended to replace British types of ornamentation with "glissandi, syncopation, and quarter tones, all deriving from African influence." Through this acculturative process emerged "a new folk music, a folk music neither African nor European, but partaking of elements of both," Joyner explained.

James Putnam, an African American born on a farm near Anderson in 1921 and later raised in Charlotte, epitomized this cross-fertilization of styles. He described his music as having been influenced by his parents and community activities. Simultaneously, like thousands of other Piedmonters, he listened to Anglo-American songs on the radio, adding his own interpretations: "Most of these people sit down and listen to music, . . . and how somebody else did it on a record or something like that; they picked it up and turned it around their way."

On the other hand, Maxine Williams (an Upstate African-American woman), preferred to keep white and black singing separate: "We were *born* to sing. And those slaves wrote those [spirituals]. . . . Their tribulations made them be composers of some of the most beautiful poetry, and carried out in song, that's ever been written. . . . When y'all [whites] went to try and sing like us, and we went to try and sing like [you], and you're making a mess of it."

Some musical traditions did remain somewhat distinct. Early African-American Piedmont blues, William Barlow suggested, evolved from the racism and segregation inherent in cotton mill labor and tenant farm work and continued along a separate path from the European derived "Appalachian tradition" into the twentieth century. The North Carolina state guidebook described these two different traditions: "A kind of music, commonly known as 'hillbilly' or string band music, is popular in most small agricultural and mill villages. Songs and instrumental selections, both old and new, are rendered in a monotonous style, varying but little in harmonization. . . . The [Negro] work song is heard often, for almost any group working by hand uses rhythmic singing to speed the task and improvises to fit the occasion."

Ralph Patrick and John Morland characterized black music as most often expressed in "the church and the tavern. . . . Both have heavy overtones of emotion and rhythm and the lyrics of songs in both places tend to be symbolically appropriate or meaningful; both have a high escapist content and reflect abandon to some degree."

By the early twentieth century, the African-American musical tradition had taken a particular shape, musicologist Bruce Bastin argued, in part created by "an environment . . . that lacks, by its very easy-going, day-to-day existence, the pace and tension of the claustrophobic, densely-packed cities. The blues of the region has a cohesive whole and yet reflects varying aspects of smaller sub-regions. . . . One may talk of the 'Virginia' sound of a John Jackson, or the 'Carolina' sound of a Blind Boy Fuller." William Barlow identified two additional areas in the Piedmont with distinctive blues styles: the Georgia Cotton Belt and the Greenville-Spartanburg area of South Carolina.

Folk music, in whatever group it has been composed, remains popular because it appeals to the hopes and concerns of the listener, as James Putnam explained: "Music carries lots of weight behind it. Because once you get words together and get a guitar ringing, . . . somebody like the way you [play], . . . and they understand what you're saying, maybe one word in a song, can hit somebody and let them know how you feel. 'Cause most all the songs that be made up, some of the words are going to pop out for me, or you, or somebody. And it's matching in with somebody's life."

The power of African-American music to touch the lives of struggling individuals stems from the origin of this music itself. Velma Childers explained: "But now the slaves . . . had a way, that when they was working down in the fields and everything, they started singing songs, and just making up songs that fit their needs, like 'Swing low, sweet chariot, coming for to carry me home,' 'Steal away, steal away to Gideon.' And white people didn't want them to sing, or pray, or do anything."

Maxine Williams noted that this music not only helped pass the time but also helped pass information. Because the slaves "couldn't get together and just communicate, . . . [they] could give signs in their singing to each other, and they understood it." For example, Velma Childers offered: " 'Steal away, steal away to Jesus' because they couldn't come out plain and sing it, they would have to go down in the bottoms or places where they couldn't be heard. But usually those songs were made up for a code. If another group was singing a song, this group over here would understand why they were singing that type song. The song meant something when they were out in the fields. But when we'd go to these churches we're just singing for the pleasure of singing."

The Civil War, though, did not end intensive black (or white) labor; such backbreaking work persisted well into the memories of many informants. "Our parents kept them [the songs] going," Velma Childers asserted. Anne Kimzey reported that Ethel Harmon, an African American born in 1898, "remembers singing in the fields when she was working in a group. She said the fields were separated with groves of trees and that when they'd be singing they could always 'hear another crowd on the other side of the woods singing.' " James Edwards, an Anglo American, stated that singing for him helped pass the time and lighten the workload: "It wasn't just the black people that sang; there was a lot of us who were singing and all. . . . I know one old song they always sing was 'Swing Low, Sweet Chariot,' 'cause it had a lot of rhythm to it. They'd sing it for hours. They'd put their own verses to it."

"Most any kind of blues would go all right with corn shucking and cotton picking," James Putnam noted. Josh White, a black blues musician from the Greenville-Spartanburg area, recorded an extremely popular work song in 1932, entitled "Pickin' Low Cotton." As William Barlow indicated, "low cotton" referred to the height of the plants and the price of the product; both oppressive to those picking for a living.

James Williams, an African American born in 1909, described another genre of work songs: those composed by workers laying rails (almost always a traditionally black occupation). Like the fieldwork songs, these also had to conform to the rhythm of the task: "You sing one that the boys like to hear, and you talk about men jumping and scatting and moving!" he recalled. As with the cotton picking songs, skilled poets would often improvise the words, following a call-response pattern, Mr. Williams noted: "When I went there [to work] they was singing them [these songs], and just a lot of fellows come on under me or since then, they would make them up. . . . A lot of them . . . had different songs. . . . Really, to tell you the truth, they would just pick out the best man in the bunch for the caller."

Mr. Williams offered several examples of verses:

> Well, when I work for L and N
> Made good money but I blow it again [sung relatively fast];
> When I work for [pause]; L and N [pause];
> Made good money [pause]; But I blowed it again [sung very slowly].

"We ought to get through before that run out," Mr. Williams explained, "but that's just doubling it in case that they didn't, you know. Sometime's it's so hard, or . . . you have to tap it [the railroad spike] again."

James Williams cautioned, though, that "we had some [songs] that is not suitable to use out in public." While he carefully edited his selections, a few lyrics were suggestive. For instance, this hoisting song he claimed to have created when he saw his girlfriend walk by:

> Yonder come Lula, heist 'em higher,
> Show her how to heist 'em; heist 'em higher.
> Everybody heist 'em, heist 'em higher.

As James Williams observed, however, African-American work songs reflected not contentment but resentment: "Spent a lot of days like that out there. Work all day long, and sundown I couldn't get home, didn't know what time I'd get there." Many of Mr. Williams's lyrics, in fact, seem to hint at indirect attacks against white employers or racist society in general. For example, one verse runs: "Well, gettin' so dark I hardly can see/Be here till I line this track," serving as a somewhat indirect request for quitting for the day. "Well, Captain can't read and Captain can't write/How can he tell when this track is right" apparently pokes carefully worded fun at the illiteracy of the white bosses. Other lyrics—such as Howard Odum and Guy Johnson's "Well, it makes no dif'unce how you make out yo' time/White man sho bring nigger out behin' "—were more barbed.

The lyrics to one of James Williams's verses are even more poignantly revealing:

> Every time I go to town
> Boys keep kicking my dog around . . .
> Well, it makes no difference if he is a hound
> Got to quit kicking my dog around.

Like the antebellum songs of the cotton fields that passed discreet messages from slave to slave, these verses reminded black singers of the legal and social injustices they faced from white society every time they too went to town.

Calendrical Holidays

In addition to the informal gatherings of friends and relatives at un-scheduled times, the lives of Upstate residents have also been enriched by celebrations at regular times of the year. These calendrical holidays involve some tied directly to the agricultural cycle of the seasons while others incorporate established days recognized by general American culture. Even these, however, often bear the unmistakable stamp of Piedmont traditions. In fact, both types of occasions reflect the values and reinforce the social institutions of Upstaters, despite often significant changes to these holidays in recent times.

NEW YEAR'S EVE AND DAY

Starting off the new year on the right foot has been a fundamental component of the belief systems of many groups, including both black and white Piedmonters. Many beliefs for good luck on this auspicious day involve the consumption of certain foods that then bring prosperity to the believer. Almost universally in the Upstate, these foods included "peas" (black-eyed peas) and greens. As "the Pearls" explained: "If you cook peas on New Year's Day indicates you will have plenty of money in change during the year, and if you cook anything green indicates you will have plenty of money in bills during the year."

The same practice held among African Americans, John Morland discovered in Kent in 1949. In Hammondville's black community, Arthur Masters noted, "Some people do that now—for good luck." His wife added, "You know, I started off with that, [but] I just give it up. That's I think an old saying." "We still do it at home sometimes," Ron Kellogg admitted.

As Mr. and Mrs. Masters observed, many people in the Upstate continue this tradition; not firmly accepting the efficacy of the belief but recognizing the value of the tradition. "I cannot remember a New Year's Day that I haven't eaten peas and collards," Maggie Nameth stated confidently. One man cautioned: "Don't play this for my mother, okay? But she [his sister] did not even like to go by my home on New Year's Day, 'cause she knows what the menu's going to be and she thinks that's silly. . . . And my mother, to this day, that's what it's gonna be. . . . And matter of fact, she's offended if she finds out that we didn't have it on New Year's Day, 'cause it's tradition."

THE FOURTH OF JULY

In part because of the welcome respite from agricultural work, residents of the Upstate traditionally welcomed the Fourth of July with significant social activities. Maxine Williams described the holiday as "a big day with farmers, because see at the time that you had your crop laid by, and you would celebrate maybe with a big picnic like that. And everybody'd have ripe watermelons, and a bunch would gather up and cut watermelons, and, oh, just have a feast, like."

Churches might also sponsor picnics, a woman from Honea Path recalled: "The young people from Chiquola Baptist Church went to Irving's Mill [?] for a picnic—an all-day affair. . . . We carried with us our picnic lunch, or drinks (tub of lemonade and a tub of iced tea), . . . and we had a big dinner, spread out on the ground at twelve o'clock."

Other activities related to the relaxation of labor and the enjoyment of ensuing leisure. Lucindy Brown added that "sometimes the men would have ball games or something like that," while Longstreet Gantt, from Winnsboro, recalled in his WPA interview barbecues and public speeches on this national holiday. In fact, the Hammondville Mill celebrated the Fourth of July 1920 by sponsoring "an *Old Time Barbecue Dinner*" [emphasis in original]. Not only did the mill shut down for that Saturday, the company also was to provide "Free all the meats, and see that they are well cooked and well served."

The Hammondville Mill had always sponsored a large Fourth of July celebration, Everett Baker recalled: "They'd have the sack races, the bicycle races, the ball throw, . . . ugliest man contest. . . . The peanut scramble was a favorite of some of the older people. They'd put peanuts . . . in a bag, and you'd put money in it. . . . One or two guys loved to . . . put a little flour in it . . . and they'd tear it just a little bit. . . . And when they'd get ready to throw it out there, they'd pick out that [older] kid and throw it a little harder right at him. And he'd reach up and grab it, that powder'd go all over him, see?"

While the festivities are no longer sponsored by the mill, Hammondville still celebrates the Fourth in much the same way. Rosemary Calder observed: "The program would be . . . at the park. And the first part of the program is for small children, like throwing out the bags of peanuts. . . . And then they have the egg race, with the egg in the spoon. And then the sack race, or the two-legged race." In other mill towns, however, now everybody "goes to the beach," Mary Gattis reported.

LAY-BY TIME

Perhaps no other holiday in the Upstate epitomized the agricultural base upon which much of the past century's folklife was established than the period of time in midsummer known in many places as lay-by time. A man at the Honea Path Senior Citizens Center explained: "Lay-by time is the time when your cotton or corn . . . has matured enough that it doesn't need any more cultivation or fertilizer. . . . At lay-by time you're waiting on it to ripen and get ready for harvest in the fall. So ordinarily, from about July the Fourth until late September you don't have anything to do on the farm much."

Consequently, lay-by time became the perfect opportunity for the numerous social activities that characterized the Upstate's folklife, such as "the huge out-door gatherings, barbecues, . . . and most popular all over the State, the family reunions," as Louise Jones DuBose noted. Ben Thomas listed "the usual round of preaching, picnics, politics, and pitched battles" in his WPA interview. Others such as Jason Lambert needed income and so sought various odd jobs "till the time came for picking."

Today, though the farm economy that supported the period has drastically changed, the association between lay-by time and family recreation still remains. Despite the oppressive heat and humidity of July and August in the Carolinas (offset to an extent by air-conditioning), the vast majority of family reunions and church revivals, two of the most important contemporary summer social activities, are held between the Fourth of July and Labor Day during the traditional lay-by time. Sometimes announcements for these activities even mention the "old-fashioned" connection. Lay-by time as an agricultural holiday no longer exists, but it still underlies the social calendar of contemporary Piedmont folklife.

CHRISTMASTIME

Besides the commercial and religious aspects of the holiday, Linda Baker related what she considered a family Christmas tradition: "Every Christmas morning he [my grandfather] came over to our house at 6:30 and shot the shotgun off under my bedroom window to wake me up . . . like an alarm clock, under my window. Every Christmas morning—bam! . . . And I'm sure it woke up all the neighbors for a mile radius."

Perhaps as a related custom, Maggie Nameth "had an uncle who . . . would bring in a box of fireworks; and we would shoot fireworks on Christmas." Ms. Baker believed that "really I think we had more fireworks at Christmas than we did Fourth of July in [Hammondville]. And people around [Hammondville] I think still buy fireworks for Christmas, which is sort of odd." This same tradition puzzled Anna Pearsall, who had moved from Maine to South Carolina in the 1930s. The creation of loud noises at New Year's Eve and Day has been noted in German-American tradition for centuries, and a related form persists in the Carolina Piedmont.

Conclusion

Whether at family gatherings around the dinner table on Sundays, on the front porch during a hot summer night, or under shady trees at a church reunion, the types of social interaction engaged in by Piedmonters, both in the past and present, reinforce group values and kin ties. The traditions of family heritage and conservative religion, expressed in so many different ways by both blacks and whites, pervade and explain the varied forms of social life that in turn support these values. Social interaction in effect links the elements of Piedmont beliefs and values by means of a network of traditionally important social institutions.

CHAPTER 9

Games and Recreations

As in every other culture, residents of the Carolina Piedmont have taken time off from cotton farming, mill work, and the other common drudgeries of their lives to enjoy various types of games and recreations. Some of these are played by children, others by adults. Some are viewed as spectator events. At times these recreations involve forms common to American culture in general; at other times they represent folk games or activities relatively unknown outside the region. Like other categories of Upstate folklife, games and recreations reflect values common to the region. Shaped in part by the passage of time and by the interweaving of traditions, these formal and informal activities constitute another segment of Piedmont folklife.

Children's Activities

BOTH GENDERS

As John Morland reported, preschool-aged children often played together. Like other Americans, Kent youngsters played tag, hide-and-seek, froggie in the millpond, drop the handkerchief, London Bridge, and ain't no bears out tonight. Informants recalled several others; some well-known from American culture, others apparently less widespread. For example, David Hawkins added hide the thimble and spin the bottle—"just simple things, games that you had to invent yourself." Everett Baker offered a form of tag called ring-a-lee-bo, in which a person tried to capture all the other players and imprison them in a circle; they could all be freed by someone running through the circle and shouting, "Ring-a-lee-bo!"

Both boys and girls also played house. Like today, observations of children playing at adult roles provide clues to children's interpretations of adult behavior. In the racially segregated Piedmont, though, children's playing house might combine not only genders but also races, particularly in social situations where whites and blacks grew up together. As Velma Childers recalled, this provided some interesting imaginary households: "Now when we would play in the playhouse, my sister would be the momma. And [name], who was white, would be the daddy. Now, we wasn't doing any 'family things,' like that, we just—we would do more whipping the children than anything else!"

As Linda Baker fondly noted, both rural and mill village children in generations past seemed to have much more freedom to enjoy each other's company. As she explained: "Now, my mother's parents worked different shifts, . . . and so when my grandmother was at work in the daytime, my grandfather was supposed to be at home with the children. But he was asleep because he worked the other shift. So they would slip off and do stuff that they weren't supposed to be doing because he was asleep and not watching them." In such situations, the social bonds between neighbors became essential, for nonworking mothers or older siblings would often safeguard "unsupervised" children.

While these games and recreations were shared by blacks and whites, a few sources have suggested that some forms of recreation may have been known only to African Americans, which created subsequent confusion in integrated play groups. Velma Childers, who had taught in the segregated black schools for decades, assisted in the desegregated system after her retirement. During one organized play session, she noticed that her white colleague introduced games unfamiliar to the black children. She responded, "Now, if you want to get some action out of *our* children, you play some little game like fruit basket." To play, she would ask each child what type of fruit they would want to be, and they would whisper their selection in her ear (one boy wanted to be "red-eye gravy"). In the center of a circle of the children sitting in chairs would be the person who was "it." When the leader would say, "Apple and orange switch," the two children with those designations would jump up and try to switch seats before the person who was "it" could take one of their places.

Alice Gassoway described another children's game not mentioned by white informants. She called it "bluebird, bluebird, in my window." To play "we'd ring up, and one would stand on the outside. . . . For the bluebird, she'd go there and tap her on the back and say, 'bluebird, bluebird in my window [repeat two more times]/Oh, Johnny, I'm tired.' Then she'd say, 'Take her, take her, patty on the shoulder [repeat two more times]/Oh, Johnny, I'm tired.' And then that one would go. We'd go all around the ring and then we'd just have a ring going around and around, singing, 'Bluebird, bluebird, in my window.' It was right interesting." She also explained another ring-sing game called "give that gal a piece of cake." To play, "one would stand in the ring, and then we'd clap hands, 'Give that gal a piece of cake, Oh momma/Give that gal a piece of cake, Oh momma/ She turned around and around three times, say/Give that gal a piece of cake!' And then the one in the ring would choose somebody to go in. And then we'll sing again. . . . That was just a little dance for us, you know."

BOY ACTIVITIES

As children in the mill villages and the cotton farms grew older, recreational activities began to segregate by gender. One extremely popular activity for boys was swimming in creeks, frequently without clothes, which created problems with community standards of decency. In fact, the Hammondville village newspaper in June 1919 printed a request "by the [mill] management that boys not go swimming in the river in sight of the village without bathing suits." Since cotton mills originally developed near sources of water power, and since creeks and rivers percolated through every countryside, Piedmont boys were rarely out of sight of swimming holes; the long hot summers of the Upstate invited their use. Ray Nameth and his friends would spend all day swimming and swinging on ropes and gigging frogs, returning home only to eat and sleep.

A rougher activity was the game known as mumblety-peg or mumble peg, played by groups of boys using sticks or broom handles. As described by several older informants, the object was to pound a stick, several feet long, into the ground and place another of approximately equal length on top. One person then hit the tip of the cross-T stick, which flipped it into the air. The player knocked the spinning stick as far as he could, with the distance determined by stepping (or "jumping" in North Carolina) it off. The person hitting the stick the shortest distance had to "root the peg": each player took one turn hammering a peg into the ground, and the loser then had to grub in the dirt to seize the peg with his teeth and gradually work it out of the ground.

Quieter recreations included various forms of games with marbles. "The knees in my overalls wore out playing marbles," Ray Nameth chuckled. "It was an art to doing it," James Edwards stated. Several informants, like Arthur Masters, played but had some difficulty remembering the rules of various games.

An interesting alternative consisted of an innovative use of the packaging from a ubiquitous Piedmont material, chewing tobacco. As Tom Davis described, tobacco plugs came fastened with tags of metal decorated with an emblem related to the brand name: a dog (for Bloodhound brand), a mule (for Brown Mule), an owl, or an apple, for example. Each player would put one tag on the ground, each on top of the other: "And you puffed real hard. If you turned them all over, you picked them all up. It's sort of like shooting marbles—puffin' tobacco tags." Alice Gassoway reported a slightly different version, where boys spun a top to knock out the tags.

As Mr. Davis's example illustrated, because of relatively low incomes from their families' mill and tenant jobs, many boys had to improvise their toys. James Putnam remembered sawing thin circular sections from cut timber, encasing these with iron rims from cotton bales, and making wheels for scrap-lumber "soapbox derby" wagons. Everett Baker enjoyed playing baseball, but he and his friends had to fashion their bats out of boards and their baseballs from wads of yarn and electrical tape, often secured from the mill. Such improvised materials added a special challenge to each game: "Well, we're playing along [toward dark] and this boy gets up to bat, a little bitty guy. . . . And he swung away mightily, you know. Throws the bat down and takes off. Everybody starts looking for the ball. . . . He just circles the bases, and we're still looking for the ball. . . . So somebody finally picks up the bat. Well, that floor plank had a nail in the end of it. So he swings—the ball sticks to the bat, he throws it down, gets a home run, the ball laying right in front of home plate!"

In mill towns, the factory became a ready and welcome source of a wide variety of materials from which children could make items for play. The paternalistic attitude of the mill's supervisory staff made this possible. Informants said they received not only scrap materials but sometimes free labor in manufacturing the toys. Tom Davis, for example, collected cloth waste from the weavers and wound it into a rope, and from the lumber shop he received leftover boards from which he and his friends made rope swings or diving boards for their favorite swimming holes. Ray Nameth and his friends used discarded wooden spindles for mumble peg. David Hawkins had the machine shop cut hoops from discarded metal drums, which he and his friends would roll down hills with old broom handles. James Edwards, although living in the country outside of Hammondville, obtained, through trade and skill, steel "marbles," actually ball bearings from the mill. Tom Davis used loom parts for little toy cars.

The prized childhood possession of several Hammondville men was a toy wagon made from mill junk. In fact, Tom Davis had a photo taken of himself in one, from 1913. These "gearwheel" or "loom-wheel" wagons were made from scrap lumber discarded and cut by the lumber shop, with a steering mechanism made from scraps of leather (from the roller shop) or cord from the mill. Axles were iron rods or broom handles. The wheels were discarded gears from the looms. "You could make good time in a iron-wheel wagon," Ray Nameth chuckled, and continued: "You grease them wheels on that thing, and it'd take off. I remember one time, the street I was living on was . . . just an old dirt road. . . . This old boy and his brother was coming down the street on their iron-wheel wagon. And he slid off the back and he had some matches in his hip pocket and they struck!" In 1971, when he worked in the old Hammondville mill parts department, one man discovered thousands of useless, outdated gears, and so he made himself an old-fashioned toy wagon. Today operated by young relatives, this gearwheel wagon still rolls through downtown Hammondville in annual Christmas parades.

GIRL ACTIVITIES

As they grew older, girls began to disassociate with boys and male activities, generally speaking. Alice Gassoway explained that "the boys wouldn't hardly play with girls no way, because they were playing ball." John Morland listed typical activities for girls, including playing hopscotch, jumping rope, playing with dolls, playing house and school, and sports such as volleyball and dodgeball. Martha Block remembered her father, a blacksmith, creating metal hoops from old wagon wheels: "We'd roll those hoops all over this place," she recalled. She also used to play a neighbor boy in marbles, "and I'd beat him every time!" Girls had less free time than boys, however, because by the age of twelve or so they often managed the households of their working mothers.

School playgrounds provided the setting for many of the activities of girls. A photograph by Jack Delano from the early 1940s depicts a girls' game on the playground of the Alexander Community School in Greene County, Georgia. The girls form two concentric circles by holding hands; one circle rotates clockwise and the other counterclockwise. Into the present generation, Linda Baker noted, jump-rope, especially "double-jumping," remained a popular schoolyard pastime: "You have to have four people—two long jump ropes and they hold them pretty close together—parallel. And then you skip back over both of them. Sort of complicated footwork."

Mary Yarbrough and her city friends used to construct "peep shows": "You dig a hole in the ground and find an old piece of glass, which was always somewhere. Then you put little flowers, or something, underneath. And then put your piece of glass over it, and have a judging contest to see whose peep show won the contest." "That was loads of fun," Lucy Wallace added.

In part serving to train for their domestic futures and in part simply to develop their own gender identity, girls frequently played with dolls. "A lot of times we'd trade doll clothes," Rosemary Calder remembered. "Our parents didn't appreciate that, but we'd trade doll clothes." Maggie Nameth and her friends "made up imaginary stories that went along with" their dolls.

Velma Childers, an African American, had two different types of dolls as a child: "I had a little doll named Geneva. . . . And she was white—had sandy hair and everything. We kept that doll, you know, just didn't play with it too much, like enjoy, we would just look at it a little bit. . . . But if we wanted to really enjoy a doll, my momma would make us rag dolls. . . . Could change their clothes, and throw them around, and pick them up when we'd get ready and what not. I don't know why the difference in those dolls." Ms. Childers believed that the contrast between the special white doll and the ordinary rag dolls was owing to the fact that Santa Claus had brought the former. Of course, subconsciously these dolls simultaneously reinforced the reality of her segregated social world.

Girls could also play house and other imaginary games by dressing up in adult clothes, drawing inspiration from parental roles or from popular media. Linda Baker recalled that she and her friends would "dress up like Cinderella or something. My mother had been in several weddings when I was a child, and she let my friends and I dress up in her high heels and the dresses that she'd had in the weddings, that sort of thing." "When we played house," Maggie Nameth reminisced, "we would always play as if somebody, another boy in first grade, were our husband."

The activities of young girls, however, were not always limited to quiet, cooperative play. Swimming in the local creeks and rivers, for example, was off-limits to "proper" young girls like Rosemary Calder: "That was a no-no, . . . [because] that's where all the boys went. And you just didn't go that way." Ray Nameth remembered groups of girls who would "put their bathing suits on and go up there [to the sand bar] and lay around on that sand bar," but they would not swim with the boys, thereby preserving the proper decorum of southern ladies.

On the other hand, Linda Baker confided: "My mother swam in the river, when she was little. Yeah, she and her brothers and sisters'd go down—or says, 'slip off to the river,' 'cause their parents didn't want them to go do that. . . . And mother thought she was 'Nioka' [a popular figure from the movies] and she'd swing on vines and land in the river. . . . I can't imagine her doing any of that." Through several generations, the imaginary play of girls often involved as much activity as male recreation and just as frequently drew upon popular media for inspiration.

Family Recreations

SHOPPING

On Saturdays throughout the Carolina Piedmont (in fact, in rural areas throughout the United States), in generations past small towns came alive with the bustle of shoppers and visitors. "Back then," Ron Kellogg recalled, "one of the main ways people had recreation was . . . going uptown . . . lot of people used to go uptown on Saturday." Payday in the mills had been the evening before, and workers now crowded into stores, often with their wives, to pass the time and obtain needed merchandise. Farmers, assuming the crops had been laid by and livestock cared for, filled their wagons with family and friends and headed into town to visit and shop. Combining southern hospitality with the individuality of small-town competition meant that the locally owned stores offered not only quality merchandise but friendly, personalized service. Larger cities like Greenville attracted thousands of people, both from the community and from surrounding towns.

Downtowns also provided many (but not all) Depression-era youngsters with inexpensive and welcome entertainment. Many sharecroppers' children, like James Edwards, received "a nickel to go to the movie and a nickel to buy popcorn, Coca-Cola with" as a special Saturday treat. As Lucindy Brown noted, however, blacks "couldn't go to the movies," or else had to sit in special sections. While Saturday socializing brought blacks and whites and farmer, merchant, and mill hand together, rules of segregation and class distinctions maintained recognizable divisions.

Hints of earlier cultural values survive in contemporary Piedmont retail behavior and restrictions. Before the 1960s, Saturday shopping was essential in part because stores closed on Sunday owing to the "blue laws" of the communities. A reflection of the conservative religious values of the Upstate, these laws left socializing with family and friends after church as practically the only permissible activity on Sundays. Today, depending on the county, most stores open by 1:30 P.M. on Sundays, but some (even in shopping malls) remain closed because of conservative corporate management. Beer and wine in grocery stores cannot be purchased at all on Sunday; clear plastic sheeting covers alcohol displays, and signs explain the ordinances. Restaurants in most cities cannot sell alcohol on Sunday either. All bars in college towns cease selling at midnight, forcing thousands of Carolina collegians to seek private parties. "Hard" liquor can only be purchased from state-owned stores in both Carolinas, and these close at seven P.M. The Bible Belt still girds the Calvinistic interpretation of alcohol-based recreation in the Carolinas.

Significant changes, though, have modified the social importance of shopping and general recreation in the downtowns of small communities today. Shoppers note with dismay the decline of personalized service, as Helen Quinnell and her friends discovered after a frustrating afternoon at a local mall. One of her friends exclaimed: " 'This place is well stocked with nothing!' And my Aunt [name] said, 'Yes, and there isn't anybody who knows where *that* is!' " In towns like Kent, mom-and-pop dry goods stores cannot compete with the massive purchasing power of discounters in shopping centers on the edge of town, one such owner noted sadly. In fact, after his recent death, his decades-old store on Kent's main street closed, adding another vacant window to downtown storefronts. "I went downtown [in Hammondville] yesterday," Vernon Randle sighed. "That's the dullest place in the world! Lord a-mercy! Don't see nobody down there." Even larger cities like Greenville, Wilma Masters observed, "don't have all that much shopping for people that live there. They all go to the malls."

Large commercial shopping malls, anchored by well-known retail stores and linked by dozens of other national chains, have directly affected the social and commercial life of the Piedmont (as well as that of the country in general). Made possible primarily by the improvements in transportation and the importance of the automobile, trips to the mall have now replaced, both socially and commercially, earlier trips to downtown. Drawing teens from both the community and neighboring towns, shopping malls provide Upstate youth with video games, fast food, designer clothes, and air-conditioned/heated venues for indoor cruising without the added expense of gasoline. Mall visits, often including meals in adjacent restaurants (as opposed to meals with family members), represent a popular form of Upstate recreation.

FLEA MARKETS

One Piedmont commercial practice has undergone some transformations but remains a significant factor in the folklife of the Upstate today: the open-air flea markets. Tracing their origin to the region's rural roots, Louise Jones DuBose, in a WPA essay, described "Sales Days" as "survivals of very old customs of the State. In days when plantations were flourishing, the people used to hold fairs at various centers when products could be exchanged and journeymen could sell their wares. . . . In the more rural counties [in the 1930s], particularly in the Up Country, Negroes and whites meet to sell and barter their products." In their casual, individualistic style of marketing as well as in their rural origins, these flea markets typify Piedmont values. Moreover, recalling the expanding postbellum economic con-

The covered booth area at the Anderson Jockey Lot
(Photo by John M. Coggeshall)

trol of town merchants over farmers' lives (discussed in chapter 2), flea
markets may also represent an attempt to escape this influence and to reas-
sert the fundamental Piedmont value of individualism.

Today lining virtually every state and national highway and many
county roads as well, flea markets consist of several tables (sometimes
merely boards on sawhorses), usually in a small parking lot near an intersection. These tables are filled with just about any item or object imagin-
able, from secondhand clothes to auto parts. Vendors most frequently are
local residents who "set up" in the same location at recognized periodic
times.

The largest and best-known flea market in the Upstate may be the "Anderson Jockey Lot," on U.S. Highway 29 between Greenville and Anderson. On Interstate 85, just north of the Georgia line and again south of the
North Carolina border, huge billboards proclaim this flea market as the
largest in the southeast; it is indeed huge. On a recent Saturday afternoon,
the Jockey Lot swarmed with thousands of shoppers from several states, all
seeking bargains and the entertainment from large crowds. The merchandise included furniture, large appliances, clothes, shoes, perfume, toys, automobile parts, farm machinery, assorted tools, animals, including dogs
and gamecocks, and locally grown and imported produce, usually from

south Georgia and Florida. Some of the items for sale seem to have come from personal collections, but many others appear damaged or soiled, giving the impression of having been railroad or warehouse salvage. Visitors occasionally question the legal acquisition or authenticity of name-brand labeling of the merchandise.

Adult Male Activities

''WOMANLESS'' CEREMONIES

One type of male-only activity involves a curious, perhaps even surprising, form of recreation, given traditional southern attitudes. Sometimes occurring at community festivals are several different types of public ceremonies where men don women's clothing, including accessories and make-up, and even "shave their legs and put stockings on," Everett Baker laughed. At the Fourth of July festival in Hammondville, Mr. Baker said, there would typically be a "womanless wedding": "Men would dress up like the brides. . . . You would always get some real tall guy and a real short guy; one of them would be the bride and the groom. And they'd have a couple of them dress up like bridesmaids—men, though. They'd always have a daddy dressed up and have his shotgun, march them in to the preacher. Usually got the school principal or somebody to be the preacher."

Anne Kimzey reported a slightly different practice from the lower Piedmont. In one family, "the brothers are into elaborate schemes for entertainment. Three of them plus one male cousin have an act they originally put together for a community center show. They dress up as women and do dance and lyp [sic] sync routines to Pointer Sister songs. They call themselves the Blunt Sisters. Their mother made the dresses for them. She said she never thought she'd be making dresses for her boys."

On a recent summer night in Travelers Rest, a small town north of Greenville, a "womanless beauty pageant" highlighted a weekend-long community festival. By 9:00 P.M. the stands in the football stadium were packed; the stage on the field was lit and decorated for the pageant. Six local men, all in drag, pranced onto the stage to the whoops and laughter of the crowd. The contestants blew kisses, hiked up their skirts, and slid their dresses down their shoulders as the emcee read their "biographies." In falsetto voices, each answered humorous questions; for example, one "woman" wanted a date with a local volunteer fireman (present in the audience) because "she" wanted to "ride that big red pumper of his." Next came the talent contest, as all danced and lip-synched their way through popular songs. Finally the two runners-up were announced and then the winner, who weighed more than 250 pounds and physically lifted the emcee off the ground in feigned delight. The queen crowned the new winner, and the contestants left the stage to mix with their friends and families in the crowd.

Few informants could offer reasons for the regional popularity of such ceremonies. These rituals could conceivably be related to the southern popularity of women's beauty pageants and might then be a male mockery of them. A younger, college-educated area resident suggested that the wearing of women's clothing by men in humorous public situations might also be connected to the long-standing British tradition of similar humor, exemplified more recently by Monty Python and Benny Hill skits. For whatever reason(s), "womanless beauty pageants" draw large crowds, and remain popular events in the Piedmont.

HUNTING

For many males (and some females) in the Upstate, hunting birds and mammals is both a necessity and a sport, and has been for generations. Mill town residents, John Morland discovered, achieved a sense of freedom and individuality from these sports, as escapes from the drudgery and regimentation of mill work. Patrick and Morland described among Kent's black community a pervasive interest in hunting, as seen through the widespread ownership of guns and dogs, food preparation habits (for example, a preference for rabbit and possum), and in the boasts and stories about a person's prowess at hunting. As the researchers explained, the emphasis on hunting fits quite well with the area's lack of urbanization, the seasonal character of cotton agriculture (with extensive lay-by and wintertime off-seasons), the need (and desire) of firearms for sport and protection, the urgency to supplement family diets, and the double function of dogs as both pets and sporting instruments. In the area, Patrick and Morland concluded, hunting provides adherents with "great satisfaction and camaraderie." Wes Young reminded his interviewer of regional bumper stickers that read: " 'When the tailgate drops the bullshit stops'; . . . serious business, then."

From an early age, young boys would accompany their fathers on hunts. Fred Alexander, for example, told his WPA interviewer that he began hunting "as soon as I could get my hand on agun [sic]." Wes Young started when he was five. William Vaughn believed that "if you got past six years old and didn't know how to shoot, it was unusual in those days." "It was probably one of the first things that a father-son did together, you know, out in the woods, started going rabbit hunting," James Edwards recalled.

As several informants have suggested, part of the enjoyment of the sport lies in the appreciation of good hunting dogs. John Morland observed in

Kent's mill communities: "Men like to own dogs. . . . They do not seem to hunt enough in many cases to justify the possession of the dogs but like to have them for their prestige value." "People in those days," Everet Boney explained in his WPA interview, "thought as much of a good fox hound as they did a fine mule." Later, the value remained high but the item of comparison changed. Everett Baker remembered his father as owning two "redbone hounds. . . . They were real good possum dogs. . . . And I never will forget it. It was long about the time the war [World War II] started, and this guy wanted them hounds so bad he offered to trade daddy a '34 Ford coupe for them two dogs, but he wouldn't trade."

An additional part of the enjoyment of hunting involves sound, for skilled hunters can determine the course of the hunt and the order of the pack based only on the baying of the hounds. Wes Young elaborated: "We know each hound by voice. And you can tell which is doing the best. . . . You always listen to which hound's in the front when they come back. . . . It's an old tradition. . . .We always try to have us some big tongues, like a choir in church. We try to have the base, the alto, sopranos. . . . If you love to hear hounds run, it's the greatest sport in the world."

According to Helen Quinnell, women would sometimes accompany their husbands, as she did. Often, she complained, the men enjoyed listening to the dogs chase the animal, but "I could not distinguish which dog was barking, or howling, or whatever they were doing. . . . [It] doesn't take too long to get boring!"

For those who love the sport, however, one of the premier animals would be a fox. "We do not go to kill fox," Wes Young explained. "We go for the chase, that's our thing—the hound music, the dogs packing up running the fox." Chasing foxes requires a great amount of canine hunting intelligence, since foxes are so clever. For example, Young has seen them dash along asphalt or along the iron rail of tracks on a bridge to lose the dogs, since "dogs can't smell on asphalt" and they fear the unsupported crossties on railroad bridges. He has also heard that foxes will deliberately plunge through cow manure to disguise their scents. When running, though, different species of foxes have varied amounts of stamina, Young continued, because grey foxes are "of the cat family and the red's the dog family—. . . I've heard many sayings on that—the canine and feline."

Raccoons would also be hunted more for the sport of the chase rather than for their meat. Like that of foxes, raccoon hunting required a specially-trained dog because of the intelligence of the quarry. Albert Wood explained: "It takes a good dog to tree a coon. . . . You know, a coon—we call it marking the tree. He'll go up a tree and come down. . . . They do that to fool the dogs—to get away from the dogs, you see." The nighttime camaraderie by the hunters would be the same as that described above, though.

Other animals would be hunted more for the table and less for the sport. "Now possum hunting—now that used to be a thing," Jason Lambert recalled. "But you don't hear tell of anybody possum hunting now." Morland described a typical possum hunt in the Kent vicinity: a group of men gathered in the woods at night and turned their dogs loose. While the men waited, they ate pecans and apples and told dirty jokes. Eventually, the dogs discovered a scent, and the party followed them through the countryside until the dogs treed a possum. The men shook it out of the tree, let the dogs "shake it" around, and then put it into a sack for later release. Few Anglo-Americans, Morland believed, actually ate possum.

Another widely hunted animal was the ubiquitous rabbit, for both the sport as well as the meat. Dale Garroway explained: "Daddy always said, 'When we run out of chickens we get rabbits.' And that's about the way it was. . . . 'Cause it wasn't any problem to go rabbit hunting for two or three hours and kill four or five." "Me and my daddy," Richard Sanders recalled proudly, "used to kill six, seven, eight, ten rabbits a day."

For those with a taste for rabbits but without the capital for rabbit dogs, one could instead trap rabbits by using "rabbit gums." These were so named, Mr. Garroway believed, because older sweet gum trees tended to be hollow inside and could be cut down and sawn into chunks. Each piece of the trunk then made a trap. Set out in old cotton fields in the wintertime, James Edwards explained, the trap "was just a little box, probably about eight inches high and eight inches wide. . . . Some of them would have a piece of screen wire on the back of them [to appear to make a tunnel], . . . and they had what they called a trap bed up front. And you had a little slot cut out where that bed can slide down and close on the front." The rabbit would enter the "tunnel," trigger a hand-carved release mechanism, and the door would slide down, trapping the animal inside.

Virtually every boy a generation ago set these, Dale Garroway felt; even into the 1950s, Louis Foster added. James Edwards believed that his son knows about rabbit gums, mostly because he "made some when he was small. Of course, he's thirty-two years old. . . . But that would be one of the arts handed down. . . . A lot of kids now don't know what a rabbit gum was."

FISHING

Another very popular sport in the Upstate, engaged in by both blacks and whites for food and for recreation, is fishing. In previous generations, fishermen (and some women) utilized the Piedmont's sluggish streams and mill ponds as often as their work would allow them to get away. J. R. Glenn, a black minister in 1930s Charlotte, reminisced: "I'll tell you another thing I love doin'. I go fishin' as often as I can. I love to sit out on the river bank even all night sometimes." When asked what he fished for, Vernon Randle replied, "Anything that'd bite my hook!"

Besides fish, Upstaters also caught turtles, frequently in baskets woven especially for the purpose by "older folks," Richard Sanders noted (see chapter 13). After baiting the turtle traps with chicken parts and submerging the traps in a creek or shallow river, Sanders explained, the trapper would kill a chicken and "let the blood go down the stream; [then] a turtle will come up" and crawl into the basket to get the chicken. The basket needs to be anchored with wire, not rope, Sanders cautioned, for "nine times out of ten they'll cut a rope in two."

In addition to using poles or baskets, Piedmonters also seined for fish, often in shallow oxbow lakes and mill ponds. To do so, one man explained, several people would walk with a long net between them to "hem up" any fish between the walkers. "We used to catch a lot of fish that way," he added; sometimes "hundreds" of pounds, according to Ray Nameth. Tom Davis caught "brim and a lot of catfish [this way]; you know, if you'd stir up the mud you'd catch a lot of catfish. [We] lived on the river, mostly," he recalled. Many of these fish ended up as picnic feasts on the lake shores, using cornmeal and cooking utensils brought for the purpose. One of the many benefits of a rural life with seasonal agricultural labor was the relative freedom to engage in leisurely activities quite frequently, a value reinforced by the region's emphasis on individualism. Rosser Taylor blamed the decline of these "exciting and hilarious seining parties" on the outlawing of seining as a method of fishing. Of course, as Maggie Nameth admitted, "They seined just the same."

Today, traditional fishing holes still yield success, especially in the spring. "Everything start moving when . . . the dogwood trees start blooming," Richard Sanders reported. Everett Baker believed that Hammondville's river remains "a good fishing river. . . . You come by here at night, you'll see three or four people fishing." Many more residents fish on the area's numerous lakes and reservoirs. So popular is Sunday afternoon fishing that ministers have decried the related decline in church attendance.

TOBACCO USE

Given the close proximity of the tobacco-growing regions of the North Carolina Piedmont as well as South Carolina's northeastern production area, it would be expected that the use of tobacco products, including chewing tobacco, would be another popular male activity. Women would "dip snuff," Ray Nameth noted, while men would chew tobacco. Tom Davis remembered that "the little ol' kids smoked and chewed tobacco. Little bitty kids. I mean, they thought that was the way. Their daddy'd give them chewing tobacco. . . . We'd watch these fellers come out of the drug store. They'd flip that cigarette butt and boy, we'd dive on it. All of us smoke it, you know—passed it around. It's a wonder we hadn't died a long time ago!"

Today, in virtually every grocery store and convenience market, the displays of chewing tobacco take up a large section, in addition to those devoted to cigarettes. Numerous brands, in brightly decorated circular cans, line shelf after shelf. The telltale circles in the backs of male pants pockets, the wadded expanse of a man's cheek, or the requisite can carried for spitting, also suggest the continued popularity of this pastime.

MOONSHINING

Numerous stereotypes in the popular media continue to feature southerners, particularly in the mountain areas, as moonshiners and hard drinkers. The origins of these perceptions may lie in the well-entrenched Scots-Irish ability and desire to transform corn on the distant frontier into a more easily transported and more commercially valuable product. Coupled with the region's emphasis on individuality and the right of free expression, the distilling of spirits has long been associated with the Piedmont as well as other southern regions.

National prohibition merely slowed but did not stop liquor production in the Upstate. By the Depression, the making of moonshine became both a means to supply thirsty family and friends and also a significant source of needed income, Mary Hammond explained. Fred Alexander, in his WPA interview, elaborated: "Peered as if I could'n make enough to pay house rent and to keep us supplied with rations at saw millin! . . . I am ashamed to say it, but I had a good corn patch and I took my corn and got a North Carolinian to show me how to make 'gully run' [moonshine]. . . . Peered funny how many demands I got at 50 cents for a half gallon." One woman felt that for many impoverished farmers, moonshine "was the biggest cash crop they had."

With such easy money to be made, many Depression-era families turned to home-produced liquor. In Hammondville, one woman admitted, bootleggers used to deliver moonshine as regularly as milkmen brought milk. Several residents knew bootleggers in the community. Even the village newspaper acknowledged their presence in August 1922. One woman described a family, originally from "Dark Corner" ("I won't call any names, now") who continued this family tradition after they had moved to town.

Another man claimed that his own grandfather "used to be a big bootlegger"; he remembered the Cadillacs, Lincolns, and Buicks stopping to fill dozens of jars in their trunks. A friend of his, as a schoolboy, would steal moonshine from his bootlegging uncle and take it to school, secreting it in the woods.

Today, despite the relatively easy access to commercially produced alcohol in the area, the long-standing tradition of self-production continues. The *Greenville News* recently reported that "the days of shotguns, 'revenooers' and liquor stills built from solder and used automobile parts might be a part of the Upstate's past, but apparently, the 'shine is still out there. [A deputy stopped a truck at a sobriety checkpoint on a U.S. highway.] . . . In the bed of the truck, he found several jars of illegal white liquor. . . . The deputies picked up twelve gallons of the stuff, the warrant says." Several months later, in the same general area, the *News* reported a raid by sheriff's deputies and federal agents on a licensed gasohol operation that had also produced three hundred gallons of illegal moonshine.

COCKFIGHTING

Another male-only activity, decidedly illegal but persistent nevertheless, is cockfighting. Long practiced on the frontier and popular enough in the Carolinas to provide the mascot for the University of South Carolina (the Fighting Gamecocks), the raising of and betting on fighting chickens has been done primarily in the rural areas for generations.

Today illegal in all states, the practice continues, one informant believed, but more so in neighboring states: "If they get caught [in South Carolina] they charge them for a misdemeanor, which is, I think, a twenty-five dollar fine. . . . They confiscate their chickens . . . and any money they find. . . . These guys that does it now, they . . . have a little society. They write a note to everybody and they know when the next fight's going to be. . . . Even now, from the way these guys talk, they still have pretty good crowds when they have them. They bet on the different types of chicken. . . . But I haven't seen one in a long time."

At the Anderson Jockey Lot, in a row of booths where animals may be purchased, a family from the Upstate still breeds and sells fighting chickens. In fact, several of the men and boys in the booth proudly wear black baseball-style caps with colorful birds on them surrounded by the words, "Till Death Do Us Part." The senior partner in the business explained that he keeps several breeds, including one he called a "Butcher." The birds had brightly colored feathers, some of varying lengths and thicknesses. To fight, two teenagers explained, sharp metal spurs are attached to the chickens' legs. Another man provided details: "They'll draw a ring on the ground, . . . that's the boundaries for 'em. They stand, hold them against each other, let them peck at each other till they get mad and turn them loose and let them go at it. Sometimes they kill each other. That's one of the reasons, I think, the Humane Society probably had a lot to do with them not being legal." Both the young teens and the booth owner had also witnessed fights and described in gory detail the bloody contests. Of course, the owner added, "I don't fight them 'cause it's cruel."

Adult Women Activities

Because of both gender segregation in American culture and the chivalry of the South, adult women in the Piedmont rarely participated with men in public forms of recreation. Generally, James Edwards summarized, women did all of the cooking, housekeeping (when female black servants were unavailable), quilting, and sewing. Women's "leisure" time, he continued, often meant the production of food, clothes, and bedding for the family. Other female "leisure" activities are discussed in other chapters. In the traditional Piedmont (as in the wider cultural setting as well), men perceived women's domestic work to be their leisure.

SEWING AND QUILTING

Girls often learned to sew, Rosemary Calder observed, by watching an older relative and by practicing on dolls: "My aunt sewed, and I used to watch (I loved to sew), so I watched her and I learned to cut them [clothes] out just like she cut out large people's clothes to make my doll's clothes." Shortly after her family first purchased a sewing machine, Elizabeth Block's mother taught her to sew by demonstrating on old flour sacks; her mother "sat right down beside me and folded the hem and pressed it with her fingers. . . . And we made doll clothes."

While Geneva Patterson's mother taught her, "I tried to teach my grand-daughter, but she's not interested. She's sixteen now. . . . But she didn't care for it. But it was a different time, I guess, when we came along."

By the early twentieth century, folklorists Laurel Horton and Lynn Myers found, women learned to quilt through several overlapping influences. Many women, particularly in the more isolated rural communities, followed the pattern of an African American from Iva who "learned how to piece quilts when I was a little girl; my mother taught me how." "My momma was a first-class quilter," Maxine Williams observed proudly. Albertha Gilchrist learned from her mother, who had learned in turn from her mother, born into slavery; Ms. Gilchrist's grandmother acquired her quilting skills from white families. Concurrently, women's magazines and newspapers began to carry patterns and instructions after World War I, and other women adopted quilting as a popular hobby, Horton and Myers wrote. County demonstration agents also taught the skill, Geneva Patterson recalled. As one WPA author noted, "At the present time, in rural communities and small towns, women meet together for the purpose of 'quilting.' "

Quilting parties, particularly for rural women, remained extremely popular social activities well into the twentieth century. Freed temporarily from domestic duties, in the home of a friend away from their husbands' scrutiny, and with child care under the usually watchful eye of older girls, women greatly enjoyed these times together. Maggie Nameth described typical topics for discussion: "All the turmoils you would tell about what happened when you had your last baby. And the gossip in the community, church." As girls, Mrs. Nameth continued, "we played in the yard while they quilted. Of course, once girls got up ten, eleven, twelve, you learned to quilt. You were really progressing in life, you getting to listen to what was said."

As Kate Flenniken recalled in her WPA interview, the relatively slack period of lay-by time often provided the freedom for quilting parties. Maxine Williams described a typical gathering: "I'd invite all the good sewing neighbors, cook big dinner, and they'd bring a covered dish . . . and sit down in unity, and . . . quilt and enjoy each other. We'd quilt five or six quilts out there a day, depending on the number you'd invite. And they'd all have a good time." "And then, you know, we might have soup for lunch . . . or in the afternoon you might have cake and coffee," Geneva Patterson added. "Some people'd just come to talk to us while we did it, and that's fun too."

As Maxine Williams noted, not every neighbor woman might be invited; or, if they all were, not all might work on the quilt. Like with all other skills, individuals differed in their abilities to stitch a quilt. Therefore, hostesses needed to organize their parties with extreme tact. Velma Childers recalled: "And if my momma thought they wasn't making the stitches neat enough, she'd say, 'Well, you can go in there and do the cooking and fix dinner for us while we do this.' "

Rosser Taylor lamented the passing of "many of the old customs . . . even quilting parties are few and far between." With alternative forms of recreation and media for communication, the necessity for female social gatherings has declined. On the other hand, women as a group still make quilts for charity auctions and church bazaars, and individuals still quilt as well. In fact, Geneva Patterson has perceived a "revival" in quilting.

Popular Team Sports

As part of the package of perks they offered communities, textile mills also supported semiprofessional sports teams. As many informants noted, these teams provided much-welcomed recreation in the otherwise drab and difficult life in these towns. Tom Davis remembered: "Now, my daddy's told me this—[they even] stopped the mill off on Saturday at twelve o'clock, and everybody went to the game." Most of the players on these teams were merely average, Everett Baker believed, but "we've had some guys that *could* have went on and played big league ball, I'm sure. But they didn't want to leave town." At least one player, "Shoeless" Joe Jackson from a mill hill in Greenville, made it to the professional ranks.

These teams, and the communities that supported them, formed deadly serious rivalries. So powerful were these challenges that, according to Everett Baker, "Champ" Osteen, a professional baseball player with the 1904 New York Highlanders (later the Yankees), supposedly told his manager that he had to return to his hometown of Hammondville over the Fourth of July weekend because they were playing their neighboring town rivals.

Despite the proliferation of community and church leagues and the increasing access to professional and collegiate sports via the mass media (as well as the expansion of such teams in the region), company-sponsored teams persist in those mills that have survived in the Upstate. For decades the textile teams in the Southeast annually met in Greenville for the Southern Textile Basketball tournament. The old hall in which the contests had been held has been destroyed, but the tournament continues, today largely overshadowed by the NCAA basketball tournaments in American popular culture. While mill teams themselves no longer form the primary means of sports recreation for Upstaters, the teams, and the interest, remain.

Several other professional sports appear to be popular in the Piedmont, perhaps more so than in other regions of the United States. A glance through the sports sections of regional newspapers reveals a relatively large amount of space devoted to golf and auto racing. Partly because of the mild climate, and perhaps also partly because of the ubiquitous sand in the Sand Hills, golf remains a very popular sport among middle- and upper-class Piedmonters. Auto racing, on the other hand, stereotypically appeals to more redneck crowds. From Charlotte to Atlanta, professional and amateur speedways host races throughout the year. Children trade cards of racing heroes while their parents collect T-shirts, caps, and posters. "For many," John Edmunds wrote about Spartanburg, "the automobile is not simply a means of transportation, but a mania that demands a passion much like love."

Conclusion

Forming additional elements in Piedmont folklife, recreations have enlivened the general pattern of life in the Upstate, providing residents with rest and relaxation. The forms of recreation adopted by area residents reflect, at least in part, the traditions of earlier times. Folk toys have been replaced by Nintendos, but other children's games persist. Many residents continue the popular pastimes of hunting and quilting, while shopping at flea markets has expanded along with the numbers of such places. Like other aspects of Piedmont folklife, games and recreations have changed through the decades but still reflect the influence of regional cultural values.

Religion and Religious Ceremonies

As one of the fundamental roots of the area's system of values, and as one of the principal forces justifying numerous social activities, religion plays a substantial role in shaping the folklife of the Carolina Piedmont. Predominantly conservative Protestant, the area's denominations support invaluable relief organizations for communities and provide important (formerly significant) types of social recreation on Sundays and during annual revivals. Church services also present a means to pass on and to enjoy spirituals and "old-timey" hymns. Despite the intrusions of Sunday football games and lake boating, religion and its expression still form a critical part of the lives of Upstate residents.

Church and Community

As discussed in chapter 4, a fundamentalist faith has influenced Piedmont social life for generations. Robert Chambers described the weekly round of church activities from his youth, characterizing his family as "focused around church." The week began with Sunday morning church services conducted by the preacher, followed by Sunday dinner and resting, including only quiet play by children. Then everyone went to Sunday evening services, again led by the preacher. On Wednesday night, Mr. Chambers continued, "was what's called prayer meeting. And that was not led by the preacher." Instead, laymen would guide the congregation in prayer and singing, others would request prayers, and then would come "testimony," where "everybody got up, just impromptu, and gave their thoughts."

Today, "churches are still very big in the South—very big," Patricia Vaughn asserted, and their hold over Upstate lives remains strong but subtle. From the blue laws limiting alcohol sales and Sunday shopping to the prayers that open high school and collegiate games to community festivals (like Hammondville's) that shut down for the Lord's Day, fundamentalism pervades the Piedmont. Common knowledge in the region is the fact that community groups, from Girl Scouts to city councils to extension demonstrations, avoid Wednesday nights, still reserved for prayer meetings.

Several informants, both in the past and present, noted (sometimes with irony) the fact that the Upstate simultaneously may be home to both the redneck and the fundamentalist. Joseph Stewart discussed this with his WPA interviewer: " 'Society had a distinct cleavage. There was a religious crowd who took things seriously and went to church every time the church had anything going on.' " This group, Stewart continued, established temperance societies and attended revivals. Their preachers thundered fire and brimstone against card playing, dancing, gambling " 'and many innocent amusements that is considered all right nowadays.' " Both perceptions persist side by side in the Piedmont: the rugged individualist subtly avoiding the law of the land and the reserved fundamentalist strictly obedient to the Law of the Lord.

Denominations

Generally speaking, as James Edwards noted: "Most of the time back then you had . . . four denominations: you had the Baptists, and the Methodists, and Wesleyan, and the Presbyterians, ordinarily. And maybe Church of God. So maybe five. You'd have within maybe a ten- or fifteen-mile radius five different churches, or five different denominations." The South Carolina state guidebook reported that about half of all South Carolinians were Baptists, with another one fourth Methodists. These figures approximate denominational membership today too.

Ben Robertson suggested that the deeply rooted predominance of the Baptist faith reflected a fundamental Upstate value: "The Baptist faith was a personal faith, Baptist prayers floated upward from the individual heart, and Baptists were responsible alone for their individual souls—Baptists belonged to a strong, lonesome religion, and the power of the church depended on the individual strength of our faith, on personal expression."

All of these Piedmont denominations, while representative of the general regional attitudes toward God and associated morality, nevertheless have remained in various stages of uneasy coexistence over the past century. Residents have long recognized subtle differences between the sects, not as much in theology but more so in sociology. That is, for each group, the creeds and regulations have often been of less importance than the placement of each church in the social hierarchy. Informants in Kent explained the difference to Ralph Patrick: " 'The Methodists take 'em out of the gutter; the Baptists wash 'em up; the Presbyterians educate 'em; and the Episcopalians introduce 'em to society.' " Another man in Kent joked to Patrick: " 'Methodists are Baptists who can read. Presbyterians are Methodists with backgrounds. And Episcopalians are Presbyterians with money.' "

Implicit in these assumptions are both a folk summary of episcopal epistemologies and a statement of social hierarchy. As in some other Upstate communities, the Episcopalians in Kent generally were in-migrants from the Low Country or their descendants. There, the English aristocrats of earlier centuries had established the Church of England, in contrast to the Baptist, Methodist, and Presbyterian faiths of the Scots-Irish settlers of the Upstate. Thus, as Patrick's informants indicated, in communities where the Episcopal church existed, attitudes toward it reflected a much deeper class division.

Traditionally in most Upstate communities, the predominant church(es) of the community could be found in the center of town and would be the ones attended by the socially prominent families. In Hammondville, the "higher uppity-ups" went to the First Baptist Church, one man commented. In fact, he recalled, one time a mill supervisor had been invited to join the town's Presbyterian congregation, with the assumption that he would thus draw in the "better" people. In Easley, another man explained that "the doctors and attorneys and professional people" mostly belonged to the Presbyterian church. "And it's real interesting how you got social stratas that branch out of certain churches," he added.

On the edges of most towns and on the edge of the traditional social hierarchy would be the more fundamentalist congregations such as the Pentecostal Holiness and Church of God. Just as fervently representative of Piedmont morality and individualism, these faiths carried with them, however, the social stigma of belonging more to the "lint heads" in the mill villages or the rednecks of the trailer courts. A regional official with the Pentecostal Holiness Church, born and raised in small South Carolina mill communities, remembered that Pentecostal churches abounded in the mill towns when he was a child but that the congregations tended to be less highly respected than the Methodists, Baptists, and Presbyterians. Ralph Patrick reported from Kent the same deep feeling of inferiority between mill and town churchgoers.

Piedmonters belong to the church of their choice in part because their church identification holds as much significance to them as does their natal family. When asked why her family has always been Baptist, Maxine Williams replied: "It's just a tradition. . . . Momma was Baptist, the children grow up and they join the Baptist church." For many area residents greeting a newcomer, the first question is "who are you related to?"; the second is "what church do you go to?" Both family and faith, crucial Upstate institutions, are often intricately joined.

Church Social Functions

One's reasons for joining a church might reflect family tradition, but they could also reflect another crucial aspect of religion in the Upstate: the social functions of churches in communities. In the recent past, the hold that churches had on the hearts and minds of white Piedmonters existed in part because of the strong religious faith of residents but equally because of the significant roles churches played in the communities. Gladys Taylor explained: "They looked after their own. There's no welfare system in those days—they were the welfare system. I don't imagine they'd ever let anybody go hungry or go in need, if they could fill it in any way. They were a caring people." In Hammondville, as in virtually all other mill towns, the company donated the land, materials, and labor to build the churches and hired and paid the ministers. Maggie Nameth remembered that, through the churches, the Hammond Manufacturing Company also donated money annually at Christmas to buy fruit baskets for all the families. After the mill was sold in the late 1940s, the money stopped, but the practice continued, "and it still is," she added.

The vital link between church and community became even more critical in African-American neighborhoods. There, generations of residents banded together to form mutual assistance organizations. Maxine Williams described these clubs as "a religious way of helping each other," succinctly linking both the social and spiritual importance of these aid groups. As ethnographer Tony Whitehead argued, these church-sponsored organizations were even more vital for blacks than for whites, because of the failure (until relatively recently) of relief agencies to assist African Americans because of racism. "Why, [when] we got where we wanted to help each other," Maxine Williams explained, "we organized and had a club," such as to help with burial expenses, to cooperate in farm labor, or to care for the sick. "I just hope we're going to keep it," she added.

Whether in larger cities such as Greenville or rural crossroads, Louis Foster explained, "Really, just about all your social life revolved around church. . . . The things that you did that were recreational . . . revolved around the church." "We didn't dare miss," Gladys Taylor recalled, "because we had a lot of socials with our church affiliation." Active church attendance, as Maggie Nameth noted, not only displayed one's faith, reinforced community solidarity, and provided Sunday enjoyment, it "was the one way you got caught up on the news too. You heard what's been going on in the community in church on Sunday."

For African Americans, Patrick and Morland observed among the blacks in Kent, "attending church and church meetings is a central activity." As Ron Kellogg recalled: "Back then, one of the main ways people had recreation was going to church, wasn't it? That's where they met, talked." Both Mr. Kellogg and Jason Lambert, as young men, admitted attending their family churches at least in part to meet young women. Because of segregation, Dale Garroway believed, "about the only fun they [blacks] were able to have was at church. That was their total social life. . . . This is probably turn of the century to the 50s. . . . That church was extremely important. And that's why they'd go at two o'clock in the afternoon and stay 'til after dark, and didn't think anything about it. 'Cause that's the big recreation."

Today, however, views about the strength of church participation differ. Ray Nameth felt that church attendance today has declined primarily because of alternate forms of Sunday recreation such as fishing on nearby lakes or watching professional sports on television. On the other hand, James Edwards argued, "The religious values and everything around this part of the country are still pretty high. . . . Especially on Sundays, I guess if you're around, you'll see more cars at church around this part of the country than you do in some of the other parts of the state."

In addition to the overt social functions that religion fulfills for Upstaters, their faith reveals their values on a more subconscious level as well. As Cash argued in 1941, "orgiastic" religions (the Church of God and other fundamentalist groups) arose to help people gain positive self-esteem regardless of their wealth or status. John Morland found that in the Kent mill villages fundamentalist sects provided believers with the psychological means to deal with the uncertainties of life as well as a hope for the future. Sociologist Harriet Herring tinted such ideas with a Marxist brush, suggesting that "a gospel of work, of gratitude for present blessings, and of patience with economic and social maladjustment" justified and supported the views of capitalistic exploitative employers. As the economic transitions from mill to service work continue to transform the Upstate, faiths that reflect these concerns continue to prosper.

Another indication of the importance of religion in the Upstate can be seen in material culture. For example, outsiders immediately note the large number of church buildings, even in relatively small towns. Many churches, even in the country, are huge, with social halls, classrooms, and recreation centers surrounding (physically and symbolically) the original sanctuary, preserved almost as a memorial (like the family's home place). In front of the church, on portable advertising marquees or permanent stands, slogans and biblical verses offer thoughts to passers-by. During a recent political primary, surrounded by a cluster of slick candidates' signs, a hand-lettered cardboard placard stated: "Vote for Jesus." Outside of Seneca, on a hillside within sight of the Blue Ridge, a sign reads: "Jesus is Lord over South Carolina." A fundamentalist faith rules as well.

Religious Services

Regardless of their functions, religious services in the Upstate adopt a variety of styles, depending on the creed, degree of ministerial education, and preferences of the congregation. While most services in the Piedmont resemble those in other parts of the United States, the stereotypical "fire and brimstone" preacher remains a feature of Upstate folklife. To become such an individual for black congregations in earlier times, Maxine Williams reported, "you just went down there and said the Lord called you and come back and make a speech. And they ordained you. And you could preach then, because your troubles and trials made you preach." Emma Kincaid lamented the fact that such "emotion" seems rarer today in services because modern preachers are more ecclesiastical and less evangelistic. "They don't have that kind of religion now," her husband added.

This fire-and-brimstone type of preaching typically elicited from the congregation another characteristic Upstate worshiping style: shouting. The preacher's enthusiasm, in fact, evoked the emotional energy to electrify a congregation. Maxine Williams offered an example from her childhood: "I remember going there [Baptist church] and all the people'd get happy. There was a Reverend Billy [name], and he would preach—oh, he could preach! And they'd get shouting. And they wore hat pins in the hat at that time to hold it on. . . . But when I'd see them shouting and clapping, I thought that hat pin's sticking them, and I'd cry too!"

While Maggie Nameth claimed that shouting more often characterized congregations in other denominations, she remembered from her childhood that one man in her church used to wail during a particular hymn: "We loved it when we were children! And the minister must have too because they used that hymn now and again, on occasion. And we knew the number of that hymn. And when the minister would call out the number of that hymn, we'd think, 'Oh, boy—gonna have some excitement now!' "

In some denominations, as religious fervor mounts, certain individuals become possessed by the Holy Spirit and begin "speaking in tongues." In what sounds to disbelievers as gibberish, the practitioners and their credulous audience hear in ancient languages the expression of God's Word and the manifestation of God's power. When done in public, the speaker assumes an aura of unearthliness and mystery. For example, Velma Childers had an aunt, Sister Ellen, "fully sanctified" in the Holiness Church. When Ms. Childers's father (a Baptist minister) debated church doctrine with Sister Ellen, she would sometimes lapse into talking "in tongue and get us all straight. . . . When she'd start talking in tongue you would be afraid of her too."

As God's power reaches an electrifying peak, sparks from that energy empower certain individuals in some congregations to receive the ability to heal, either themselves or others. One man offered a personal experience narrative to explain how he had regained the use of his hand, mangled in a mill accident: "But there was a miracle happened in all this. I went to prayer meeting that night. . . . And, oh I was feeling so good and religious over there. I was beating my fist on the sinner [?] table over there. . . , wasn't no feeling or hurting a-tal there. But, boy, I got back home, the right feeling I reckon was a-getting back in there. I begin to hurt, and my mother and dad, they was praying people, . . . and I asked them, I said, 'Pray for me.' I said, 'I'm hurting awful.' And they came in there and prayed with me. Now this sounds like a fake, but I never have woke up with that hand hurting [again]."

For the uninitiated, witnessing a congregation shouting during a service, speaking in tongues, and asking for physical healing can be somewhat unsettling. During a recent annual revival at an Upstate Pentecostal Holiness Church that I attended, numerous members of the virtually all-white congregation began with clapping and joyful singing to upbeat hymns. Then came a period for personal prayer, delivered out loud by the congregation in a cacophony of voices. Booming out over the others, an elderly man connected to an oxygen tank shouted in a patterned but unintelligible tongue. After the visiting preacher spoke in tongues and the band and choir performed several upbeat pieces, the congregation responded with even greater intensity. Soon the shouting and dancing peaked: some literally raced around the auditorium at top speed; others danced and played tambourines in the aisles. Eventually the altar area filled with sobbing, laughing, shouting, praying people; some standing, some kneeling, and others completely prostrate on the floor. With no clear-cut ending to the service, the minister gradually slowed the pace of his delivery, and the audience filed slowly outside into the warm summer night.

Religious Songs and Hymns

Besides the folk songs of secular life, those songs associated with religious worship form another significant component of Piedmont folklife. Maxine Williams suggested that most religious songs had been composed originally by slaves, "and we've brought them on down and changed them up a little bit." In slavery times, Velma Childers noted, the spirituals reflected not only religious belief but also served as a covert code for communication. Today, though, she added, "we're just singing for the pleasure of singing."

Because fewer people in past generations could play (or even had access to) a piano, the earlier songs frequently were sung a capella but in a different manner than today. "There's a old-time way and then there's a new way" to sing the hymns, Albertha Gilchrist explained. While recent songs are faster paced because of piano accompaniment, older hymns were longer and slower. They sounded, Ms. Gilchrist explained, more sing-songy because they were sung in a wavering voice. Elizabeth and Mary Block, as children, listened to the singing from a neighborhood black church but had difficulty describing it. The songs "didn't come out the same way," Elizabeth Block felt. "It had a different melody to the singing," her sister added. "The rhythm is altogether different."

As Albertha Gilchrist noted, the lyrics and music for these sacred songs may have been accessible in hymnals, but many congregations did not have printed texts while others might have been illiterate. Consequently, she continued, "People just made those hymns up, more or less." "I'm sure we have plenty good composers," Maxine Williams commented, "but it wasn't recorded it was composed, but just as we felt."

Even in her church today, Ms. Williams continued, parishioners spontaneously compose hymns about immediate events, such as the death of a minister: "And when you got it in words, and in tune with the music they wanted . . . lyrics. Well, you'd sound it and you could rhyme it, and it's beautiful. And it had a meaning to it."

These songs, especially when sung in the context of deeply emotional services, energized the congregations just like workers' songs used to do, James Williams observed. "You can sing some songs in church," he continued, "and even like the benches will seem like a-move. And them that's on the benches, they'll sure move if they feel it." Maxine Williams noted that in her congregation "this old sister'd get happy and say, 'Come on, children, and let's go home.' You see, you done it from feelings. . . . You get your . . . emotions from your feelings. . . . When you think of the words, and apply it, and I think that's what the whole thing's about. . . . There's something in there, I tell you, that I learnt as a child, that brings back that feeling to you. . . . And even after two hundred years . . . it brings out the same reaction and emotions."

Revivals and Camp Meetings

Perhaps one of the most traditional forms of religious worship in the Upstate are revivals, usually held in conjunction with camp meetings during mid- to late summer (often lay-by time), "when the farmers were not so busy," Helen Quinnell explained. At the designated location, families from a wide region would camp out in tents or (in later years) small cabins. Louise Jones DuBose described a typical camp: "A hundred or so huts or 'tents' are grouped around a central auditorium locally called the arbor. The latter is built with a large roof but no sides. . . . Members of the congregation camp in the huts for a various length of time during the revival and attend the services. . . . The social activities arising from these meetings are significant." Maxine Williams elaborated: "They'd be cooking, and, you know, enjoying, fellowshipping. But then the preachers would come in, they'd start singing and shouting and have the good revivals." After a week of spiritual and social renewal, the families, now refreshed, would again disperse to their mill homes and cotton farms.

While perhaps not conducted with the same fervor as in earlier times, camp meetings and revivals are still held in the Upstate. Gladys Taylor suggested that such celebrations have become "just a sort of a custom that has been known down through the years." Every summer, in fact, newspapers contain special sections listing all the area revivals and camp meetings. Notified through a similar announcement, I attended the Beech Springs Pentecostal Holiness Camp Meeting, held during late July near a small country crossroads.

According to the host minister, the Pentecostal Holiness Church has conducted camp meetings at Beech Springs since 1915. In earlier days, he explained, families camped for a week on the grounds because transportation was relatively poor and facilities virtually nonexistent. Today, he said, some families still stay on the grounds, but most of the worshipers commute each day, especially after work in the evenings. Some attend the morning breakfasts and services and then reserve the afternoon for socializing and relaxing. The largest crowds, though, arrive for the evening services.

The grounds and buildings were extensive. Behind the huge brick church and smaller cemetery ran a long, one-story gray and white brick building that contained men's and women's lounges, a large cafeteria (capable of seating perhaps two hundred people), and a series of motel-like cabins extending another two hundred yards. In front of the building lay a wide, macadam lot surrounding two large shade trees. Around each tree were built raised wooden platforms with benches, for people to sit and enjoy the shade. To the left of the church, in front of the cafeteria and lounges, stood an enormous cement-block auditorium, the tabernacle where nightly meetings occurred. Behind the cafeteria spread the campground, with water and sewer connections for trailers; about fifteen campers sat on cement pads. On the other side of the asphalt lot was a wide field

Beech Springs Pentecostal Holiness camp meeting site; rooms for overnight guests (Photo by John M. Coggeshall)

containing children's playground equipment, a baseball diamond, a teen recreation house, the church office, and the superintendent's residence.

According to participants, the annual camp meeting served several functions. While the feeding and housing of the thousands of attenders cost the church more than they received in donations, the superintendent firmly believed that the benefits outweighed the expense. He described the camp meeting as a "thermometer of the year," a way to gauge and strengthen the congregation's enthusiasm. The superintendent also perceived the camp meeting as similar to the Old Testament calling of the "Tribes of Israel" together; despite the diversity of lives and backgrounds, all can share in one common annual event, thereby building fellowship. One older participant, in fact, has attended religiously for years, renewing old friendships and making new ones. As Emma Kincaid observed about another camp meeting, "There's a warmth and a informality and, just a closeness and a fellowship, in a camp meeting."

All-Day Singings and Homecomings

Another bond of fellowship, reinforced with food and song, is created by church homecomings and all-day singings, also frequently held in the hot and humid summer months during lay-by time. "The first sign of spring," William Vaughn joked, "was the date of the . . . first ADSDOG—all-day singing and dinner on the grounds." Homecomings represented important church anniversaries; since these celebrations often featured gospel singings as well, both types thereby became stronger through their association. As Gladys Taylor explained:

> Back in those days, everybody would bring their food, you know. And you set tables outside, in some shade. . . . Beautiful tables, full of every kind of food that you could imagine. And then you had drinks, and cakes and pies, that were the specialties of all the women in the congregation. And, normally, they had the service just like always, and then after that was "dinner on the grounds," they called it. Then, lots of times in the afternoon they would have singing. They would invite people to come with their groups, like quartets and soloists. . . . That took up a good bit of the afternoon. Nowadays, a lot of times, our members have to get home and watch the ball game. So that's different. That is right much of a difference too.

All-day singings frequently featured "shape-note" singing, where the shape of the note, rather than the line or space, indicated the pitch. Popularized by Piedmonters William Walker and Benjamin White, shape-note singing of southern folk and sacred songs spread throughout the Midwest and South by the late nineteenth century. The notation style was developed by music teachers to enable everyone, regardless of education, to be able to read music and thus enjoy hymn singing. Performed a capella in harmony, the music wavers and fluctuates, blending together with an underlying drone almost like an organ. A listener can easily imagine these same songs drifting heavenward from a plain, clapboard country chapel in the antebellum South.

Velma Childers described an annual singing convention that her father had helped to manage: "And they would come to this convention all day long. One group would sing, and he [her father] would rate them on how they held to the music. . . . And then another group would sing. . . . And at the end of the session, . . . [a] group won the prize for being the best singers in the group." Typical songs, Ms. Childers added, would be " 'get to heaven' songs; . . . all religious songs; all looking for a better day."

As with other church-related events, those who attended did so for various reasons. Some went for the uplifting religious music; children went for different reasons. Velma Childers offered an anecdote from her past: she and her friends had nicknamed one conductor from a neighboring church " 'Cyclone,' because he'd get up there and he'd make all kinds of motions. . . . When he wanted the voices to go up he'd throw his hands

Revival and gospel singing advertisement (Photo by John M. Coggeshall)

way up in the air—they called him 'Cyclone Williams' 'cause he'd do all kinds of things."

Singing conventions persist in the Upstate today, although with much less of the social and religious significance than in previous generations. James Harbin, current president of the Anderson County (South Carolina) Singing Convention (which began in 1868), still performs the traditional songs for area churches. He described a typical convention, which usually opens on Saturday night: "We'll have an opening song, we'll have a prayer. And then we'll sing to roughly ten o'clock. . . . On Sunday morning, . . . just before twelve o'clock or thereabouts the pastor, we'll ask him to have a devotional. . . . Then we'll sing two or three more songs and have dinner on the grounds, and then start back immediately after we eat, and go to around three, three-fifteen." Mr. Harbin has appeared at these conventions "since I was a teenager. . . . I enjoy it—nothing like it as far as I'm concerned."

Homecomings also persist today, although with some modifications. Gladys Taylor explained that meals rarely are eaten outside now; "so many of the churches these days have big buildings that are gyms." Also, "since very few of our members even cook any more," she continued, "a lot of times we have things catered." Lucy Wallace had served on a centennial committee for her church and had joked about replacing the time-honored phrase "dinner on the grounds" with "dinner in the air conditioning," but soon realized that no other phrase captured the traditional idea and sentiment.

The deeply entrenched Piedmont values of family and faith become reinforced further through the serving of family-donated foods at church-related functions. Gladys Taylor neatly summarized these sentiments as she explained typical foods: "Any kind of vegetable that you'd have at home you'd bring a dish of those for the reunion or homecoming at the church. It was the same kind of thing, you know—it was the larger family—the church family."

To examine the social importance of these ceremonies, I attended the Union Grove United Methodist Church homecoming, held in late September on the church grounds. Rather than have "dinner on the grounds" on concrete tables under a shady grove, the hosts served the meal in the air-conditioned fellowship hall, which accommodated the crowd in more comfortable surroundings. About one hundred attended, mostly adults, sitting at long tables upon folding chairs. Foods today are less often homemade, and participants do not stay as long as they used to. Too many eat and run to other Sunday activities such as boating on the nearby lakes. Younger folks, their elders admonished, become bored and restless and do not visit as they themselves used to do.

Despite these changes, the basic functions of the church homecoming remain much the same as they had for previous generations. Older parishioners linger to tell family stories about founding members, still a popular pastime. The minister said he listens to these tales religiously, for he implied that family history recapitulates church history. This tie is recognized by participants, for one woman specifically compared this church reunion to a family one. At both types of get-togethers, regardless of contemporary modifications, family stories reinforce history for the next generations, while all share a communal meal of traditional and contemporary foods. One woman summarized the significance of these homecomings; she feels "this warm sense of belonging."

Conclusion

Piedmont religious ceremonies and beliefs form a significant part of Upstate folklife. Strands of deeply held values about family and fundamentalism cling to, and are reinforced by, religious gatherings. Traditional foods, served at church reunions and revivals, draw additional meanings from the context in which they are offered and consumed. The very act of gathering together with like-minded individuals solidifies both the institutions they represent and the values they uphold. As these behaviors and beliefs intertwine with the historic strands of long-standing social institutions, Piedmont folklife takes its distinctive shape.

CHAPTER II

Foods and Food Traditions

Adding flavor and aroma to Upstate folklife are the foods that typify the region and its people. In fact, these foods play a significant role in numerous social activities in the Piedmont. Whether grown by moon signs in backyard gardens, served at family-based Sunday dinners, or consumed as snacks during storytelling sessions, the types of foods eaten and the context in which consumption occurs are important parts of Piedmont folklife. For Upstate residents, traditional foods, traditional activities, and traditional values remain inseparable.

Foodways in General

The sights and smells of cornbread cooking in a stove or gravy spread over warm biscuits always create powerful images of days gone by for Upstaters. Even as long ago as 1936, John Wigington waxed nostalgic when describing his own favorite childhood foods: "Poke sallet, hog's jowl, buttermilk and cornbread. What a flood of pleasant memories the mention of such things release. Barefoot days, plowboy days, the rush to get through planting, an appetite 100 plus, and the mid-day meal in which . . . fresh buttermilk from the spring house, and corn bread were the big features."

Due to the rural atmosphere of the area today, Tony Whitehead argued, many food traditions persist because residents can still supplement grocery items with food from gardens, hunts, and rivers. In addition, foods also retrieve memories of enjoyable family gatherings, from church and family reunions to Sunday dinners with country ministers. Moreover, since foodways tend to be private, John M. Vlach believed, they would be expected to persist while more public expressions of identity might fade.

Both the foods and their social context serve to reinforce traditional values and, ultimately, a sense of place. Gladys Taylor, whose family hosted soldiers from a nearby military base to Sunday dinners during World War II, discovered that northerners "had never had fried okra. A lot of things that were southern to them that were different to them, that we would have had. And grits, of course. A lot of the boys from the northern states had never had our kind of cooking. . . . And sometimes they had to get accustomed to it before they would even say they liked it."

Besides regional variations, foodways may also distinguish racial, class, and occupational boundaries, extremely important to maintain in the traditional Piedmont. Thus, Whitehead noted, pork neckbones were seen by higher-income whites as "poor peoples food," while lower-class whites saw them as black foods. Rupert Vance described differences in foods between landowning farmers and tenants, with the former consuming better cuts of meat and a more diversified diet of fruits and vegetables. As income declined, though, cornbread, pork, beans, molasses, potatoes, and greens became more common. As might be expected, Lois MacDonald noticed that mill workers generally ate less nutritious foods than town dwellers.

While foodways served at least partially to distinguish classes and occupations, food traditions between races blurred much more than these groups mixed in everyday life. While differential income continued to dictate at least some of the variation between African- and Anglo-American foods, these groups shared much in common. As with many other elements of Piedmont folklife (such as family and religious values), the strands of black and white foodways have blended together so thoroughly that it has become virtually impossible to disentangle them.

Much of this interweaving stemmed from the former relationship between black and white women, traditionally those responsible for preparing family and group meals. Whether in the country or city, mill village or uptown neighborhood, many white families employed a black woman as cook. Dale Garroway explained: "A lot of our traditional foods came from black people, because before this century, during slave days, they did all the cooking. And so fried chicken and all those things, . . . it came from them. And I'd say a high percentage of the white women were taught to cook by black women."

If many white foodways derive from African Americans, where did their preferences come from? Tony Whitehead suggested that black foodways were shaped primarily by the political economy of slavery and then perpetuated under the sharecropping system. From there, the emphasis on pork, fatback, collard and turnip greens, black-eyed peas, potatoes, grits, and cornbread, along with the tradition of frying meats, passed into Anglo-American subculture by means of black cooks for white families.

Regardless of the sources of food traditions, social interaction blended them, ultimately creating the distinctive traditions that mark this region today. Mary Willis recalled eating: " 'a lot of beans, fat back, gravy, grits, . . . buttermilk and cornbread. . . . We ate a lot of fat meat just fried out real crisp and you'd have that with gravy and biscuits. . . . We always had plenty of food but it was a typical Southern diet.' " Moreover, despite cholesterol warnings and weight concerns, many of these traditional foods, and the contexts in which they are consumed, remain important regional indicators.

Foodways about Meat

PORK AND PORK PRODUCTS

For most Piedmont families, one of the least expensive types of domesticated meats came from hogs. Dale Garroway remembered that "when I was a boy, there wasn't much beef. It was pork. People who lived in town had beef." "Always try to have a little hogs, so as to eat a little hog and hominy, as the old saying goes," George Tanner commented in his WPA interview. Preferably, Jason Lambert remarked, these animals would have been fed corn, because "a corn-fed hog tastes better than any hog; . . . makes . . . the meat more harder." During his childhood in a mill village, Tom Davis recalled, "most everybody had a hog back then. . . . And they'd kill that hog."

Arthur Masters tried to avoid the annual early winter hog slaughter because he did not like to see them killed: "I don't think I've ever actually watched them kill one," he admitted. Maxine Williams remembered: "Wasn't nothing for my daddy to kill four or five hogs in the cold weather. We'd start by Thanksgiving. And then you had your meat for the year. You see, you'd salt that slab meat down, and it got cured. . . . You'd go in anybody's [smokehouse], of the industrious people, white and black, and he'd have hams, shoulder meat, the year round. . . . And you got ready to put on a pot of beans, you'd go out there and . . . cut a slab of meat and put it in that big black pot, and boil them." George Jackson fondly recollected slices of those salt-cured hams cooking in a pan: "You can go on out across yonder, you can smell it before you get back to the house."

The butchering process, as Ron Kellogg observed, "became a kind of a community affair, 'cause several people come to help you." In his WPA article, L. E. Cogburn described these traditional activities as taking place just before Christmas, if the weather permitted. Everyone on the farm assembled for the task: men butchered and cleaned, women rendered the

While fatback is popular, not everyone enjoys it. (Photo by John M. Coggeshall)

lard, cooked the meat, and prepared the chitlins. The black field hands assisted the women, Cogburn wrote. Neighbors from other farms also assembled to help as well, James Putnam added, thereby reinforcing reciprocal ties.

Besides hams and the choice cuts of pork, thrifty farm families utilized other portions of their hogs as well. These cuts also formed distinctive features of Upstate foodways. For example, Jason Lambert described the "middlin's": "Some of them call it 'fatback.' . . . And the side, we call that the middlin's. And the back is the fatback. But you can call it all fatback, you know. You see, that back ain't got no lean in it; it's all fat." "How you expect to live to be an old man, you never eat that?" David Hawkins chided me. "People will say fat meat will hurt if they want to," Martha Block noted, "but our grandmother lived to be ninety years old." Of course, as Velma Childers confessed: "That's why we all have [high] cholesterol now!"

Fatback would be utilized to create additional taste treats, as Ray Nameth noted: "But I'll tell you one thing—you get you some good fatback, fry it out good . . . and crisp, where that skin'd be good and crisp." The crispy skin would be mixed into cornbread while the grease would be used to make biscuits. Fatback could also be used to cook along with vegetables.

Minnie Dunn commented: "The older people—they never boiled a pot without putting a chunk of meat in it. And when they was eating the vegetables, they'd have a chunk of that meat on their plate like that." Dale Garroway conceded that "it was delicious, but it's pretty high cholesterol."

Fatback today, Maggie Nameth felt, has shrunk in size from two inches to less than an inch thick: "But you know people who are on the health kick now. And because they [farmers] are not growing pork anymore, they try to grow it leaner." Still, her husband continued, "You'll see it piled up in the grocery stores somewhere or other—this old white meat laying there." Quite common, in fact, near the meat section in most area grocery stores are displays of packaged fatback: large slabs of pure white lard with a piece of pork skin attached. Today "they call it salt pork," David Hawkins noted.

Besides other types of meat, the hog's intestines would also be utilized to make chitlins. As Arthur Masters warned, though, "they smells!" The intestines would be cleaned by emptying out the undigested food and rinsing them thoroughly for several days in cold water. Then the intestines were turned inside-out, scraped, and washed again. Sometimes, Minnie Dunn stated, the "chitalins" would be salted and stored for several days. L. E. Cogburn noted: "After another good washing, they are ready to cook. They are prepared for boiling by looping in continuous knots, and when done, may be served as they are, or fried after being rolled in flour, similar to oysters."

Perhaps the similarity between oysters and chitlins does not end with their preparation; they may also resemble each other by their effects. "Chitlins make you feel like a new man," a black security guard once told me. When pressed for a further explanation, he replied that they will make a person stronger. By the twinkle in his eye and slight smile on his face, I assumed that he meant as an aphrodisiac.

Many Anglo-American informants admitted rather sheepishly that they had tried chitlins, but few acknowledged that they enjoyed them. Most said this food was eaten more by blacks than whites, primarily owing to class differences. Somewhat rare today, chitlins remain a well-known (if not widely consumed) food. "You can actually buy them in the supermarket around here," Arthur Masters commented, "but that smell is still in them; you never get that smell out of them." Those desirous of tasting (and smelling) the real thing might consider attending the weekend-long "Chitlin Strut" held every fall in the Sand Hills community of Salley, south of Columbia.

Most informants today recognize that the consumption of large amounts of pork negatively affects health, but the traditional tug of foodways remains strong. Minnie Dunn, for example, had heard such admonitions for years: "And hog meat didn't hurt nobody that I know of in those days. But hog meat will kill you now." A doctor had warned Ms. Dunn to quit eating pork in order to keep her blood pressure down back in 1952, "and he died in 1953!"

WILD GAME

Piedmonters hunted for both sport and subsistence, but only certain animals were consumed. Perhaps the one most associated with the South in general was the ubiquitous and lowly possum. Dale Garroway and Louis Foster, now academic professionals, reflected on eating possum when they were children. They described the meat as greasy and not associated with higher-status families. "Lord, I can't hardly tell you" what that meat tastes like, Richard Sanders laughed. For numerous Upstate residents, though, possums provided vital protein during lean years of the Depression. "You see, back then, what your parents put on the table, you had to eat it," Mr. Sanders explained.

The problem with possums, Louis Foster conceded, was that they had to be raised properly: "You'd catch a possum, they'd put it up and feed it sweet potatoes . . . for about a month, and they claimed that cleaned him out. See, 'cause they're basically a scavenger." As a child, Ron Kellogg forever lost interest in possum consumption after overhearing an unsettling conversation: "I can remember laying in bed, my parents and some of their friends be talking, late at night talking about possums in the graveyard. Turned me off on them!"

After being properly cleaned out, possums would be cooked with sweet potatoes and barbecue sauce, Albert Wood recalled. Jason Lambert agreed: "Ol' possum was a good thing, you know, if you fix them right. Put them taters around it. But after I quit hunting them, though, I quit eating them. And that's been at least thirty-five years ago."

Raccoons would be prepared in a similar way to possums, Richard Sanders explained: "People catch coon every so often. And that's extra good meat. . . . See, you take them and boil them first, then put them in the stove and bake them, put you some sweet potatoes around there, two or three pieces of bacon on it, and you got you some good eating."

Rabbits were another readily available source of meat protein for Depression-era families. These animals provided many winter meals, James Edwards recalled, because "the meat of the rabbit is not any good in the hot weather; that's what I've always heard them say." Mr. Edwards, raised as a tenant farmer, remembered his mother boiling rabbits in stews or else frying them like chicken. The half-inch of grease left over from cooking would then be used to make gravy. Rabbits are still hunted today, of course, and are still consumed.

Besides fish, turtles also proved to be popular food items, particularly in the past. According to Dale Garroway, though, turtles like snappers presented much the same problem as possums: they had to be cleaned out because they were scavengers. "We fed them cantaloupe," he added. To clean a turtle for consumption, Richard Sanders explained, "You take and put him in some hot water, . . . all that shell will come off of it. Then you have to lay him down on his back, and take a sharp knife, and take that [guts?] out of there. Then that ain't nothing but plain meat. Cut his feets off, head off, you got plenty of meat. You parboil it and bake it." "Momma cooked them just like chicken," Dale Garroway observed.

Several informants noted that turtle meat possessed an odd quality. Richard Sanders elaborated: "But they say a turtle got all kind of different meat—you heard of that? Yeah, they got all kind of meat—beef, pork, any kind of meat. They say they got part of it in his [body]. . . . Every time you get your turtle, . . . when you eat this end it taste a little different; you eat this end it taste a little different."

BARBECUES

It is no coincidence that the Quinnell family reunion, like thousands of others throughout the Piedmont, featured barbecued chicken, ribs, and hash. As the cook himself stated, "Everybody in the South knows chicken and ribs." Both the North and South Carolina state guidebooks noted that barbecuing has a long history in the area: "Usually such a feast is prepared for throngs of people at a celebration, anniversary, or political meeting," the South Carolina guide continued. Farmhands, relaxing during lay-by time, might also be given a barbecue by the landowner as a reward for a productive season. Wesley Jones, a former slave, described a similar event for his WPA interview: "'Dem days barbecues was de mos' source of amusement fer ev'ybody, all de white folks and de darkies de whole day long. All de fiddlers from ev'ywhars come to Sardis and fiddle fer de dances at de barbecues."

Mr. Jones knew the process of barbecuing intimately: "I used to stay up all night a-cooking and basting de meats wid barbecue sass (sauce). It made of vinegar, black and red pepper, salt, butter, a little sage, coriander, basil, onion, and garlic. Some folks drops a little sugar in it. On a long pronged stick I wraps a soft rag or cotton fer a swab, and all de night long I swabs dat meat 'till it drip into de fire. Dem drippings change de smoke into seasoned fumes dat smoke de meat. We turn de meat over and swab it dat way all night long 'till it ooze seasoning and bake all through." "The secret was slow cooking," William Vaughn asserted.

After the meat had been cooked, the preparers removed it from the fire

Homemade barbecue cooker (Photo by John M. Coggeshall)

and shredded it into two forms: "barbecue" and "hash." The former consists of slices of pork, pieces of chicken, or beef or pork ribs, all seasoned with the sauce and cooked slowly over the open fire. Hash, perhaps more common south of the Carolinas border, is made from finely shredded pork and mixed with a thicker sauce. The hash, similar to a thick stew, then is served over rice or eaten as a separate dish.

Traditional barbecuers today are highly valued for their skills. At the Quinnell family reunion, several older family members volunteered to stay up the night before in order to prepare the barbecued chicken, hams, and ribs. They utilized a portable cooker made out of a large milk storage container about the size of an oil drum. The cylinder was cut in half lengthwise, and the metal lid was counterweighed so that it would open more slowly and easily. The maker also mentioned that he had had to remove the can's insulated lining first because otherwise it would have burned. The charcoal fire was placed inside the drum and the meats cooked slowly all night long. The result, consumed the next afternoon, proved to be "finger-licking good."

Today, the love of good barbecue in the Carolinas has not diminished, but the social context has changed. A few skilled cooks still prepare meats for political rallies of hundreds of patrons, as Anne Kimzey reported from

McCormick. Others, such as the Quinnell relatives, prepare smaller feasts for family reunions. Some may even be catered by professionals. Most Piedmonters savor barbecue in restaurants, serving a generalized menu characterized by Kovacik and Winberry for South Carolina: pork, rice, hash (on the rice), sauce (on the hash), sliced white bread, presweetened iced tea, and various vegetables. While contemporary Piedmont residents may vigorously disagree as to specific locations, virtually all could indicate to hungry visitors the "best place in the state" to get real, old-fashioned barbecue.

Foodways about Plants and Plant Products

GRITS OR HOMINY GRITS

The most well-known southern food item from a northerner's perspective must be ground corn, or grits. Ben Robertson elaborated: "At breakfast we had a big bowl of water-ground hominy grits that had simmered for an hour over a slow fire; we never missed having hominy and we never tired of it, . . . and we were never able to understand why people in the Middle West, in the corn country, did not eat hominy too. Hominy was such a good food, eaten with butter or with sliced tomatoes or with red gravy, and it was so cheap. We do not know what we would do in the South, white folks or black folks, if there were no hominy grits."

Informants like Geneva Patterson, who have ventured above the Mason-Dixon line, would agree with Robertson. Mrs. Patterson "always looked forward to getting back to where we could have grits and eggs and bacon or ham for breakfast." As I discovered in a restaurant recently, northerners who request grits stick out like cornstalks in a potato field. When the waitress asked if I would prefer grits or hash browns, I replied "grits," and she smiled at my response. Later she explained that most people with "your accent" refuse the grits that come with the plate, and so she always clarifies the order with customers who have "a different accent" to make sure they understand. Grocery stores throughout the Upstate display sizable volumes of both yellow and white grits, under several labels, on their shelves. The largest packages sold contain fifty pounds, attesting to their continued popularity.

BEANS

Dried beans, usually "pintos" or "field peas," form another important part of Piedmont diets. Maggie Nameth, raised in the country, remembered eating a lot of dried beans such as "butter beans" (lima beans) and black-eyed peas. Tom Davis joked that his family "had beans and bread one day and bread and beans the next." These legumes were commonly prepared, as David Hawkins noted, with "a little piece of salt pork in there." Today, Tom Davis commented, he and his wife still "put on a pot of beans—we have beans, we cook a pot about every other week or something. I love them—they're good for you."

PEANUTS

This legume draws its regional significance not as much from the fact that it is known in the Piedmont but much more so from the traditional methods of preparation. H. W. Corley, in a WPA interview, offered one of the most widely known processes: "In the late summer when the peanuts mature they are pulled and washed and while in the green state are boiled in the shell. . . . As the peanuts cook salt is added to the water. When done, they are not only tender and delicious, but very easily digested."

Boiled peanuts remain widely available throughout the Upstate, particularly in South Carolina. In the fall of the year one sees numerous roadside stands offering them for sale; hand-lettered signs attest to less formal vendors. Frequently a homemade operation, the boiler consists of a large oil drum from which a metal dipper extracts large cupfuls of steaming, soft peanuts. One can also purchase green peanuts in grocery stores and boil them at home.

Boiled peanuts have a unique taste and smell that not everyone appreciates. To those more familiar with hard peanuts, the first touch and bite is disconcerting. The shells after boiling are soft and pliable, slightly slick from the salty water. The mushy softness of the meat tastes very much like a slightly harder navy bean. Consumers simply discard the shells, and at community festivals or flea markets one can locate the peanut vendors by retracing the trails of telltale shells.

Another distinctive way of preparing peanuts is by "parching" them or drying them in some way. Miemy Johnson, an African American interviewed by the WPA, hinted that this practice may be group-specific: " 'Let me fetch you a plate of boil [sic] peanuts, which I just is set off de fire,' " she said to the interviewer. " 'You lak them? . . . Most white folks love them dat way, 'stead of parched.' "

Richard Sanders provided a contemporary recipe: "You get your stove up to four hundred [degrees], put your pan of peanuts in a pan, put them in, and cut your stove off. When it cool down, the peanuts is parched." Jason Lambert's wife offered Ron Kellogg and me some of her homegrown parched peanuts during a recent field trip. Freshly picked from the garden and then roasted by the sun, the peanuts were of various sizes and shapes and slightly smaller than those commercially grown. The nuts had an unusual, coffeelike flavor.

Boiled and roasted peanut vendor (Photo by John M. Coggeshall)

GREENS

The North Carolina state guidebook offered another very typical regional food: "Dear to the heart and the health of every southerner are the greens or 'sallet,' turnip, mustard, poke, and water cress, or 'creases,' according to the section from which one comes. A 'mess of turnip sallet' boiled with hog jowl or fat meat is a common dish." Both collards and turnip greens may be purchased in the produce sections of major grocery chains as well as from farmer's markets. Many people also grow them in their home vegetable gardens.

Collard greens provide important nutrition during times when other garden vegetables cannot be obtained, for they grow well in cooler months. In fact, they need frost, according to Corrie Wingard, a black WPA informant: "These is nice collards. Ma brought 'em to me last night. I always boils 'em with a piece of fat back. That sho' gives 'em a good flavor. All of us loves collards. They's heaps better after the frost hits 'em." Wilma Masters added a more practical consideration, however: "That's to kill all them little ants and things that's in there." "Boy, they good then," she emphasized, "but they ain't better when you cook them, though. . . . They stinks, but they good!"

Thinking about the smell of cooking collard greens then reminded Ar-

Greens for sale (Photo by
John M. Coggeshall)

thur Masters and his wife about "poke sallet": "You ever hear of poke sallet? It's something kind of like a turnip green, but it grows wild. Everybody
don't like it, but when you cook it, it really puts out a smell in the house. . . .
A lot of people cook them with a lot of onions in them, don't they?" Wilma
Masters added: "And then they sit and eat that nasty mess, and I don't see
how they can eat that stuff!" Richard Sanders countered: "It's good. One
mess of it a year will do me, 'cause I've had my share."

Today, Mr. Masters observed, "You see some of the old people going
around picking it." His wife believed that this may be for folk medicinal
purposes as well as for nutrition: "They say that a mess of poke sallet is a
dose of medicine for your kidneys. But I guess maybe I'll stay sick all the
time!"

OKRA

Another unusual southern plant (from the perspective of Yankees) is
okra, which grows on long, waist-high stalks. The vegetable itself is shaped
like a green cone several inches long. "You're not a southerner," Gladys
Taylor chided me, "so you don't know too much about this, but fried okra
is a very popular dish through this part of the country!" "Okra's a good
food for you, for your stomach," James Lambert believed.

Okra may be prepared in several ways, Arthur Masters continued: "You can boil it, or you can even fry it. You ever eat tomato soup? You never made it with okra in it? Well, that's one of the things people around here put in tomato soup. . . . Basically, that's something that you eat mostly in winter months, when it's cold." Ron Kellogg cautioned that when okra is boiled, it becomes "a slimy kind of food"; thus, "most people fry it."

POTATOES AND RICE

Common foods at Sunday dinners, potatoes (both sweet and "Irish"— white) also appeared as snacks or as dinnertime fillers for hungry but poor families. We would have starved, Tom Davis asserted, "if it wasn't for Irish potatoes and pinto beans." In earlier times, after working all day in the field, Jason Lambert explained, "that's all we'd get at night—baked potatoes and milk. . . . When you get full, you're full. . . . You know, people now don't know about that." In mill communities, sweet potatoes were handy after-school snacks, Ray Nameth recalled: "You'd come home in the afternoon, after school, get you a biscuit and a fried sweet potato (my mother used to slice sweet potatoes and fry them in grease, put a little sugar on them—just a little). Get you a biscuit, put that stuff in there; man, that was good."

Rice, while used in the Upstate, was much more prevalent in the Low Country, primarily owing to the earlier attempts to cultivate rice on plantations. Ron Kellogg, raised in the Piedmont, attended college in the Low Country: "I can remember when I was in college, the kids from the lower part of the state, they always wanted two scoops of rice—every one of them. Whereas kids from the upper part of the state, they'd only want one. Most people downstate eat a *whole* lot more rice than people in this part of the country."

Particularly in South Carolina, rice serves mainly as a vehicle to deliver barbecued hash. When rice is mixed with either black-eyed peas or "cowpeas," the combination becomes "hoppin' John," the traditional New Year's Day meal. In area grocery stores, bulk packages of rice may be purchased, attesting to its continuing importance in Upstate diets.

Fruits, Snacks, and Sweetenings

WILD GRAPES

David Copeland, traveling through the Piedmont in late September 1884, described his consumption of a widely known southern fruit: "I came on, as far as Mr. Pitts and spent the evening there, eating muscadines" [wild grapes]. Ray Nameth explained: "Now, you know what a muscadine is? . . . Muscadines grow out in the woods, mostly. A pine tree's usually the best bet for a muscadine vine to grow on. . . . Muscadines don't get ripe until fall, September. They get plumb white-looking when they get ripe. . . . It's got a sweet flavor. . . . You just wash them things and get that inside out—they're good."

A relative is the scuppernong, another wild grape. Robert DeCoin provided an 1864 description: "The most delicious table grape we ever tasted was the Scuppernong, which was discovered on the Scuppernong River, near the Albemarle Sound, in North Carolina." The North Carolina state guidebook cited an eighteenth-century description of North Carolina fare, including "the scuppernong, a white grape native to the State, [which] furnished an especially fine-flavored sweet wine." Maggie Nameth described this grape and its use: "Scuppernongs were a smaller grape [than muscadines], and they don't grow in bunches. . . . And they have seeds in them. . . . People would build an arbor, and you'd have scuppernongs on it. And they'd make scuppernong hull pies. . . . They would use just the hulls, not the inside pulp, . . . and cook them until they were tender."

Today, both scuppernongs and muscadines may be purchased in area grocery stores and at numerous roadside stands, becoming widely available in the early fall. As informants noted, scuppernongs contain several small seeds in a sticky sweet pulp, but they do make an enjoyable snack by themselves. Many Upstaters also process them into preserves or even wine.

MOON PIES

Moon Pies—a classic southern treat—remain extremely popular in the region. Consisting of two saucer-sized wafers of white cake covered with chocolate or yellow icing and sandwiching a layer of marshmallow filling, moon pies help to define the South in general as well as the Piedmont in particular. Everyone recognizes them and many consume them, but most would rather not embrace them as definitive. A character in a Pat Conroy essay suggested their humble context: " 'Why, I've see the mill kids come into school year after year having had nothin' for breakfast except a moon pie and a pepsi-cola.' "

The combination of a soft drink and a moon pie is widely known in the South as well as the Piedmont region. For example, for almost a year, the yellow marquee sign at a convenience store at the edge of Hammondville advertised as a special: "RC Cola and moon pie 47¢." At a recent meeting of the Greenville County School Board, the chairman "handed out Moon Pies and RC colas at a board workshop Monday as part of a long-running joke between himself and [another member. She] . . . said the combination of Moon Pies and 'R-O-C' cola was popular in her native Arkansas." Moon pies may be purchased at virtually all grocery and convenience stores today.

MOLASSES

Molasses can rarely be purchased in stores today, at least not the home-grown kind. The North Carolina state guidebook identified "sorghum molasses, as the southerner calls it, [as] . . . an amber-colored, thick syrup to be eaten with hot biscuits and butter, or with buttermilk, or used in making desserts and candies."

In order to obtain this widely used sweetening, Jason Lambert indicated that, in earlier times, "everybody who was on the farm just about tried to plant some [sugar] cane, you know—that's the way you got 'lasses." Olivia Timms Landreth, describing her farm childhood in the Upstate before World War I, remembered that "we always had a large cane patch. And we very seldom ever bought any sugar. When we used this syrup, you know, to sweeten our pies with."

The process of producing molasses from cane was described by Elbridge Wright:

> When the molassey cane matured, . . . they would strip all the leaves off of the stalk; they would cut the stalk down, cut the top out of it, load these on wagons, and they'd carry wagon-loads to the mill. The mill consisted of two items—the press (from which the juice was squeezed from the stalks) and the cooker. . . . The press involved some big steel rollers that were turned by a mule walkin' in a circle. . . . As the mule . . . turned the rollers, a man stood there and fed stalks of cane into the press, and of course that squeezed the juice out. The juice ran into a container. When you had enough juice to start cooking the juice, then you transferred it over into a big pan . . . something like about eight feet long and about four or five feet wide, and probably six inches deep. Course the fire was built up under this pan. . . . They'd boil the juice. . . . The water evaporated as it boiled.

George Jackson, who made his own molasses until his recent death, described the traditional cooking process: "When you were making syrup like that, . . . the man take it off (or whoever cook it—everybody couldn't cook), he'd take it off too quick, it wasn't exactly done, it would spoil. . . . But he cook it down to where it supposed to be, to where it would just drip. . . . And he could hold it up that-a-way and tell when it's ready to take off. But now you'd have to know . . . something about making up syrup to be doing that. . . . But some people just take it off dead right."

Jason Lambert still grows his own cane and makes his own molasses with a mule-driven press. In fact, on the day Ron Kellogg and I visited, he had several jars in his kitchen that his wife invited us to taste. To me, the sweet, honey-colored liquid tasted rather salty, to which Mrs. Lambert replied, "Maybe it's your mouth!" The Pickens County Director of Public Works Roy Collins enlisted the aid of county employees and prisoners to make molasses the traditional way every fall. At "dinnertime" the workers get to "sample the fruit of their labor, slopped over homemade biscuits and country ham on paper plates." "It keeps an old Southern tradition alive," Mr. Collins commented.

Breads and Gravies

BISCUITS

In most southern homes, Rupert Vance observed, "failure to provide hot biscuits three times a day almost vies with Scriptural grounds as sanction for divorce." Geneva Patterson recalled, "My daddy until he died, wanted fatback—fry it out and you make cream gravy, . . . and hot biscuits. . . . And a lot of people didn't have anything *but* that for breakfast." "I'll tell you," Ron Kellogg reminisced fondly, my mother "couldn't cook enough biscuits."

One time Martha Block nearly faced that predicament. During a wake at her home, nine men had stayed up all night talking. That group ate one hundred and twenty biscuits, which she had baked to feed them. "And our father never eat less than eight biscuits when he'd sit down at the table, when he was working," she continued; "and he never weighed more than one hundred sixty-five pounds."

Some Yankees even risked eternal damnation in order to feast on real southern biscuits, Gladys Taylor joked. During World War II, local families like hers hosted soldiers from a nearby military base for Sunday dinners in order to dispel homesickness. She continued: "One boy in particular was Catholic, and he assured us that if his church ever found out he was coming to worship in a Baptist church, that he would be excommunicated. But he said he'd take that chance 'cause he loved my mother's biscuits!"

Today, though, Ron Kellogg and Jason Lambert agreed that their respective spouses do not make biscuits quite as good as their mothers used to; nevertheless they still love their spouses and their biscuits. In fact, Mr. Lambert added, "I don't eat no 'lasses if I ain't got some biscuits." Ray Nameth appreciated his wife's biscuit-making effort: "What she does that I like, a lot of times, she'll maybe cook some biscuits for supper at night. And she might have a little ball of that dough left over, and in the morning

. . . she'll roll that out," and cook it in a pan full of bacon grease. "It's full of grease," he admitted, "but it's good."

Numerous informants mentioned the biscuits and gravy breakfasts in Hardees as exemplifying the next best thing to homemade, traditional biscuits. "Every local will tell you that," Robert Chambers asserted. "Go into Hardees and get you a biscuit and gravy one morning, and see how you like it," Ray Nameth invited. Thus a traditional southern foodway persists but in an altered form.

Informants also agreed that biscuits taste best with butter, jam, or molasses, but particularly smothered in gravy. After frying ham or other pork, Maggie Nameth described, "you put your flour in some of your grease and you kept stirring it . . . until it's brown. And then you put milk, or milk and water, in there and make the gravy." "It'd thicken up," her husband added. "It's delicious." Biscuits would then be "sopped," or dunked, in this gravy, Mr. Nameth continued. Despite health concerns, this tradition persists.

CORNBREAD

In addition to biscuits, David Hawkins commented, "we eat a lot of cornbread. . . . I'd rather have cornbread than a biscuit." The North Carolina state guidebook noted that "cornbread in some form is served every day in some homes." Not only in the Piedmont but throughout the South, cornbread is quite popular. Rupert Vance, in fact, observed that while northern families annually consumed about fifty pounds of cornmeal, southern families consumed about five hundred pounds per year.

As Arthur Masters observed, "I like cornbread with turnip greens. . . . People cook it with beans—not green beans. They were called dry beans—pinto beans and black-eyed peas, things like that. People usually cooked cornbread with that type of thing. . . . We'd always eat it with greens."

Excellent cornbread, though, also contains the little pieces of hog skin left over from the frying of fatback, L. E. Cogburn wrote for the WPA: "They are removed from the boiling grease, and are placed in a container where they are pressed and as much of the grease removed as can be. They are called cracklings, and are used with corn meal to make crackling, or fatty bread."

While very few people today slaughter hogs and render out the lard in the traditional manner, one may still acquire old-fashioned cracklings, Tom Davis related: "You can get the cracklings (they call them meat skins at the Jockey Lot) and they're fresh—they render them out right there. And you can crumble those up and put it in corn meal and it's really good." Ray Nameth often makes his own cornbread today, "and right before I get ready to put it in the pan I'll stir the cracklings in. . . . I chop them up real fine." His wife Maggie cooks her cornbread, with or without cracklings, in the traditional way: "In fact, *all* cornbread I make, I make in a cast-iron skillet."

Conscious of contemporary concepts of health and nutrition, many informants characterized their current eating and cooking habits with some mild self-reproachings. For example, when describing her preparation of crackling cornbread, Maggie Nameth joked, "Don't go out and tell I still cook like this! I don't care that much for cracklings." She continued, "And you're not going to believe this—when we [she and her husband] go to have physicals, our cholesterol runs low!"

Traditionally, informants in the Piedmont often consumed their cornbread in another widely popular manner. Arthur Masters explained: "My wife said that she used to like to crumble it up in buttermilk. I like it okay like that. I have actually ate cornbread in sweet [whole] milk. Some people like it that way—I liked it okay, though she don't. . . . She wants it in buttermilk. . . . Years back, people used to do a lot of that." Many informants agreed with Ray Nameth, however, who admitted that "we still do that some too." "Good buttermilk and bread is tasty," Tom Davis related.

Iced Tea

In the Piedmont, the characteristic foodway associated with one type of liquid refreshment involves not a particular type of drink but the way in which it is served. John Morland explained: "A favorite, almost year-round drink in the mill villages is iced tea. Except on the coldest days we had iced tea at the boarding house. Each time I have eaten in mill homes, iced tea has been served. . . . Hot tea is unknown as a drink." As Morland also noted, the ubiquitous iced tea is universally presweetened quite liberally, a trait Tony Whitehead attributed to an African-American origin.

Today, presweetened iced tea remains the overwhelming drink of choice for Piedmonters, whether dining formally or informally and whether consuming lunch or dinner. At a family-style cafeteria in Kent one afternoon, the counter waitress took my order and then asked, "Tea?" as if that was what she assumed I would have to drink. At family and church reunions too, huge tubs of iced tea provide the vast bulk of liquid refreshment. Inevitably, the larger container holds the presweetened tea. Even at fast-food pizza restaurants, servers assume that one would like tea, and alert northerners must specify "unsweetened," for the default type is sweet. With a knowing glance, the server will return with a glass of unsweetened tea and four or five bags of artificial sweetener, thereby helping the visitor to preserve the tradition.

Traditional Forms of Food Preservation

Whether mill or farm resident and whether black or white, most Depression-era families practically lived out of family gardens. As James Miles noted, "My mother was very frugal and she canned fruits and vegetables, and we ate from the garden." George Jackson's wife, as with most Piedmonters, learned to can from her mother. Velma Childers's sister worked as the first black home demonstration agent in an Upstate county and helped organize canning groups during the Depression, "so she taught the mothers how to can fruit and how to preserve different things that they might be able to survive on." In a photograph from 1930s Upstate Georgia, several farm women are depicted hoeing in their garden; another photo shows a huge pantry filled with thousands of jars of canned and preserved materials. The art of canning and preserving enabled thousands of families to survive leaner times.

Today, as Arthur Masters observed, some traditions have changed: "I don't ever remember [my wife] preserving any. Well, we do preserve if you want to say freezing it; . . . we do that now. Back years ago you didn't see many freezers. People used to know how to put it in jars and keep it that way. . . . My parents used to put it in jars and put tops on it. . . . But basically most people now just use freezers."

While home freezers have undercut earlier forms of food preservation, they have not completely replaced them either. Many women in the Upstate today combine both forms of food preservation. Albertha Gilchrist, for example, cans certain vegetables like beans with a pressure cooker while freezing other items like corn and okra. Her garden provides almost all her needs: "In fact, right now, I don't buy no beans, no butter [lima] beans, no peas. . . . I have all that right there."

As Jason Lambert and his wife have discovered, though, well-stocked freezers might have their drawbacks too. In their home they keep three different freezers and several pantries full of preserved garden items to sustain them throughout the year. However, their adult children have not acquired the traditional methods of food preservation. Thus, Mr. Lambert scolded, "The children of mine, . . . they come here and get it! They don't know how to put up most of the stuff."

Foods might also be stored by other processes. A more traditional method, described by Albertha Gilchrist, involved sun drying. First, fruits like apples, peaches, and pears would be peeled and cut into chunks, which would then be laid on large pieces of tin out in the Carolina sun. The fruit had to be protected from the evening dew, but within a few days it would be completely dry. Mrs. Gilchrist's family would "dry it by the sacks full," she observed.

The other widely used method of processing fruit, preserving it, is still commonly done today. Mattie Pullin, for example, grows pears in her backyard near Troy and preserves them each year. First, she slices a peck and stores them in five pounds of sugar overnight; the sugar draws the syrup from the pears. Then she cooks the entire mixture down into a syrup in a two-gallon pot and cans the preserves for later use. Freezers can also be used to store fruits without necessarily preserving them in the traditional manner.

Curing meats, another method of food preservation, provided many Piedmont families with delicious meats. L. E. Cogburn, in a WPA essay, explained that after the pigs were slaughtered, the hams and shoulders were cured by being covered in a coating made from black pepper, molasses, and corn meal. The meats were hung up for several days and then wrapped in a flour sack or other cloth. The meat was salted and stored for a month or more until it was ready to be smoked. Then the meats were soaked in water to remove the salt, dried, and smoked with green hickory. A pepper and molasses mixture might be added to prevent excessive drying.

This process, once widespread, has virtually disappeared from the Upstate, a victim of stricter health ordinances and "improved" food quality. George Jackson, however, regretted the change: "I used to have some nice hams out hanging. They'd cure out there. . . . You could just cut one slice of it off, cook it. You'd be out across yonder, you could smell that ham. But now you go up there [to the store] and buy a slice, you can't hardly smell it. . . . I don't know what go wrong. It don't eat like it used to."

Food Consumption Practices

As described in chapter 8, social occasions have played a significant part of the customary routines of Piedmont residents. As might be expected, at large family gatherings elaborate meals were prepared. The overall goal, John Morland noted, was to display "conspicuous consumption" by overwhelming the guests with food. Minnie Dunn remembered that on family holidays "there'd be plenty to eat around. . . . And as I used to tell my mother, I'd say, 'There was so much to eat yesterday, I just filled up looking at it.' "

During revivals, when the visiting preacher ate at several different homes in rotation, Maggie Nameth observed that each family desperately tried to outdo their neighbors: "You could not *dare* put a meal on the table that was less than what they had the day before at somebody else's house. You know, there was a rivalry there."

Part of the purpose for a table groaning with delights was an almost unavoidable outcome of southern hospitality: everyone within relative calling distance might be invited after church on Sunday afternoon. Thus, Maggie Nameth related, "You never knew how many people were going to be at your house for a meal. You prepared for a large number." "When we came home from church," Gladys Taylor recalled, "a lot of times we'd have company there." The Piedmont pattern of a large midday meal followed by evening leftovers or a lighter meal, typical of Sunday afternoons, may have its roots in an agricultural past. The contemporary custom of bountiful feasts for special occasions might reflect this past as well.

One other southern consumption practice is widely known in the Piedmont as well: the almost panic-stricken purchasing of bread and milk from grocery stores at the slightest suggestion of imminent, inclement winter weather. So well known is the practice that television forecasters joke about owning shares in food or store stocks. Shelves empty within hours as puzzled northerners stare with amazement and amusement. This particular behavior might find its origins in the traditional basic southern meal of cornbread and buttermilk. On the other hand, a southern colleague scoffed at that idea, reminding me that bread and milk are staples that one might soon deplete. For whatever reason, the practice is quite common.

Transformation and Persistence of Foodways

As discussed with the various types of foods served, nutritional concerns have modified traditions in the Upstate. At the same time, however, many Upstate residents still enjoy the "bad" foods they ate from their childhoods. David Hawkins explained, "You know, it's a funny thing. Most of the time what you eat as a child, in later years you still eat and enjoy."

In part, Tony Whitehead noted, the persistence of regional foodways is owing to the fact that most residents still have direct or indirect (through relatives) access to gardens, wild game, or home-processed pork. More important, though, Whitehead believed that this continuity can best be explained by viewing foodways as part of culture. In other words, cultural traditions like foodways persist because they meet significant "sociocultural, psychological, and biological" needs. For example, Whitehead has observed that older cooks still prepare the greasy, high-cholesterol foods for a very important reason: they enjoy the pleasure of compliments received when cooking the traditional way. Mattie Pullin, for example, proudly showed her interviewer her recipe box. She had formulated these recipes by cooking the way her mother had taught her, without written directions, while her grandchildren watched, measured, and copied the instructions down on cards. Thus, traditional foodways serve as an extremely valuable link between generations as well as supporting the self-esteem of elderly residents.

Conclusion

From the family reunions at the home place to the RC and Moon Pie at the country store, foodways reinforce and intertwine with forms of social interaction and typical Upstate values. This synergistic blend, Whitehead argued, further explains the persistence of certain southern consumption practices. As people gather around the church social hall or the Sunday dinner table, the taste and smell of traditional foods recapture fond memories and establish new ones. These practices simultaneously support both social institutions and the values they represent, linking families together during summertime reunions, supporting religious values during church homecomings, and tying generations of cooks and their descendants through webs of family heritage. Foods create a powerful bond uniting generations and activities across time and space. Because of this multisensory potency, foodways serve today as an extremely important part of Piedmont folklife.

CHAPTER 12

Traditional Occupational Culture

Four principal areas of work have long constituted a division of labor and class that has consistently shaped social interaction in the Upstate for the past century. Farmers, both tenants and owners and blacks and whites, form one general group, with their long-standing traditions and stereotypes distinct from the workers of the mill hills, a second group, and the local elites of the small towns and cities, a third category. Urban African Americans, originally segregated from most mill work and many city occupations, constitute another group. These men and women traditionally performed menial tasks such as construction or served as the maids and cooks for white elites, forming significant conduits for folklife passing between blacks and whites. Together, the social interaction of all of these groups helped shape the pattern of contemporary Piedmont folklife.

Farming

All farmers and former farmers agreed that the work involved a tremendous amount of traditional knowledge, as James Edwards explained: "I tell ya—it was a art to being a farmer; you had to really know what to do." Many informants began learning the trade at an extremely young age (like their comrades in the mills). Like other farm boys, Vernon Randle was "about nine years old when I first started plowing a mule. Turning land, and laying off land, planting cotton and planting corn." Girls would also contribute as soon as possible. One woman recalled: "The first that I remember was carrying water to the boys in the field in a jug. And I was so small that I had to take the jug and roll it over the terrace, and then crawl over the terrace to get the water to the boys that was . . . plowing."

Regardless of age, field work was extremely laborious. George Jackson complained: "Now I farmed all of my life—*all* my life. . . . My daddy—I didn't want to do it, but he *made* me do it. But then when I got out on my own, I *had* to do it. I didn't like the hard work." "Life on the farm sho' keeps you stirring," George Tanner reported in his WPA interview, "but I don't reckon nothing else would suit me, being that was my raising." Roy Elrod, raised as a farmer in the Hammondville vicinity, agreed: "My daddy learned me to work, but I said there's one thing he didn't learn me. . . . He didn't learn me to like it."

TENANT FARMING AND SHARECROPPING

Since landownership determined economic and social status, those Up-state residents without a land base formed a separate class, subdivided further by race. As discussed in chapter 2, the institution of trading labor for either money (tenant farming) or crops (sharecropping) had become well established in the Piedmont by the late nineteenth century. By the beginning of the Depression, writers like W. C. Hendricks described the existence of farm tenancy as "the most crucial social problem in North Carolina and throughout the South." As Cash observed, the gap between owner and tenant, like that between mill worker and owner, increased tremendously. Ben Robertson, from a family of landowners, described tenancy by this time as "a caste. . . . Tenants had begun to be born into tenancy, to marry into tenancy, and to die in tenancy."

This developing caste consisted of both blacks and whites, who (despite segregation) often lived, worked, and socialized nearly together. This was because, as the South Carolina state guidebook observed, "living conditions among Negroes and whites of the lowest economic class are not as different as is generally supposed." Later, the guidebook described both groups as "thoroughly acquainted with neighborhood customs and ways of tenancy." Thus, Rupert Vance believed that "croppers, tenants, and small owners, whether white or black, have developed pretty much the same practices and ways of living in the eastern portion of the Cotton Belt." As noted in previous chapters, folklife traditions of both blacks and whites shared much in common.

TENANT/SHARECROPPING WORK

Life as a tenant/sharecropper presented difficult challenges for both Anglo and African Americans; however, because of segregation and prejudice, life was even harder for the latter group. For example, the WPA interviewer W. Dixon described the home of Jesse Davis, an eighty-five-year-old former slave in Winnsboro, South Carolina. Davis, his wife, and son all

Never-ending cotton rows
(Photo by John M.
Coggeshall)

live "in one of the ordinary two-room frame houses that dot, with painful monotony, the country farms of white land owners. The three attempt to carry on a one-horse farm of forty acres. . . . The standard of living is low." Hours were long and tedious, George Jackson recalled: "When I was out there sharecropping, you didn't have time to do nothing but catch that mule, go on out there in the field. . . . Plow him to twelve o'clock. . . . Come home and get them beans . . . or whatever it was. . . . One o'clock get on back out there in the field again. [Plow until] that sun get to where you can't see. . . . When that sun goes to peeping up, you better get up and get on about him [the mule] again."

While men did the plowing, women worked just as long and at equally challenging labor. Besides field work, women traditionally cared for children, prepared meals, cooked, cleaned the home, canned and preserved garden foods in the fall, and sewed and quilted all the family's soft goods. Colie Craft, like many other Depression-era impoverished women, married early not to avoid work but to attain relative independence. Mrs. Craft married her husband Daniel when she was sixteen and he was thirty-four. She told her WPA interviewer: " 'We were poor, and there didn't seem anything else for me to do. We lived in the country and all of we [sic] children had to work in the field. So I figured I had just as well marry Daniel and have a home of my own.' "

A North Carolina prostitute described her pre-Depression life to a WPA interviewer similarly: " 'I was the eleventh child of a sharecropper. We lived at two or three different places and we never had more than three rooms. . . . We was supposed to get half of the crop [but] . . . we never got a thing out of our money crop; never. We did usually get the corn and pea vines to feed the stock on, and we cleared new ground and done other outside work to buy our rations in the winter months. Mama used to take in washing for the few in the neighborhood who could afford to have it done.' "

Velma Childers adopted a more philosophical approach to the poverty from farming. Her father, a minister, always counseled his family to live by the Bible: "That was one reason he never did accomplish anything any more than he did because he always said, 'It's just as easy for a camel to go through an eye of a needle than for a rich man to get to heaven.' So we all wanted to go to heaven so we rather stay poor and go to heaven than accumulate anything and miss it. . . . But I always thought, 'I don't think God had any objections to your being comfortable!' "

Because of the tremendous need for labor in cotton farming, many informants helped on the farm as children rather than attend school. "Out there in that field—that was my school," George Jackson recalled. Jason Lambert, several decades younger, remembered bitterly: "Went to school maybe month or two out of the year. . . . Sometime around November and December we'd go to school. . . . But the time'd come to plant, had to go to the field and break up the land. . . . They'd take us out of school before school was out. When we should have been getting more schooling, we were working." Ron Kellogg, born a generation later, added: "I can remember when we were living on the farm, . . . you get to stay out of school to pick some cotton. And you'd see the bus'd go by so we'd lay down in the field so the other kids wouldn't see us." This differential access to education not only exacerbated the class distinctions between landowners/elites and tenants/sharecroppers, it also enhanced the gulf between blacks and whites.

A benefit to this type of annual contractual labor between landlord and sharecropper/tenant was that the latter group ostensibly could choose for whom to work, reflecting the importance of individuality as a basic Piedmont value. Potentially, James Edwards suggested, this might create a "buyer's" market for tenants: "And it was a competitive field, I guess, because I remember several people coming to my house trying to lure my dad away. He had a name for a pretty good farmer, you know. And people would come to try to lure you away and offer you a better deal, or a little better house, or more acres to farm, or maybe they might furnish your cotton seed." Martha Block cautioned, though, that "it was not like that at all places—you might as well know. . . . But if you had some good ones somebody'd try to steal them away from you."

Simultaneously, tenants had the individual right to avoid unscrupulous owners, Vernon Randle noted: "Used to be a fella, . . . had a big farm. . . . Well, they say that man'd take everything them people made. . . . You go there and farm his land, you wasn't going to get nothing but just what you owe and what you ate. When you leave there, you be owing him." Likewise, Jason Lambert felt that one of his employers had not given him "a fair deal. And so I married and then I moved with the other one 'cause that where my wife was born. And . . . I got a little better deal with the other one."

In part, the honesty of an owner depended upon their estimation of goods bought on credit, for all basic and ordinary living expenses had to be purchased without cash from town merchants (see chapter 2). Maxine Williams explained, "And during the summer, if you needed clothes, dry goods, . . . you could go there [to the store] and get what they call allowance, you know—you could buy so much on credit. . . . Farmers could buy . . . fertilizer. They could buy . . . groceries, tubs of lard, barrels of flour."

When the crop came in and tenants/croppers received their shares, Vernon Randle observed, "Some'd get out of debt and some wouldn't." Those who could not pay off everything, Ron Kellogg noted, "had to find them something else to do during the winter months. . . . 'Cause I can remember my father . . . going to Florida to work during the winter months. . . . You had a poor year, by the time he paid the bills there wasn't nothing left—if he paid them all."

Throughout the South in general gradually developed by the 1930s an agricultural system frighteningly similar to that of a century earlier. As discussed in chapter 2, African Americans were forbidden by law to work in the region's expanding textile industry, which increasingly siphoned off white tenants into the factories and mill towns. Coupled with this were the Jim Crow laws of segregation, preventing most blacks from obtaining even a minimum equivalent education and virtually excluding them from the voting booths where real political change might otherwise have occurred. The region's deeply rooted tradition of paternalism too supported the assumption by elite whites that blacks were incapable of caring for themselves and needed well-meaning caretakers to safeguard their rights. In return, blacks were to feel thankful and submissive for the largesse. In effect, virtual slavery had returned to the Piedmont.

Numerous social reformers, as well as the tenants themselves, recognized the potential for exploitation inherent in this system. Cash discovered that

Abandoned tenant house with landowner's home in background
(Photo by John M. Coggeshall)

landlords viewed such exploitation not as dishonesty but "simply a part of the natural right of the man of property" to claim all residual income from his land; in effect, the persistence of the antebellum attitude of paternalism. Henry Ketchin, a Winnsboro area farmer in 1938, described the evolution of the situation: "After the [Civil] war, . . . a Lien Law was devised to gain credit for the farmer. . . . The landlord had a lien for the rent of the land, and the merchant had a lien for the supplies furnished to make the crop. The merchant . . . set the price of the cotton. Could a tenant, usually a Negro, be in a more hopeless situation?"

In fact, Rosser Taylor noted, "many landlords preferred honest, industrious Negro tenants to shiftless white tenants. They were, as a rule, more tractable and obliging and were generally content to submit to a lower standard of living. White tenants required more 'fixings' and were sometimes squeamish about living in houses which formerly had been occupied by Negroes."

While some white landowners undoubtedly were honest, many others were not. Vernon Randle offered this assessment: "Yeah, they'd cheat you. Some of them'd cheat you if you *could* write. . . . There used to be some dirty old farmers—you know, people that own the land. If you go to him, farm his land, he going to take everything you got. Never would get out of debt with him. He'd cheat you. He could beat you counting."

"Some of them [landowners]," James Benson said, "they'd take advantage of you, because you didn't keep no figures." When sharecroppers like Jason Lambert's father settled up, the employer kept the books and set the prices for loans during the year, such as for clothing, food, and fertilizer. At harvest time, the employer also sold the cotton, so sometimes the worker might never learn the actual selling price. Finally, the landowner or his agent also did all the computations to figure the entire debt and the ultimate profit, if any.

By the end of the year, after everything had been calculated, it was entirely possible that nothing might remain. George Tanner, for example, produced a huge crop every year but admitted "we commonly uses what we makes a year on this place for what we're obliged to get." Manda Walker, a former slave from the Winnsboro area in 1937, described to a WPA interviewer the situation of her early marriage: " 'When de children come on, us try rentin' a farm and got our supplies on a crop lien, twenty-five percent on de cash price of de supplies and paid in cotton in de fall. After de last bale was sold, every year, him [her husband] come home wid de same sick smile and de same sad tale: "Well, Mandy, as usual, I settled up and it was—'Naught is naught and figger is a figger, all for de white man and none for de nigger.' " ' "

Other stories depict the cruel injustices often inflicted on black tenants by white landowners. George Burris provided a poignant example:

Us had all kinds of chickens, and one time us had a mule and cow, but you know how it is with poor ol' niggers. Every year the white man would come 'round with the year book and sorta figure up how we stood. Well, sometimes he would give us a little money. . . . Then the next year when the man would come back, he would tell us that we hadn't made nothing that year. . . . Then he would take the calf that Pa had saved for a young cow. . . . [Eventually] Pa kinder got on to what that white man was doing; . . . he made us move right out. . . . [Later, on a farm in "Kent" County] we made nothing the first year. . . . In the fall of the year the man came and took our cow away from us. . . . Ma was sick and needed milk then, more than ever, but that man didn't care nothing about that. He told us if we didn't make nothing the next year, he was going to take them mules back. . . . Ma died that summer and Pa give the man the mules.

With the law virtually always on the side of the whites, blacks were almost always doomed. As Leon Berry bitterly exclaimed, "How you going to get anywhere, the other man take it all? That's the way they done you. . . . That's the way the other man got so far in front of the Black man."

With the massive transformations to the political economy and agricultural base of the Piedmont following World War II, and with the gradual awakening to social equality of the area's residents, it would seem that the older paternalistic sharecropping system would have disappeared completely from the region. However, it persists today in small, isolated pockets. In southern "Kent" County, where cotton is still grown on large farms with tenant help, many hired hands live in ramshackle buildings scattered throughout the fields. Other homes remain occupied by older black inhabitants, who had worked for years for landowning families and now have retired to live rent-free for the rest of their lives. Comparisons between these houses and the more modern home places reflect traditional ideas of paternalistic concern as well.

Mill Work

For most of the Anglo-American residents of the Piedmont over the past century, two principal occupations influenced their lives and continue to shape those of their descendants. One of these jobs was cotton farming; the other task was mill work. This latter occupation implied not just income but in effect an entire lifestyle for the workers and their families: one's standard of living, one's social position, one's values and outlook on life, one's forms of recreation, and perhaps even one's religious background. Mill work, like cotton farming, formed a significant subculture in the past century's heritage of the Upstate.

TRADITIONAL TYPES OF WORKERS

At the very top of the mill hierarchy (and in fact most likely living in the largest house on the highest hill) was the superintendent of the factory. Below him (women supervisors were virtually nonexistent before the 1970s) was an overseer of each department or "room," such as carding, spinning, or weaving. "Second hands" were their assistants. Departments were subdivided into sections, headed by section hands. "You was kind of a little old boss yourself when you got to be a section hand over your department," Ray Nameth observed. "Fixers" repaired any disabled machines and, because of their mechanical knowledge, ranked relatively high. "Hands" (the traditional farming term) operated the machines, while "doffers" transported spindles from machine to machine. On the bottom of the rung were the "sweepers," who removed the loose lint from the floors.

To mill hands, just as within their neighborhoods, their colleagues were "like a family." Edna Hargett explained: "In the mill, it was hard work and aggravating work, and we all complained a lot. . . . But still, I think that ones living now would say, in a way, they'd love for times to be something like that. Of course, the wages was awful low back then, but still we had a comradeship we don't have now. We had the love for one another we don't have now." Icy Norman, a former textile worker from Burlington, North Carolina, described her sentiments upon retirement: " 'When I retired it was like leaving my family, because I felt like they was all my family. . . . Every time I go back up there I feel like I'm going back home.' "

Mill positions inherently had the assumption of class ranking among them; those individuals with the more prestigious jobs, in other words, felt themselves to be, and were seen by others, as slightly better than those below. However, any supervisory position based on an internal promotion immediately created a potential anomaly: equals overseeing equals. In the South, with a value system emphasizing individualism, and in mill villages emphasizing familial bonds between neighbors, workers promoted from within faced awkward challenges.

To help reestablish a sense of family and equality between employer and employee on the job, workers often resorted to practical jokes. At other times, supervisors like Everett Baker manipulated another southern trait, the importance of family ties: "Everybody knew my family; everybody knew me, . . . I was a pretty good guy, and everybody liked me. . . . I knew a lot of the people, most of them, and everybody knew me. It was pretty easy for me to go in and check them on the job." Wit and tact also proved indispensable.

Another internal mill division was that of one's shift (first, second, or third), an economically irrelevant but socially important categorization. John Morland elaborated: "Almost in the same breath with a person's name is mentioned the shift he works on. One's shift indicates when he has spare time, when he eats, and to some extent his prestige, since the first shift carries highest prestige."

Gender formed another internal division. Women worked in the mills as well but rarely in direct competition with men; in earlier times women were never fixers or supervisors, the higher paying positions. "There was [gender] segregation as far as jobs were concerned," David Hawkins admitted. Both Mr. Hawkins and Everett Baker agreed that women might be sweepers or doffers, but it was much more common to find women in the spinning or weaving departments. Perhaps, as Mr. Baker suggested, this was because these duties required "a little finger dexterity," which women tended to have more than men, he felt.

For a generation or so, children formed another category of workers. Children had traditionally labored alongside adults on the farm, so they logically continued doing so when families first moved to the mill villages. Alexander Batchelor discovered that in 1926, on the average, two children from each mill family worked in the factory and would rather work than attend school. Some, he continued, helped support a sick parent or worked in place of a deceased or absent parent while others contributed income to increase the family's standard of living. "It took two or three salaries to keep up," Gladys Taylor noted.

Upstate residents who worked as children, or whose parents worked, painted a fairly bleak picture. Ray Nameth's mother, he recalled, entered the mill when she was ten, working a twelve-hour shift to help the family finances. Esther Phillips began work when she was twelve, for ten cents a day, and turned all of her earnings over to her father. James Miles "didn't get along in school" and begged his mother "to let me drop out" so he could work in the mill; she agreed.

By the time youngsters reached high school age, only a tiny percentage continued on in school, Allen Tullos found. Even after child labor laws had taken effect, required attendance only continued into the middle teens. Even for those in school, mill labor had a profound impact. Maggie Nameth commented: "I can remember when I was teaching . . . we would have boys who would come to school for a full day and then go to work at four o'clock, get off at twelve, and be back at school the next morning."

Because of the segregation discussed in chapter 2, "nobody working in that mill but the white folks," Vernon Randle observed. Thus, Arthur Masters noted, blacks could only work in the warehouse, as janitors, or as groundskeepers. One man, until desegregation, worked both in the warehouse and as a groundskeeper; in fact, during slower times he was required to cut his supervisor's grass as well as that around the mills.

MILL WORKING CONDITIONS

In mill towns throughout the Piedmont, factory whistles signaled shift changes: for Oliver Wilson in the late 1930s, these typically were forty-eight hours per week, an improvement over the earlier fifty-five hours per week. Colie Craft, a mill worker in Columbia in 1938, worked until midnight: " 'but I don't get to sleep till after 1 o'clock. When I get home every night, I wake mother up and we kindle a fire and sit around and talk for an hour or more. We make coffee and eat something, if we can find anything to eat. . . . Hours in the mill and my family duties at home wear me down sometimes.' "

Not only were the hours long and wearisome, but working conditions made them even harder to endure. James Miles recalled a particular job-related handicap: "Life in a textile plant was . . . especially hard for me because of my height. . . . For years I was stooped much more than I am now. . . . I was stooped by working in a stooped position for years and years and years."

Informants also described other occupational hazards: the loose lint and dust from the cotton fibers as well as the excessive noise of constantly running machinery. Grover Hardin, from one South Carolina mill town, remembered: "When you hit the mill on Monday morning, you'd have a tough time a-coughing. You'd cough, and sneeze, and cough, and fill your mouth full of tobacco and anything else to try to keep this dust from strangling you." Ethel Hilliard faced similar difficulties: "One thing I remember. I coughed the whole time I was in there. There was too much hot lint in it. And the machines was noisy running, and just a-flying." Everett Baker's mother-in-law, who had devoted her entire life to mill work, had become hard of hearing from having worked in the weave room. The noise, Mr. Baker added wryly, "bothered some people."

Besides the dirt, noise, and lint, the machines themselves created an even more treacherous occupational hazard. The rows between moving parts were quite narrow, the machines themselves full of spinning, sharp projections, and the workers were often young, tired, or careless. "It wasn't unknown to lose a hand or an arm," Mr. Baker noted. Carl Thompson, a Charlotte-area mill worker, offered an example: "I'd seen so many get hurt on them [the machines], get their arms broke. That was when they had overhead pulleys. . . . There was one man, his shirt or something or other got caught in that belt, and that belt throwed him to the top of the mill and busted his brains out. He just hit the ceiling of the mill. . . . It killed him." For workers who became too disabled (by losing a hand or arm), Mr. Baker noted, the company gave them other jobs, such as watchmen: "in the old days this happened quite often."

MILL WORKER ATTITUDES

As discussed in chapter 3, mill workers shared a common worldview, shaped by their relative social isolation, the social interaction of their mill hill neighbors, the stereotypes of other groups, and their boring, underpaid, and sometimes hazardous jobs. In part to relieve the stress of these dangers, and in part to retaliate against a paternalistic company that underpaid and overworked them, employees sought surreptitious ways to fight back. Like workers in many other service occupations, mill hands mastered what Tullos described as "tricks of the trade." Some of these were relatively serious, such as the occasional theft of material by throwing cloth out the mill window and retrieving it later. Other "tricks" were more innocent, like the practical jokes and other forms of recreation during slow or down times.

Clever workers might also "steal" time, as Ray Nameth explained: "You learn shortcuts in that type work. . . . When you been on the job pretty long awhile, and you figured it out, made the shortcuts where you could get more rest out of it."

These "shortcuts" then became extremely useful when mills adopted the notorious "stretch-out system," where supervisors applied time management studies to laborers, getting more work from fewer people; hence "stretching out" the workers. In order to evaluate efficiency, however, each job had to be timed initially. Mr. Nameth was ready: "Well, now, a good smart worker could outsmart the man with a stop clock. You could do the same job, and just be sure you were just a tad slower. You know, you . . . made your job look like you were really staying busy all the time. . . . What I did, the time they checked me, I went back to my long ways. I didn't do my shortcuts."

Such worker retaliations, innocent or not, reflected the growing frustration of mill laborers toward their occupations and their lives. As "lint heads" became identified as a stereotypical social type, their values and attitudes also came under scrutiny by social reformers, trying to understand their particular attributes.

All agreed that mill workers were becoming increasingly poor; in turn, this poverty bred despair. " 'Mill folks is too busy scufflin' to think about anything but bread, meat, and work,' " one man commented to Lois MacDonald. This poverty, historian Susan Willis believed, led to apathy and complacency: " 'When you don't know there's anything much better in life, you don't miss it,' " one woman related. John Morland summarized worker attitudes: acceptance of life as it is; no desire for improvement; noncompetitiveness with neighbors; repression of emotions, especially around strangers; and feelings of inferiority and inadequacy. Even in sports and recreation, Morland added, "a person who brags or shows much self-confidence . . . comes under censure" (note then the role of practical jokes as crucial leveling mechanisms).

Related to these values was that of living for today; mill people, Morland found, spend their money as soon as they receive payment. Abel Starnes, a mill worker interviewed in 1939, reflected this apathetic sentiment: " 'But, shucks, we couldn't save anything—Didn't even try much. You know how most mill people do. They spend everything they make.' " Reflecting the paternalistic concern and control of management, the Hammondville newspaper exhorted workers to "buy only what you really need. Save something every day."

John Morland associated these worker attitudes with several cultural practices, such as the feeling of insecurity about affection (carried into adulthood) created when infants were forced to leave their parents' beds, replaced by younger siblings. He also observed that in mill churches "the sermons, . . . [and] their emphasis on the authority of the Scriptures, give

Sewing Center advertisement for textile workers (Photo by John M. Coggeshall)

sanction and support" to mill attitudes of humility, passivity, and inferiority. On the other hand, some observers have argued that these feelings of complacency and hopelessness ultimately stemmed from the workers' increasing recognition of their own impoverished condition.

MILL WORK AND WORKERS TODAY

Despite improvements in facilities, older cotton mills remain noisy, dusty, and dreary places to work. The noise level continues to be deafening; in fact, for both tours I have been on I was issued earplugs. The amount of loose lint and thread swirling about the machines and in the air, too, is alarming, since that material might drift into one's lungs. As Allen Tullos discovered, many former textile workers, some with only meager pensions, suffer today from byssinosis, "brown lung disease," their lungs so clogged from years of inhaling lint that they no longer function properly. To me, the most frightening aspect of the workplace was also the least avoidable: the rows of whirling, open machines with thousands of movable, entangling parts. Textile mills, I decided, have always required a very determined group of men, women, and (in the past) children to seek their living in this manner.

Corporate consolidations, plant downsizings, and overseas production have limited mill employment opportunities in the Piedmont today. However, the textile industry persists, often in a different form. Springing up throughout the region in the past generation have been long, low, nondescript buildings. These "sewing halls" or "sewing centers," depending on their size, may employ as many as three hundred workers, frequently women, often blacks, and always for minimal wages. In these small factories, cloth is shipped in to the employees, who sit at rows of machines and cut the pieces out and then stitch them together. Others press the clothes, package them, and ship them to distributors. Wilma Masters, who has worked at several of these centers, described her duties as extremely taxing: "You just go and go all time. Only time you sit down is when you're eating your lunch. After you get through with your lunch you get right back up." The desperation and hopelessness of mill work has, in some ways, persisted.

Traditional African-American Labor

Forbidden by law and by custom from working as equals in the mills until desegregation in the 1970s, blacks leaving the hard labor of the farm had few other opportunities. Like the poorest social groups in other times and places, African Americans did "the most strenuous and hazardous of jobs," Allen Tullos noted. Men worked on railroad crews, as janitors, and as laborers, while women worked in white homes as cooks, maids, or child-care providers. As the Anglo Americans themselves recognized, these occupations perpetuated the antebellum slavery pattern. Ben Robertson, for example, noted that on his family's farm "we live like Job of old in our country, with cooks to do our cooking and washwomen to do our washing." Ralph Patrick and John Morland, likewise, recorded from the Kent elites a deep-seated antipathy toward manual labor, such as cooking and cleaning, fitting the "Old South" attitude that such work should be reserved for black servants, which explains why many whites could maintain their traditionally slow-paced lifestyles.

AFRICAN-AMERICAN WOMEN

Like women in many other cultures, working African-American women in the Piedmont faced some very difficult choices. Velma Childers elaborated: "Wasn't any jobs open to black women only in these white people's kitchens. They cooked for them and cleaned their houses and tended their babies and did that while the white women worked in the stores and places like that. And they all had maids."

Training for these tasks began at a very early age, Lucindy Brown recalled: "I worked as a domestic help all of the time. And when I was a little girl, I remember a lady gave me a dollar a month to stay with her. . . . And my mother let me stay there with her. And I just grew up doing domestic work like that."

Black mothers then faced some heartrending decisions, for it might mean the benefits of much-needed additional family income weighed against the drawbacks of losing a daughter (and the pleasures of her childhood) as she moved out of the home at a very early age. For example, Minnie Dunn recalled: "I stayed with one [white] family years before I married and helped raise children with them. . . . I was right there with them, day and night. And so, I'd just come home to my people once, oh, come home Sunday afternoon a little while and then once in awhile we'd have a Sunday off and then come home, say, on Saturday night and then right back there Sunday evening." Wilma Masters, too, worked as a domestic for a white family about eight miles from her family home and returned to see her parents and siblings only on the weekends. Even after Vernon Randle had married, his wife had to leave their home at five every morning in order to walk to Hammondville and cook breakfast for her white employers.

On the other hand, Alice Gassoway stayed home because of her mother's pride—still employed, but also "free": "My mother never hired any of her children out to work for white people. She washed and ironed, and what we could do here to help her, well, that's what we did. . . . So she always said, 'They'll do what *I* want them to do instead of going off.' "

For African-American women, these service occupations proved to be difficult and disruptive, forcing them from the comfort of their own homes and families, often at unbearably early hours or for long periods of time, for very low wages. One Greenville woman described her family's cook's responsibilities: "those days, . . . the cooks . . . came in time to fix breakfast. We had mid-day dinner. And then she would leave in the afternoon with supper prepared in the refrigerator." Virtually all black informants recognized the hardships inherent in these long hours.

White employers, however, rarely acknowledged these difficulties. Black cooks in Kent loved their work, John Morland reported their white employers as believing, because "all they had to do was to turn on the radio and cook pinto beans." To whites, black nurses or cooks were "almost like one of the family," which generally reflected a sincere feeling of care coupled with a paternalistic sense of social distance. "I've had blacks working in my home," a Hammondville woman commented, "and I just really loved them dearly, and appreciated them." Another Hammondville woman elaborated: "We had a lady who . . . came as a maid every day, and cooked and what-not. And we were crazy about her. . . . [She] used to go with us to the mountains a lot. And we had a maid's room on the house in the mountains." The informant had even saved a photograph from her girlhood that showed this black caregiver, in a white uniform, keeping a watchful but distant eye on her and her cousin.

In the Piedmont (in fact, for all of the South), this familial concern permitted private exchanges of emotion while simultaneously forbidding any public interaction as equals. For whites, the children of their African-American nurses may have been playmates, but both groups also recognized and dared not violate the immense social gulf dividing them, and thus perhaps making certain types of relationships more acceptable. Each lived in different neighborhoods, went to different schools, worshiped in different churches, married in different groups, utilized different public facilities, and had entirely different opportunities for the future. As discussed in chapter 3, the traditional relationship between whites and blacks consisted of a complex theater of social interaction, with certain roles permitted and others absolutely forbidden. As long as both knew their scripts, the performance was an (unequal) success.

If these black domestics were old enough, they might also watch their employers' children as well as clean the house. African Americans like Alice Gassoway described this occupation as one of the few available to black women before desegregation. Maxine Williams noted, however, that only nurses who could read would be hired "and got what they call good pay," especially when compared with picking cotton.

Black mothers, with their own children to watch but with the necessity of caring for their white charges as well, may have been forced to place their own children in the hands of relatives or neighbors, potentially undermining the solidarity of the black family. Much more commonly, however, these working mothers simply brought their own children, especially when preschoolers, along with them to the white household. Maxine Williams, for example, grew up in this way: "And those [white] children was put to bed with us, eat with us till their mommas come back. And then we'd play together."

As discussed in chapter 3, the continuing interaction between these black domestics and their white employers or charges fostered the constant exchange of folk (and other) information between groups who otherwise did not mix in public. Ralph Patrick and John Morland, for example, noted that black cooks in Kent occupied positions of trust and intimacy in white households and served as conduits to pass information from the black to the white world and vice versa. Likewise, the social and emotional interchange between adult black women and white children provided another extremely important vector by which African-American traditions entered Anglo-American culture.

Cooking traditions, too, often passed from group to group. Minnie Dunn had to learn how to cook what her white employer wanted: "I didn't know how to do anything but cook the country way. You know what I mean—just put on a pot of cabbage, and a pot of beans." Alice Gassoway, though, could not bluff her way through her first cooking job, even by invoking time-honored southern tradition. As she explained, she had fled the South and sought employment as a domestic in New York, using her friend's references to land a job. Told by her white employer (who was leaving on an errand) to make apple dumplings, she tried to prepare them "just like my mother made chicken dumplings . . . and it was just a mess!" When her employer returned and opened the pot: "she said, 'My goodness! What kind of mess is this?' I said, 'that's the way my mother make apple dumplings down South!' "

According to William Vaughn, one perk of being a black cook was the tradition of "toting"—carrying home leftovers from the meal she had already prepared for her white employers. Rosser Taylor described the practice: "The Negro cooks, poorly paid, supplemented their wages by 'toting.' It would be unfair, doubtless, to state that all colored cooks around Carolina Crossroads 'toted,' but the majority of them did, and with the tacit knowledge and consent of the white folks. A little sugar or cold biscuit was always in demand in the Negro cabins where the larder was lean and the family large."

For African-American women without much education who were unable or unwilling to work as domestics, one of the only remaining jobs was that of washerwoman. "My mother," Richard Sanders stated, "she washed clothes and ironed them, for people; . . . that's all they [black women] had to do was cook, wash clothes for people." Not only did these women wash clothes in a large iron kettle, they also had to rinse them in other tubs, iron them, and redistribute the clothes throughout the neighborhood. Judy Adams recalled seeing black women carrying large bundles of laundry on their heads, often walking several miles in order to transport the clothes.

Alice Gassoway's mother operated her own laundry service at home. With all the clothes hanging on lines in their backyard, Ms. Gassoway exclaimed, "It looked like snow around here." Her mother washed and ironed everything by hand, including all the pleats and collars. She also had to know exactly how much starch to add for each piece. Finally, with no method of tagging or labeling, the clothes had to be returned to the rightful owners: "She knew everybody's clothes; . . . just remembered it in her head," Ms. Gassoway noted proudly.

As a child, Ms. Gassoway's job was to return the clothes, relying on the help of a friend: "She'd take one side of the basket. And momma would always say, 'Don't you wrinkle those clothes!' . . . And we'd start across the railroad, across the overhead bridge to take the ladies' clothes. And then come back and get another basket and take them." She would also help her mother wash during lunch recess "until I'd hear the bell . . . and then I'd have to run back to school."

Black cooks and washerwomen gradually disappeared as greater employment opportunities developed for African-American women and as household appliances became much less expensive. Unfortunately for the whites who had depended on that relatively inexpensive labor, this created a concomitant decline in traditional southern hospitality and elegant entertaining, as three Greenville women admitted.

AFRICAN-AMERICAN MEN

Nonfarm occupations for most black males differed from those of women but were just as strenuous and limited. Those who did not (or could not) become teachers or ministers had few other choices. Simon Gallman, a former slave from Newberry in 1937, recalled his options: " 'When freedom come, de slaves hired out. . . . De ones dat moved to town worked at odd jobs, some at carpenter work, janitor work or street work.' " Richard Sander's father worked as a janitor at the white school in Hammondville: "Because it was large, they didn't have but one janitor there, so he had to do it all. So I used to go help him" after school, Sanders stated. Black men might also work on the railroad, Velma Childers noted, but "the most work that they did was just working for other people—common labor, you might say."

A very characteristic black work pattern, Ralph Patrick and John Morland related, was the skilled laborer who "agrees to perform [a] certain service at a stipulated rate and he will usually furnish a crew of helpers who will be paid by the person wanting the job at the going rate. . . . It means there are innumerable informal work bands who 'go out on jobs.' "

As discussed in chapter 4, this pattern might account for several aspects of traditional and contemporary labor attitudes in the Piedmont. First of all, much urban manual labor traditionally had been done by blacks, which might explain the antipathy among many white groups toward hand labor. Second, given the general southern rejection of unionized labor, craftspeople take a lower position on the social scale and might work with a more casual attitude, reflecting in turn the region's emphasis on individualism. Third, the pattern fits the very deep-rooted traditional hierarchy of owner/employer, overseer/contractor, and slave/worker. While large numbers of both blacks and whites serve on various labor crews today, these same attitudes persist.

Many African Americans became carpenters. Velma Childers's uncle learned his craft in trade school; most others learned on the job. Jason Lambert, for example, simply observed others during lay-by time, gradually acquiring his skills in that manner. To this day, he still works during nonfarming months on a crew operating in his rural district. Vernon Randle had worked for decades on the railroad and learned carpentry and construction from "the boss man" as they built trestles and bridges.

Sometimes, skilled carpenters built more than houses. Velma Childers knew of one man who made coffins for his neighbors: "He had dressed lumber that he would make, and he had different cloth that he would put a lining, padding in and make a little pillow. And on the outside he would put some type of flowered material, or whatever the people could afford. And they buried grown people in these homemade caskets. . . . He was a carpenter. . . . He could build houses, and different things by special measurements, make it neat."

Many other African Americans, like Arthur Master's father, worked on the railroad. He was a "section man," whose task it was, as part of a crew, to maintain a section of track under the watchful eyes of white supervisors. The crew would repair the railroad bed, tear out the old ties and replace them, driving in spikes by hand. If the weather was bad, no one worked (and thus no one got paid). On the other hand, he felt, the overall salary was better than blacks could have received virtually anywhere else, in part because they belonged to a union (founded in the North, of course); the family also received free travel.

Vernon Randle worked as a section hand himself and recalled the extremely difficult conditions: "I done everything, . . . ten cents a hour, ten hours a day . . . and I thought I was making some money! . . . I was young; I didn't mind it. After you got used to it, caught the sleight of it, why, you do all right. But now, you got to catch that sleight; didn't, it'd catch you. . . . My hand was blistered up so bad I couldn't hardly fold them up like that. Didn't have no gloves." With his first paycheck, however, he bought a pair of work gloves.

Contrary to popular images, when asked if his crew sang as they worked, Mr. Randle responded: "Sang? Cussed all the time! . . . Some of us would get hollering in the morning, and some of us'd be hollering when we quit— arguing about something. . . . Well, that made the day pass on. Yes, sir— everybody wouldn't say nothing, look like that was the longest day. . . . Oh, yeah—talk, keep up something all the time. Some kind of old devilment, foolishness, something or other. . . . Yeah, some of them could tell some mighty big tales. I enjoyed it." (See chapter 8 for accounts of workers' songs.)

Conclusion

Urban labor, like that of farming or mill work, created a class of workers who saw themselves as different from their fellow Upstaters as the latter two groups did of them. Segregated by law and by fact from equality, African Americans in the cities became a distinct group as well. At the same time, however, all these segments of Piedmont society interacted in a variety of interconnected ways: mill hands purchased produce from farmers; white and black tenant children played together; the wives of black railroad workers cooked for overworked white mill wives; and tenant farmers perennially sought employment in, and fled the entrapment of, mill work. While these distinct occupations partially differentiated categories, social interaction continually rewove them into an intertwined whole. In this way, folklife traditions constantly flowed between groups, reinforcing the common basis of Upstate traditions.

CHAPTER 13

Material Culture

The ways in which people organized their personal spaces—the houses in which they lived, the objects they created, and the cemeteries in which they reposed—form the final elements of Piedmont folklife. Some of these elements represent part of the background of traditions: the mill houses and tenant cabins, for example, were the places where the creation process has occurred. Other elements form segments of the traditions themselves: colorful quilts and utilitarian baskets, for example, display the interweaving of black and white ideas that has characterized Piedmont folklife for over a century. Today the material landscape and the cultural objects of the Upstate still reflect the area's history.

Countryside Cultural Use of Space

THE HOME PLACE

Dotting the landscape throughout the Piedmont, often on hillsides with magnificent views or adjacent to country crossroads, sit large, porticoed houses, the cores of former estates. Surrounding the "big house" (regardless of size) would have been farm outbuildings, barns, and the rental cabins for white and black tenant farmers. As discussed in earlier chapters, the spatial organization of the farm reflected the social relationship between owner and tenant and between black and white.

Many of these beautiful old houses still exist for a very significant reason: they represent what families term "the old home place." This house, Michael Ann Williams proposed, symbolically represents the physical place of family origins. For Kent's elite, Ralph Patrick discovered, "there is a sentimental attachment to 'old home places' and a great deal of concern with ancestors." Similarly, Maxine Williams commented that, as African Americans, "we didn't know to make history books. See, we kept history by . . . where we used to live." The home place becomes a physical expression and conjoining of the fundamental Upstate values of heritage and family, thus imbuing the building and/or its location with extremely powerful meanings.

Rarely, the power of the home place to attract descendants dissipates because of modernization trends. Much more commonly, Upstate residents continue to live in, or to visit regularly, the home of their birth. Jennings Rhyne, for example, discussed the ties between mill and farm: "Occasionally we may find the mill worker and his family journeying out to the farm for the week-end to the 'old home place' where perhaps a married brother or sister or 'the old folks' still live."

Sometimes relatives would be interred "on the place," thereby strengthening the connections between past, present, and future even more deeply. This was done, Marjorie Potwin continued, not to save money but to retain the sentimental association between the loved one and "familiar surroundings." Ben Robertson reported a conversation with his family's African American cook, in which she chastised blacks who went North: "That's one reason I don't want go north—I'd hate get caught sick way off there and die and have to be buried away from home—it's bad enough have live 'way from home and it's worse be buried away."

As Michael Ann Williams noted, the means by which families maintain the old home place vary. Some build a new home and use the old one for another purpose or perhaps incorporate it into a newer structure. For example, John Culberton, interviewed by a WPA worker in 1939, told the researcher that he had been born on the same farm on which he still worked, in an old two-story frame house now part of his barn. This apparent disrespect of a sacred symbol, Williams concluded, occurs because the ultimate power of the home place lies not in the physical structure itself but in its ability to evoke memories of family heritage.

At other times, the association between family memory and physical place is much more direct. Many Upstate residents, Williams observed, preserve the old home place virtually intact, even furnished, as a site for family reunions. A recent article in the *Greenville News* described the efforts of three cousins to repair their grandparents' home and furnish it with period furniture "to give family members a gathering place filled with memories." One cousin remarked, "it's something that my kids and maybe their grandchildren will come visit."

As families inevitably expand, however, who inherits the home place? Louise Jones DuBose, in a 1941 WPA essay, summarized this potential conflict between two basic southern values: that of rugged individualism and private property versus family heritage and corporate possession. Ralph Patrick offered his views on this association between private and symbolic ownership: "The relationship of the present generation to highly valued property and heirlooms of the lineage is . . . that of custodian rather than outright owner. The individual is not 'free' to dispose of property symbolic of the position of his lineage, he is duty bound to preserve it and to pass it on to the next generation. The South is perhaps one of the few places in America where it makes sense to keep and maintain an unprofitable 'old homeplace,' or to work and save in order to buy back into the family an unprofitable 'old homeplace' which had been lost to a mortgage holder."

To bypass this potential conflict, many Upstate residents follow the settlement pattern outlined by Michael Ann Williams: despite the pulls of urban living, children tend to live near their parents in rural clusters. Thus, Williams continued, "in keeping with tradition, new ranch houses and mobile homes encircle the bungalows and other dwellings built by the parents' generation in mid-century."

Throughout the Upstate, rural informants frequently live surrounded by relatives. For example, Mary Brown, raised near Piercetown, South Carolina, described her life: "I was happy growing up out there on the farm. . . . My sister lived in one house, my brother in the other house, and my other sister in the other house—there were four houses on this farm. But we lived in the big house. . . . And every time one of us would get married, they'd let us go there and stay free of charge. We didn't have to pay any rent."

For Piedmonters, residence near an aging parent directly reflects the significance of family. For example, Richard Sanders felt the pull of filial devotion after he retired from the service and noticed that his brothers and sisters had virtually abandoned his aging parents: "As they got old, somebody had to be close by them some way. They wanted me to stay with them. . . . If you care anything about your parents, yeah, the children stay with them. . . . They got to go to the store, they got to have food, . . . got to go to the doctor. . . . Somebody got to be around to take care of them."

Rather than building brick or frame homes on parental property, many Upstate residents today rely on cheaper, more mobile trailers. To many Piedmont residents, these impermanent homes signal a less welcome, "trashy" population and thus become a blight on the landscape. However, Michael Ann Williams proposed that the Upstate's well-established preference for mobile homes may reflect some deeper regional traditions. First, early pioneers often constructed "small, replaceable buildings," a trend that trailers continue. Second, the traditional log house "provided some freedom from the cash economy," matched today by the relative low cost of trailers and a preference meshing with the area's value on individualism. Finally, Williams felt, even the older practice of adding on to a house (with attached kitchens and enclosed porches) may be seen today in the frequent extensions to mobile homes. Thus, rather than serving as a blight on the Piedmont landscape, trailer parks may represent the continuation of older traditions.

TENANT HOUSES

Before World War II, the living conditions of sharecroppers and tenant farmers, especially the African Americans, were abysmal. A WPA interviewer described the home of Moses Lyles, a former slave then living in Winnsboro, South Carolina: "He lives in a two-room house, of the 'saddlebag' type. . . . The home is the ordinary tenant house of a Negro in the South. . . . There are two windows to each room, which are closed with plank shutters. The floors are clean and yellowed from much scouring and sweeping. On the outside is a tiny walk to the house, bordered on either side by rows of jonquils." Velma Childers, a preacher's daughter, acknowledged that her father's occupation allowed them to live in a relatively nice home, but she did recognize that "a lot of people lived in what they call shanty-type houses."

Since the landowner rarely invested much effort in these homes, interior decoration depended solely on the occupants. When asked if she had had any books at home as a child, Maxine Williams replied: "catalogs—Sears, Roebuck, Montgomery [Ward]. When you got through sealing the house with them, I learned to read by reading the advertisements—spell the words. I learned my ABCs off the wall."

Homes for white sharecroppers were often larger, somewhat better maintained by the landowner, and also usually closer to the "big house." Still, the rental property inhabited by whites was often spartan, as James Edwards remembered: "I know two of them [houses] that we lived in that I can remember were tin-roof houses. One of them didn't even have electricity when we first moved in; they wired it up after we moved in. . . . Most of them, most of the time, were in very rundown type conditions." Although cheaper to build and maintain, tin roofs absorbed sunshine in the summer, thereby heating the home almost unbearably, while in the winter these same roofs dissipated heat, allowing the colder air to penetrate.

Farmhouses, whether those of the elites or their tenants, shared several features with homes in mill villages. One of these traits, Ben Robertson explained, was that "all of our [farm] houses . . . had bare sanded yards surrounded by gardens of flowers. We did not care for green grass in our yards, . . . and white sand to us was more restful and quieter-looking than grass. . . . Every Saturday morning, with corn-shuck brooms, we carefully swept the yard." "At that time," Maggie Nameth related, "if you had grass in your yard, that was a sign of laziness."

Another feature shared between mill and farm were gardens, commonplace for both tenant and owner, black and white. Many times, in fact, gardens supplied welcome produce to Depression-era families. Olivia Landreth explained: "And we always had a garden, of course, and we had plenty to eat and all. We didn't know what it was to go to the grocery store and buy anything."

Because many mills were located in rural areas, farmers found a ready market for their extra garden produce in the adjacent mill villages. Transforming vegetables into much-needed cash, tenant families like James Edwards would "load it up on a wagon, take it to town. . . . You go down through the mill village . . . and peddle vegetables and things like that off the wagon." "In the summertime we made it better than we did any other time" in the mill village, Tom Davis recalled, "because . . . these farmers would come in town with wagonloads of vegetables you could get cheap." While much less common today, Everett Baker felt, farmers still sometimes "peddle" vegetables in towns or at many crossroads and flea markets, where not only residents of mill villages but also those in the encroaching suburbs may purchase fresh produce.

Today, most of the older tenant houses have fallen into disrepair or kudzu patches, while the better-built ones have been modernized and remain occupied. On the outskirts of Hammondville, for example, along the main highway into town on both sides of the road cluster about a dozen small, four-room homes in varied states of upkeep. Most have had porches and other rooms added. Down a side road at right angles to the highway, sited close to the pavement, sit several unpainted four-room homes disintegrating into scrap lumber. Since landowners must pay taxes on all buildings, George Adams commented, most of the vacant tenant homes have by now been destroyed.

Still, a very characteristic feature of the Upstate landscape today is the clustering of several homes (vacant or occupied) in outlying rural areas. Occasionally a vacant house may be seen sitting out in the middle of a field, but most line the highways or country roads. These groupings of former tenant houses, in fact, often account for the tiny, unincorporated communities with rural-sounding place names discussed in chapter 5. In effect, these homes are fossils of an earlier time, physical reminders of an entire set of traditions, from agricultural practices to lay-by time recreations, that have changed through time, just as the homes have.

Contemporary tenant house (Photo by John M. Coggeshall)

COUNTRY STORES

Another formerly common feature of the Upstate landscape was country stores, conveniently located at rural crossroads. While farmers secured their major purchases on infrequent trips to town, outlying stores offered many items relatively close at hand. As discussed in earlier chapters, these commercial establishments also offered convenient places for community social interaction. Larger chain stores, Arthur Masters lamented, have eradicated many of the older general stores. In some instances, however, the convenience markets associated with modern gas stations serve the same function of earlier times but offer different products. On the other hand, some general stores like that at Slabtown (near Greenville) have survived by offering the best of both the present and the past: convenient foods and convenient company. In fact, this store had been suggested by several informants as epitomizing the "classic" general store.

Mill Community Cultural Use of Space

As discussed in chapter 2, the communities surrounding mills constituted what Jennings Rhyne termed "a traditional part of the industry" and a very typical part of the Upstate landscape. Generally speaking, industry-sponsored sources tended to paint glowingly positive, almost quaint pictures of "mill hills." Contemporary residents, however, depicted a different image. For example, in his WPA interview, William Buchanan described "the Winnsboro Mill Village of my childhood. It was a dreary lot of unkempt, unpainted houses on a hilly spot south of the town. . . . The persons making their way through its unkempt streets sometimes would have to hold their noses to keep out the stench of pig pens or cow stalls. . . . The officials [sic] main idea seemed to be to make money and had no regard for health and sanitation."

The spatial organization of mill villages, like the ergonomics within mills, reflected a basic concern for corporate profits as the ultimate driving force. For example, in 1918 the editor of the Hammondville community paper wrote: "Few persons aside from the managers of a mill have any idea of the difficulty experienced in arranging a cotton mill village so that every family will be convenient to the mill, the stores, the churches, schools, lodges, and railroads. The Mill management do the best they can for their people."

Often "the best" translated into standardization, as even the promanagement William Jacobs admitted. Harriet Herring, like many of those who actually lived in these communities, found the duplication to be overwhelmingly depressing: "the monotony of the average mill village is not alone due to identical houses but to similarity in many details of the village pattern: the houses are all about the same size; they are set back precisely the same distance from the street; they are all in about the same state of repair or disrepair; [and] they often have no flower gardens or other touches of individuality." Compounding the dreariness of the carbon-copy mediocrity of mill villages even more, John Morland observed, was the fact that those located adjacent to already established towns such as Kent starkly contrasted to the homes of the elite, a physical expression of the social contrast as well.

Depending solely on the largesse of the mill owner and/or his company, each mill hill came equipped with utilities. Often the homes had electricity provided by the mill's generator, in contrast to those on outlying farms. Sometimes, as Marjorie Potwin reported, the homes might not have any indoor plumbing. In other communities, such as in one of Kent's villages, the houses had running (cold) water (usually a spigot on the back porch), or they may have had community wells; all had outhouses in the back with no internal sewage systems.

In other urban amenities, too, mill workers perceived the corporate influence of the mill on their lives. Streets, for example, preserved the names of those important to the community, especially managers. Even commu-

Contemporary mill houses (Photo by John M. Coggeshall)

nity sidewalks reflected the corporate concern for optimal spatial organization. In Hammondville, two local historians noted that, "since transportation was scarce, or non-existent for many people, paved walkways provided easy walking to the various destinations in town. The walkways . . . lead to churches, stores, schools and the mill, and they deviated away from the streets when necessary in order to provide the most direct pathway." "And when they turned out at the mill" on these pathways, Tom Davis observed, "it was like ants crawling all over the hillside."

In general, mill management constructed the town and shaped its occupants to suit their corporate needs, physically and even morally. Helen Quinnell, raised in Hammondville, described this situation: "They took care of everything, I mean, and poked their noses into everything. They kept people on Main Street . . . that they knew would keep up their houses and yards, and would act decent and all that. And there were a few streets . . . where they put the people who were not as careful about all that sort of thing."

Mill houses themselves were almost always built of wood and "in the same style, a few at a time as the mill expanded, until finally a small village surrounded the factory," John Morland noted. Again, cost dictated the materials, Robert Adams felt: "Wood, for instance, was used because it was the cheapest thing that you could use for the building. And the mechanics knew how to work with wood." Houses might differ in size and facades according to the decade in which they were built, the company providing them, and the types of workers who would live there.

The dreariness stemming from the similarity of architecture and proximity to the street was exaggerated even further by other company attempts at uniformity. Maggie Nameth explained: "I'll tell you this—every house in town had the same color walls, same color woodwork. They used *one* color, painted everything. Nobody had anything different. They all looked alike."

To combat this boring similarity, renters occasionally added their own artistic touches. Ollie Farrington, a textile mill worker in one of Charlotte's mill villages in 1939, proudly told her WPA interviewer: "Did you notice my flower box on the front porch when you come in? Its [sic] made out of pop bottle caps. I sorted out the colors and kinder put them together so they would match up. . . . There are several thousand caps in it. . . . I made it myself and I am kinder proud of it."

Flower and vegetable gardens served the same purpose. In addition, Gladys Taylor observed, gardens reflected the rural backgrounds of many mill families. Pauline Griffith said that, after moving to a Greenville mill village, her mother "had a garden. . . . Coming from the country, they used to allow us to have a place where we could have a hog pen. . . . And we had a cow, too. We had our own milk and butter. She grew a lot of vegetables in the garden. . . . We canned up food, you know, and helped out, just like in the country, only it was on a smaller scale."

Very often, mill villagers (like their rural neighbors) despised grass in their front yards and worked vigorously to remove any vestiges of vegetation, Tom Davis explained: "If there's any grass in the yard, you take a hoe and shave it up—it wasn't like it is now. You didn't have no lawn mower or anything. So, the little bit of grass, you'd just take the hoe and—you didn't want that in your yard."

For many families, especially those recently arrived from the farms, life in mill houses required some significant adjustments in concepts of personal space. For one thing, Lois MacDonald observed, farmers usually lived great distances between neighbors in the country and now had to reside within hearing distance. Reinforcing this feeling of crowding, Rosemary Calder noted, was that "most of the houses were built for two families anyway. They had the two front doors, had the one bath, . . . and had two kitchens, and then [one room upstairs]—it'd be three rooms per couple."

Crowding might, of course, enhance even more the social benefits of life in a mill village. Tom Davis explained: "But I was born and raised in three rooms of a six-room house. And my uncle had the other three rooms. So me and my first cousin were born in the same house."

While average workers lived in small, relatively cramped houses or duplexes, their supervisors resided in roomier and more ornate homes. Most of the time these better houses lined a busier street or clustered nearer to the mill, but in other villages they might be scattered among the workers' homes.

Inevitably, though, crowning the height above the river, the mill, and the community would be the supervisor's (or owner's) house, paternalistically overlooking his industrial plantation. In Hammondville, for example, the *Greenville News* of January 24, 1889, described the "handsome two-story house being built for [the] Assistant Superintendent. . . . The house will be large, containing seven rooms and conveniently arranged. Broad piazzas surround two sides of it from which a pleasant bird's eye view of the busy village is to be had."

While this home still stands above Hammondville today, the community, like all others in the Upstate, has undergone significant changes. As the company sold the houses and ceased the community perks, newcomers moved in while the factories deteriorated. Landscaping and lawns have transformed many mill towns into more typical suburbs, and outhouses and outbuildings disappeared as utilities and zoning modernized towns. On former cotton fields, housing developments now encroach on the outskirts of these previously isolated villages while interstate highways and telecommunications improve ties.

At the same time, however, Upstate mill villages retain many physical and social traces of earlier eras. In most, the mill (whether operating or not) still dominates the town physically and spatially. Streets, although paved and often with sidewalks, frequently meander from the mill in a nongrid pattern that confuses and misleads drivers. Despite individualizing landscaping and siding, the uniformity of mill homes cannot be disguised. Gardens may still be seen, although today serving more a function of nutrition and recreation rather than as a connection to an older, rural way of life.

Many of the earlier social stereotypes and antagonisms continue to affect spatial organization, for in cities like Greenville, despite urbanization and urbanity, the mill villages that used to ring sections of the city and have now been completely absorbed by it, officially lie outside the city limits. Kent's mill villages still reflect the social class distinctions described four decades earlier by Morland and his researchers: some back streets remain unpaved, with weeds in ill-kept yards of dilapidated houses; a laundromat indicates a lack of purchasing power for consumer appliances; and tiny tenement apartments cluster in an unzoned area of empty lots, abandoned cars, and a greasy filling station. Even in tiny Hammondville, Linda Baker related, a newer housing development inside the town has maintained a separate grid system of streets rather than connecting into the existing one because (she felt) the occupants of the new houses did not want to live in a mill town.

African-American Urban Communities

As discussed in chapter 3, social and legal segregation prevented blacks and whites from sharing certain aspects of social interaction during the past century. Thus, in most Upstate communities today (as is true of virtually the entire country), separate neighborhoods exist for African and Anglo Americans, especially for those in the middle- to lower-income groups. Because of the South's long history of formal segregation, however, many of these black neighborhoods have remained quite stable for over a century. African Americans often appreciate the continuity associated with these well-established communities. To most white residents, especially in the smaller towns such as Kent and Hammondville, the black neighborhoods have been locally known by disparaging names since their great-grandparents' day.

Despite segregation, however, urban blacks have long associated with whites in the same town, as servants, washerwomen, and cooks. With urban transportation expensive or nonexistent, the necessity to work in white homes coupled with the reality of segregation created in many larger cities a checkerboard settlement pattern: large, spacious white-owned mansions interspersed with smaller black homes. Patricia Vaughn noted about Greenville: "One thing, back in our childhood, there would be a white neighborhood, and immediately behind it would be the black neighborhood, so the help could always walk to work. We still have that to a degree."

Mattie Jamison lived in a house along a Charlotte alley in 1939 when she was interviewed by a WPA worker. More specifically, the researcher continued, she lived in "one of the type known locally as 'shotgun houses' because they are said to be a stack of boards held together with nails shot haphazard from a gun." Ralph Patrick and John Morland described the same general type from Kent; virtually all Upstate communities (both rural and urban) contain numerous examples.

John M. Vlach argued that the shotgun house exists throughout the United States in black neighborhoods. Notably distinct because the gable side, rather than the long side, faces the road, the house type represents a major break with Anglo-American tradition and probably represents a continuation of an African style. The configuration of rooms, Vlach continued, forces the inhabitants into one of two directions: interaction within the family internally or interaction on the porch and thus with the entire community. Front porches, and the social interaction they make possible, are extremely important to Piedmonters and to southerners in general. In fact, one of the specific architectural features Vernon Randle missed in northern cities was that the people up there "ain't got no porch to sit on."

In the Upstate today, many houses—rural or urban, black-owned or white-owned, large or small—have porches upon which are several comfortable chairs, often filled with family and friends in the evening catching cool breezes, watching the traffic, or just talking. The architectural innovation of a porch, Vlach believed, stemmed not from European but ultimately from African tradition. Like many other Piedmont traditions, those from the black community have blended completely into contemporary Upstate folklife.

Folk Arts and Crafts

Like people everywhere, Upstate residents manufactured many commonplace, practical items from everyday materials, using methods and styles handed down from one generation to the next. Quite commonly women's social activities and the materials they simultaneously produced received less public attention than primarily male crafts such as basketry. Perhaps this was because women's crafts were much more often done in private (or with a small apprenticing audience), or perhaps because women's tasks were seen as more utilitarian and thus less "important." Regardless of the perceptions, Piedmont folk utilized local materials to construct needed objects for their everyday lives; many of these items reflect Upstate traditions.

CLOTHING

In earlier generations, especially among impoverished tenant farmers and mill workers, cash for ordinary items such as clothing was often scarce. Thus, innovative mothers utilized every available scrap of material to make their families' clothes. One woman explained: "We didn't know what store-bought clothes were. . . . She [mother] made all our clothes just out of anything that probably she could pick up. And they used to buy feed in these feed sacks. . . . Well, I knowed her to make many dresses out of those feed sacks." Another woman recalled that her grandmother made dresses from flour sacks; whenever the family bought flour "we was always excited to see what sacks we was going to get." "There was no stigma," Maggie Nameth noted, "in wearing a dress to school made out of flour sacks."

On the other hand, Alice Gassoway sighed, sometimes this sack clothing did create embarrassment. Her mother made her underwear out of hog feed sacks, "and I hated to wear them because the other children would have nice, good-looking panties. And mine was made out of the sacks. Sometimes the letters would be on there but I never would go and be excused [to the bathroom] with the other children 'cause I was afraid they might see those letters on my panties."

No informants remembered using any natural dyes to disguise the utilitarian origins of this material. However, Maggie Nameth did recall that the extra white cloth that mills sometimes distributed to village residents could be dyed by soaking it in the ubiquitous red clay mud of the Piedmont. After washing, the material would have a permanent pinkish-orange tint.

Ralph Patrick and John Morland observed one distinction in dress between African and Anglo Americans: head scarves. The researchers described these as quite common on older black women (usually those from a rural background) and made from several types of cloth. Head scarves would be worn in one's home or on the front porch, never in public. Patrick and Morland further noted that each woman used her individual creativity in tying her scarf. Folklorist Helen Griebel has argued that this tradition, frequently depicted in American popular culture (for example, "Aunt Jemima"), probably stemmed from European customs, but black women modified the practice in order to emphasize elements of African aesthetics: a focus on the head and face; stylistic individuality (paralleling artistic improvisation); and the desire for audience compliments (similar to musical call-response).

QUILTING

A more specialized type of sewing was that done to piece together and back quilts. The social enjoyment of piecing quilts has been discussed in chapter 8. Quilts, though, may also be seen as folk art and as social commentary, as Laurel Horton and Lynn Myers have argued.

As social commentary, quilts reveal much about the cultural background of their creators. As Horton and others have observed, African-American quilts utilize different artistic patterns than Anglo-American ones from the same time period. For example, black quilt makers often piece the tops in strips, not blocks; their patterns are often asymmetrical; and one pattern often overlays another. In effect, the tendency of African-American quilters to improvise is directly analogous to black improvisation in music, particularly blues and jazz. Horton, Myers and Vlach agreed that this African-American tradition stems directly from West Africa.

As folk art, quilts can express the individuality of their creators in a number of interconnected ways. The artist, for example, needs to select a pattern for the block, one which she will also visualize as a recurring theme on the entire object. Secondly, the materials selected for the individual blocks will be chosen for either their contrast or coalescence, and the artist must also be assured that she will have enough of the material to complete the project. Geneva Patterson carefully lays out the blocks and pieces to see exactly how the colors will appear together. Cleora Cunningham "chooses her colors by what she thinks looks good together: 'something that makes it show up pretty,' " Anne Kimzey reported.

Even the stitching linking the blocks together serves an artistic function, scrutinized carefully by critical eyes. Geneva Patterson noted: "The closer together the stitching—a real good quilter can get ten stitches to an inch. An average is seven to an inch. Mine's like about five or six or maybe four—you know, I'm not a good quilter." On the other hand, Mrs. Patterson confessed: "I do them for my grandchildren; 'cause if they're going to put them on a dorm bed, what does it matter?"

About the time she and her husband married in the late 1940s, Maggie Nameth recalled, blankets began to replace quilts, mostly because the latter were seen as "old fashioned." Quilting parties also faded. However, quilting has persisted, in part, Mrs. Nameth believed, because of the tremendous value in well-made quilts. Some, she felt, might earn their makers as much as six hundred dollars. On the other hand, craftswomen like Cleora Cunningham quilt "because it is 'something to keep my mind busy.' "

Regardless of why they continue to quilt, many informants mentioned that their quilts, whether made today or in the past, have become treasured family heirlooms. Mary Hammond displayed an appliqued quilt that had been handed down through at least three generations; she estimated it to be two hundred years old. The Block sisters owned a quilt that at one time had contained the name of their uncle's childhood girlfriend; as a boy he had excised the name with his pocketknife, but his mother (the sisters' grandmother) had patched the hole. An Anglo-American woman from Iva commented that her grandchildren and great-grandchildren want her to make them quilts: "They say they want to remember me when I'm gone. They want to look at that quilt."

In addition to all the other functions of quilts, from warming young children to representing artistic creativity to reflecting cultural values, quilts as heirlooms also reinforce fundamental Piedmont values: heritage and family. Composed of scraps of people's clothing, quilts thereby contain scraps of people's lives: grandpa's overalls, mother's doll clothes, or one's own prom dress, woven together in a patchwork of ancestral memories. In this sense, quilts become icons of a family, stitching generations to each other, supported by a backing of stories and traditions. While men may often dominate the public histories replayed at family reunions, women preserve their family's heritage through a different but equally effective medium—their quilts.

CANING AND BASKETRY

Wooden strips, carefully split from straight poles, have long been used by Native-, African- and Anglo-American Upstate residents to make utilitarian objects. Upstate baskets differed markedly in materials, styles, methods, and cultural origins from those made (primarily by African American women) on the Sea Islands in the Low Country; they also differ from those made by Native-American groups. In the Upstate, however, as Indian, black, and white continually interacted, Horton wrote, the tradition of split-oak baskets eventually formed another strand of Piedmont folklife shared among these groups.

The skill could be handed down through several generations, but evidently mostly by men. Leon Berry's wife, he admitted, knew how to make baskets and cane chairs, but "she didn't have time to fool with that—she piecing quilts." Albert Wood, an Anglo American, learned "from an old colored fellow, . . . [who] carried me out in the woods and showed me." James Edwards's father had known how to make baskets "just handed down along, you know; one family to the next, or one generation to the next." Mr. Berry, whose family has been making baskets for more than one hundred forty-five years, also learned by experience: "After I done learned to make baskets, I can come in there and look at a basket, what somebody else has done made, . . . and I can just take it and turn it right round and come back home . . . and set down and make that basket."

Baskets ranged in size from small to huge. "Uncle" George Briggs, interviewed in 1937 at the age of eighty-eight, explained that " 'we made fish baskets, feed baskets and wood baskets and sewing baskets and all kinds of baskets fer de Missus'[sic]. All de chair bottoms of straight chairs wuz made from white oak splits and den de straight chairs wuz made in de shop.' " Large square or circular hampers or "cotton baskets," Laurel Horton noted, were commonly employed for a variety of farming tasks. Long conical tubes containing another, inner cone served as fish traps. Leon Berry has made square or round "dinner baskets" and also made one for a person's dog to sleep in. James Edwards, raised on a farm, used baskets for gathering vegetables, storing fruit, and carrying food on picnics.

Laurel Horton described the process by which logs are carefully split into "billets" which are then shaved into long "paper-thin splits," eventually to be woven into baskets. Ribs formed the basic shape of the basket, which may be either round or square. Strips were woven either "over and under" or "twill"—over two and under one. The top of the basket acted to preserve the shape and to even out the tops of the ribs.

The process of basket weaving combined both technical skill and artistry, as Elbert Brown described to Horton: " 'I can have a pile of ribs down there. If I want a sixteenth of an inch, I can just take my hand and go through them; I can feel them and tell what they are. In oak, when you're working and splitting it, you get that feeling in your hands, it's just like, almost sort of like electricity.' "

Increasing age, declining health, and scarcity of materials have all contributed to the increasing rarity of basket making today, Horton observed. "The old generation of the people . . . like that, they're gone, and the . . . younger generation never did take it up much," a mill worker from Bynum, North Carolina sighed. "Basketmakers now about as scarce as hen's teeth," Leon Berry admitted. Despite experimental new shapes owing to market pressures and ideas from books and magazines, Horton noted, basketmakers retain traditional construction elements, weaving the past into the present.

POTTERY AND CERAMICS

This traditional folk craft has a long history in the Piedmont, and presently persists in pockets. One ceramic tradition began with the Native Americans, including the ancestors of Cherokee and Catawba Indians who continued their styles well afterwards. Folklorist John Burrison traced the origins of lead-glazed earthenware to Anglo-American settlers in the mid-eighteenth-century Piedmont. Another tradition developed independently, Charles Zug noted, introduced by Moravian immigrants. John M. Vlach described the development of a third stoneware pottery tradition among African and Anglo Americans that began in the Edgefield County area of the southern South Carolina Piedmont in the early nineteenth century and later disseminated elsewhere. Of particular curiosity were "face jugs," some stylistic and others somewhat realistic, probably stemming ultimately from a Euro-American background but with African elements as well. At the present, both Zug and Vlach have observed, few folk potters remain in the area.

ADDITIONAL CRAFTS

Although not recorded during my Piedmont fieldwork, wood carving has a well-established place in southern folklife. Many of these carvings are intricate pieces of art and whimsy. Anne Kimzey, for example, described the contemporary work of Ike Carpenter, of Edgefield County: "Ike's woodcarving involved a lot of 'trick' pieces like a ball inside a ball inside a box. . . . He had some chains and boxes and rings all carved out of a single piece of wood. . . . He carved a 'short timer stick' when he knew his tour [in Vietnam] was almost up. It is a walking stick with 'Quangtree' (his location) carved on it and the dates he was there. . . . The tip of the cane is an artillery shell."

A few informants, both in the past and present, worked with iron, having learned either as blacksmiths or as mill machinists. Fred Alexander, interviewed in 1938, described his skills: "But I am best at machine work. . . . You take iron for instance. I can make almost anything out of iron that can be made. . . . Yes sir I took the iron right down to Bob Bailey's blacksmith shop and made those hinges right there." Tom Davis, a former machinist in the Hammondville mill, maintains his skills as a hobbyist in a small shop behind his house. Using the traditional split wooden pattern, he has made fish baskets out of wire, among other objects.

CEMETERY INSCRIPTIONS AND DECORATIONS

In death as in life, Upstate folklife reveals certain aspects of Piedmont traditions. First of all, prior to widespread desegregation, burials in cemeteries reflected the social discrimination of life in general; blacks were interred in separate locations. Most of the time, this was at least in part owing to the segregation of church congregations. Since most cemeteries were located adjacent to churches, the burials simply reflected the constitution of the constituencies. On the other hand, city cemeteries also remained segregated even if African Americans lived in the same community. In Hammondville, for example, the small community cemetery contains the graves of mill supervisors, workers, and their families, while deceased blacks (who lived within a few blocks but "across the tracks") were buried in their own church cemeteries. More recent cemeteries, of course, have been integrated.

In the older black graveyards, some tombstones also reflect aspects of traditional daily life. Maxine Williams recalled that "there wasn't many real tombstones in the colored [section]. They'd use flat rock and they would write on there." Other graves might be marked by concrete slabs into which had been pressed stencils or hand inscriptions of significant names and dates. Obviously done as cost-saving practices (or less obviously as improvisation?), fieldstones and concrete slabs seem to be quite common in older cemeteries.

A few African-American graves in the Hammondville cemeteries, however, bore more expensive marble markers. Based on the inscriptions, these appeared to have been donations by white families for their servants, re-

Cement tombstone from an African-American cemetery
(Photo by John M. Coggeshall)

flecting the complex social relationship of genuine love and patronizing protection described in chapter 4. The stone of one woman, for example, read: "Served faithfully the Trowbridge family many years, respected and trusted by all/Rest from thy labors." The epitaphs of a woman and her husband might have reflected their roles in life as servant and field hand: "Having finished life's duty/She now sweetly rests; His toils are past/His work is done/He fought the fight/The victory won."

Conclusion

As with other aspects of Piedmont folklife, the ways in which Upstate residents have organized the space around them and the materials with which they have filled that space in part reflect the past and mark the present for residents today. Mill towns and tenant houses, even if abandoned, still represent for most people a very recent heritage. The "home place," likewise, offers a symbolic location to renew significant Upstate values as well as to partake of traditional foods in a familiar setting. Quilts, cotton baskets, and effigy jugs, whether as antiques or as tourist souvenirs, continue a deep stream of traditional Upstate crafts. Serving as the background for Piedmont traditions, the cultural landscape of houses and villages has in turn helped to preserve and to shape Piedmont folklife.

CHAPTER 14

Synthesis

The gravel road stretched to the horizon, running due north along the township line. On both sides, aligned in perfect rows like green soldiers, marched tall cornstalks, genetically engineered and thus almost precisely the same size. Black soil, perfectly free of any rocks, anchored the golden-tasseled corn, framing the fields with a dark border. On the distant horizon, along low ridges, grain elevators marked the locations of small country towns, strung like beads along railroad lines. Like the cotton Piedmont, southwestern Illinois presents a marked contrast of vivid colors. However, unlike the Upstate, the prairie's pattern consists of different squares, symmetrically organized into sections of contrasting crops, bordered by perfectly aligned roads. As I stood by the lane in the warm, humid afternoon, I thought about the intersection of geography, history, and culture that combine to create distinct regions in the United States.

In southwestern Illinois, heavily glaciated during North America's ice ages, no mountains edge the horizon. Instead, above the limestone and loess bluffs of the Mississippi River, extensive prairies lay between long ridges, the remains of glacial moraines. Otherwise the land has been bull-dozed flat by the power of prehistoric ice, presenting farmers with ideal plowing conditions. The coal-black soil, partly a by-product of that same glaciation, provides an extremely fertile medium for crops. With distinct growing seasons and severe winters, fields yield valuable crops of corn and soybeans, much of which serve as feed for the region's hog and cattle farmers. Bumper crops are stored in the "prairie skyscrapers" of grain silos, which (along with church steeples) punctuate the skylines of every town in the area. Shipped by rail or road, most agricultural products arrive at another gift of the glaciers, the prairie rivers—flat, muddy interstates for inexpensive transportation.

The geography of the Upstate offers a distinct contrast to that of south-western Illinois. Never glaciated, the region's bright orange clays have formed near the Blue Ridge, whose foothills constitute the Piedmont itself. Generally blocking colder continental weather, the mountains help provide milder winters and a longer growing season. With a different settlement history and less fertile soils, the area succumbed earlier to agricultural disaster, exacerbated by monocrop overproduction of cotton. To help stem disastrous erosion during the Depression, sages advised importing kudzu, too sensitive to northern frosts but which thrived in the Piedmont's hot, humid summers. Above the Fall Line and below the Blue Ridge, Piedmont farms remained less accessible to easy transportation until the arrival of railroads and (later) highways.

Virtually unsettled frontier until a decade or so after the Revolutionary War, the southwestern Illinois prairie attracted a few French from the Mississippi bottomlands across from St. Louis, many emigrants from the Old Southwest (Kentucky and Tennessee), and also some from eastern communities in Ohio and Pennsylvania. Surveyed after President Jefferson's land-division system in the early 1800s, most farms were based on township and range lines that ran due east-west and north-south. Thus, many roads in Illinois, particularly the country lanes, follow these land division lines. By the eve of the Civil War, thousands of German immigrants had selected the region for settlement as well. As the home state of Abraham Lincoln and Ulysses Grant, Illinois remained in the Union; after 1865, most communities erected monuments to local heroes who had fought in the War of the Rebellion. Today, over a century later, the war and its monuments lie overlooked in city cemeteries and in northern memories.

The Carolina Piedmont, with Scots-Irish and other Europeans having already eliminated Native Americans from the region before American Independence, has a much longer history. As part of the original Thirteen Colonies, the area had been surveyed using the English metes and bounds system, which divided fields on the basis of landmarks rather than mathematical units. Thus, farms and roads take apparently haphazard twists and turns or cut diagonally and directly from one place to another, unbound by imaginary geometric lines. As the home state of Fort Sumter and the first to secede, South Carolina boldly led the others out of the Union, while at Bennett Place in North Carolina Joseph Johnston surrendered to William T. Sherman after Appomattox. Following the disasters of the War of Northern Aggression and the equally ruinous Reconstruction, the states raised monuments to their heroes of the "late unpleasantness." Today, as the Confederate battle flag flies from homes and adorns bumper stickers, monuments to "the War" designate for many white Upstaters a grand ancestral period and one that most will never forget.

After an uncertain beginning, slavery was outlawed in Illinois. On the southwestern prairies, farmers from both North and South staked claims and established farms without slave labor. Later German immigrants, although steeped in Old World class rankings, abhorred slavery and selected free states for settlement. Fighting to free the slaves and to preserve the Union during the Civil War, prairie farmers (speaking both English and German) welcomed the idea but not the freed slaves themselves. As quiet towns industrialized under German muscle and organization and Yankee know-how and capital, southern blacks fled North following Reconstruction. Several prairie towns acquired African-American residents, but they lived in segregated neighborhoods while attending public schools along with whites. With relatively small numbers of blacks to distinguish, separate but equal facilities never appeared. Today, racism and differential settlement patterns keep most southwestern Illinois communities virtually all white, a situation most white residents prefer.

Slavery had a long and bitter history in the Upstate, and many farmers (both plantation and independent) owned slaves. Fighting for the right of their own states to determine slavery's legitimacy and legality, Piedmont farmers lost the struggle but retained their black workers, now freed but continuing to work at slave wages. As the sharecropping/tenant system developed after the War Between the States, most whites retained personal relationships with their black neighbors but required that they remain segregated in their own neighborhoods, schools, and churches. A complex system of separate facilities evolved alongside the mutual friendships between blacks and whites. Despite federally mandated integration, feelings by most whites for their black neighbors have changed little today.

Economically, German immigration to southwestern Illinois drastically altered the landscape. An antebellum area of small farms evolved as the postwar boom brought more immigration as well as the development of the area's coal resources, fueling a related boom in small industries. German and Irish labor organized into unions, still ubiquitous in the area today. With an infrastructure tied to the St. Louis and Chicago markets, some communities of southwestern Illinois became small urban centers while others remained farming towns supplying meat and produce. As blue-collar labor evolved in recent decades into service sector jobs, the region's economy also changed. Today anchored by retail, banking, medical, and government employment, southwestern Illinois retains a solid agricultural foundation as well.

Alongside agriculture in the Upstate developed the textile industry. Fueled by cheap supplies, labor, and power, mill villages sprang up like mushrooms throughout the Piedmont region. Drawing labor from the mountains and farms, the villages also helped to unite these different groups and their perceptions into a new group, the "lint heads," with associated stereotypes and behaviors recognized by themselves and other groups. In turn, the textile industry influenced attitudes toward work and recreation, including antiunion sentiments. As the mills metamorphosed into other industries after World War II, new groups and new ideas infiltrated the Upstate. Today, though, mill villages and mill people, together with cotton farmers, still form distinctive components of the cotton Piedmont.

While geography and history account for many contrasts between Illinois prairie towns and those of the Piedmont, other differences occur because of culture. German immigrants drastically altered the eponymous landscape of their new homeland, so that southwestern Illinois contains place names like New Baden and Darmstadt. German accents flavor the speech in these towns, while a distinct southern dialect echoes throughout the Piedmont. The conservative, fundamentalist faiths of Methodists and Baptists in the Piedmont denounce the widespread consumption of alcohol, while Roman Catholic and Lutheran church festivals in southwestern Illinois invariably serve beer, even on Sundays. Taverns dot many street corners in southwestern Illinois while supermarkets forbid Sunday beer sales in most communities in the Piedmont. Sauerkraut, bratwurst, and potato pancakes are replaced with fried okra, biscuits, and grits in the Upstate. While wedding reception bands in both places may play country-western music, chances are that those in southwestern Illinois will also feature polkas.

Other cultural distinctions are more difficult to explain. Illinoisans certainly honor and respect their families, but they do not place memorials to loved ones in newspapers. Family reunions seem to have more organization and more significance in the Upstate than in southwestern Illinois. Religious faith is as strong in both regions, but Illinoisans typically do not hold revivals, reunions, and gospel sings in their congregations. Farmers in both areas worry about the weather and may plant by the same traditional solar and lunar signs, but the black prairie soil does not produce okra, black-eyed peas, or peanuts, which are *never* boiled in Illinois.

This contrast between two regions of the United States illustrates some key features that distinguish the Piedmont from other areas. Some of these features, such as the soil and the crops it produces, depend mostly on geophysical characteristics but also partly on historical and cultural trends. Other features, such as the Upstate's black/white interactions, have in large part been shaped by historical forces but also depend to an extent on cultural attitudes and values. Then, features such as traditional foods stem largely from cultural factors, in part influenced by historical and even geophysical influences. Climate and culture, history and industry, chance and change, interact and intertwine to create the characteristic elements that together distinguish the Piedmont from other American regions.

Robert Chambers summarized most of these components as he described the past century of the Upstate, reflected by his own family history: "I'd like to go on a real crash tour . . . just to show you how this, in the last fifty years, has taken place. . . . There's an old home place . . . where my dad stayed, and . . . you could see how the family farm was laid out, and how they lived their lives. . . . And then you can go . . . right up the road for about five miles to the church where my mother met my dad and my grandfather was a preacher. So there . . . you can see an old, old church, and the way they had their meetings, and the way it was the focus of the social happenings. And then you'd drive on up to . . . a couple of the cotton mill communities. . . . Now they're [the mills are] bricked up and all."

Many older informants, when reflecting on the modifications they had witnessed, then connected their own memories to their family's past, creating an even longer chain of recollections and an even greater accumulation of changes. Most informants, like Elizabeth Block, were almost overwhelmed at the Upstate's transformation within their own lifetimes: "Grandpa was born in 1841, and Granny was born in 1846. And to me it's just almost unbelievable that I grew up in a house with those people from that era."

As Ms. Block indicated, Upstate residents alive today grew up with, and listened to, grandparents born before slavery had been abolished. These people lived as slaves or as masters (directly or indirectly), and passed these stories of antebellum times to their grandchildren on front porches or by family hearths. In turn, these individuals witnessed the metamorphosis of cotton agriculture into fields dotted with mill towns as they sweated in those humid mills or labored in those cotton fields that fed the factories. Now these same Upstaters have grandchildren of their own, who microwave snacks in air-conditioned suburbs and who listen to their grandparents as they rest on benches in the shade of shopping malls. In a sense, those "with a little age on them" view their lives as living links between a past almost so distant as to have been a dream and a future almost so amazing as to be a mirage.

Middle-aged Upstate residents, those born before the 1960s, grew up in a segregated society where black and white friendships (some genuine and some paternalistic) were commonplace. Most African Americans toiled long, weary hours as tenants or general laborers or as maids or laundresses. They played with their employers' children but attended different churches and schools. Their white companions, often working alongside them, shared stories and beliefs about ghosts and gardens and often ate the same foods prepared by the same black cook. Other whites, both men and women, sweated in mill factories, leaving before high school graduation in order to help first their birth families and then their own children have a better life. Now, as these same Piedmonters organize their family reunions and attend to their aging parents, they reflect with nostalgia on the church socials and community activities of their youth, but also recognize decided social and material improvements in their own lives.

Those Upstaters who barely remember desegregation have been raised in a decidedly different world than even their own parents. Blacks no longer attend segregated schools and may legally eat in any restaurant or swim in any community pool they choose. Whites, of course, acknowledge this right even if a few secretly dislike it. Most likely, these Piedmonters have never genuflected before endless rows of cotton or kowtowed before whirling spindles of thread; they are much more likely to have achieved the relatively comfortable lifestyles their parents had labored so long and hard to achieve. Now with young children of their own, they worship at huge suburban churches but attend homecomings at their parents' country churches. As they boat on lakes on Sunday afternoons and cloister their families before television, they regret the loss of community ties and neighborly visits from their parents' childhoods but also welcome the broadened horizons from new industries and new people.

To the children of these Upstate baby boomers belong the heritage of the past and the constellation of traits that still constitute a regional identity. These youngest Piedmonters fidget restlessly at family reunions but listen politely to their grandparents tell stories about mill work or cotton farming. They watch their mothers prepare traditional foods and input the recipes into their computers. They lovingly care for grandma's quilts and learn (perhaps through videotapes) how to repair and replace blocks. They accompany their fathers and grandfathers on hunting and fishing trips and humor their mothers about planting gardens by the light of the moon. They learn prejudice and stereotypes but also pride and tolerance as they attend public schools and summer Bible camps. Improved education brings new ideas about the equality of women and the reality of God, but children then hear at home about the importance of tradition and the identity of Jesus.

Sometimes, though, the gap between generations seems almost insurmountable, as Elizabeth Block discovered with her grandchildren: "They can't understand if we tell them what it was like when we were growing up. They can hear it. But they don't really know what it was really like, because they grew up in a whole different world. None of them got out and hoed cotton. . . . And I'm not so sure they always believe what we say!"

As can be seen over and over again, however, grandchildren not only have listened attentively but they have learned their lessons well. On many Sunday afternoons after church, families gather at a relative's house to

Family, food, and faith: a community church, picnic benches for "dinner on the grounds," and a local cemetery (Photo by John M. Coggeshall)

weave several of the most important elements of a Piedmont identity together: family, food, and faith. The women may have had "the Colonel" prepare their chicken and the men may discuss football instead of cotton prices, but the collective prayers and family stories reflect the same pride and emotion of a century earlier. Each new generation interprets and modifies traditional elements of Piedmont folklife in its own way while inevitable social and cultural transformations make others obsolete. However, the key characteristics of family, food, and faith, defined by geography and history and remodeled through time, continue to distinguish residents of the Upstate from those in other regions of the United States.

In the beginning of the book I utilized a weaving metaphor to describe the process that has created, and that continually transforms, the folklife of the Carolina cotton country. It is important to remember that the cloth of Piedmont folklife is not an antique stored in the attic of the past. Instead, this cloth continues to be woven, with new threads sometimes replacing older ones, with the warp sometimes modifying the pattern, and with the loom itself sometimes adjusting speeds. Precisely because traditions change, Upstate folklife persists through time; the cloth does not wear out but continues to be produced and is even reinforced where and when necessary. This dynamic historical process has spun from cotton and woven through time an extremely durable and colorful cloth.

Andrews, Ray. An Anglo American, Mr. Andrews owns his own business in Greenville, South Carolina, where he also lives. Although a "southerner," he did confess that his mother was born in the North. Mr. Andrews was suggested to me by Lucy Wallace.

Baker, Everett. Mr. Baker, an Anglo American, was born in 1934 and has worked for textile mills in and around Hammondville, and still works as a supervisor in an area mill. An avid local historian, he and his wife have one child, Linda. Mr. Baker was referred to me by several Hammondville-area residents.

Baker, Linda. Everett Baker's daughter, she lives in Hammondville with her maternal grandmother and was born in the mid-1950s. Ms. Baker obtained a master's degree from a regional university and now works as a professional in an area business. She was suggested as an informant by her father.

Block, Elizabeth and Martha. Martha (b. 1915) and her sister Elizabeth (b. 1918) live today on their "home place" outside of Hammondville, which their Anglo-American grandparents bought in 1841. Elizabeth, an armed services retiree, had lived at various locations throughout the United States and now lives with her sister, who has operated small businesses in the Upstate, including a nearby crossroads convenience store. Martha was contacted for the study during a visit to her store, and she then introduced me to her sister.

Calder, Rosemary. Born in the late 1920s, Ms. Calder, an Anglo American, works as a professional in a Hammondville business. She also serves as a local historian and was referred to me by Mr. Baker and other Hammondville residents.

Chambers, Robert. Born in the Greenville area in the early 1940s, this Anglo-American professional is also a local historian and amateur musician, playing banjo in area groups. While his grandparents had once farmed, Mr. Chambers's father left the farm to work in area mills; he grew up in a mill village and became a businessman. Mr. Chambers was referred to the study by another local historian.

Davis, Tom. Born in 1924, this Anglo American's relatives came originally from the mountains of North Carolina to work in the Hammondville mill. Now retired from mill work, he and his wife still live in town. He was referred to me by Mr. Baker.

Edwards, James. Mr. Edwards's father's family has lived in the Hammondville vicinity for several generations. An Anglo American, Mr. Edwards was born in 1936 and worked as a sharecropper until entering
the service in the mid-1950s. Retired from the military, he now operates a small business in Hammondville with his wife. I met Mr. Edwards without a referral and invited him to participate.

Foster, Louis. Raised during the 1940s on a Piedmont farm owned by his
Anglo-American grandfather, Dr. Foster now serves as a state official.
I had met Dr. Foster several years before, and invited him to partici-
pate in this study.

Garroway, Dale. Mr. Garrison's grandfather had been a landowner in the
Hammondville general vicinity; later, Mr. Garroway's father worked
in area mills and rented his farm. Mr. Garroway, an Anglo American
born in the late 1930s, has worked for the state since 1964. He was
asked to participate by Louis Foster.

Hawkins, David. Born in 1913, Mr. Hawkins has lived in Hammondville
all his life, except for service during World War II. Mr. Hawkins's
Anglo-American family is originally from the mountains of North
Carolina, while his wife's family had been farmers in the Hammondville vicinity. Mr. Hawkins is now a retired mill supervisor. He was
referred to the study by Mr. Baker.

Jackson, George. An African American born in 1908, Mr. Jackson had been
honored as a centennial farmer by the county extension agency. He
passed away in 1993. Mr. Jackson's family had been sharecroppers, but
he eventually bought his own farm, which his son still operates. He
also worked at factory and janitorial jobs. Mr. Jackson was contacted
for the study by Ron Kellogg.

Kellogg, Ron. An African American from a downstate South Carolina
farming family, Mr. Kellogg now works as a state employee. Born in
the 1940s, Mr. Kellogg was recommended by Dr. Foster to assist in
identifying additional informants.

Lambert, Jason. An African American born before the Depression and
raised in the southern Piedmont, Mr. Lambert has been a sharecropper and farmer all his life. While still farming today, Mr. Lambert also
works various construction jobs during the winter. He was suggested
for the study by Mr. Kellogg.

Masters, Arthur and Wilma. African Americans living in the black neighborhood of Hammondville, Mr. and Mrs. Masters were both born in
the area in the early 1940s. Mr. Masters works in a nearby textile mill,
while his wife works part-time in a Hammondville business. Mr. Masters was suggested for the study by Mr. Baker.

Nameth, Ray and Maggie. This Anglo-American couple lives in a small mill town about five miles from Hammondville. Mr. Nameth, born in 1920 in Hammondville, worked in the mill for a short time but then served as a town official. Mrs. Nameth, born in the mid-1920s in a small farming community in an adjacent county, taught in the Hammondville school after 1944, where she eventually met her husband. Mrs. Nameth had been contacted during my talk to a women's club in the Hammondville area, and she invited her husband to participate.

Patterson, Geneva. Born in 1909, this Anglo-American woman grew up on a farm in northern Greenville County. Recently widowed, she now lives in Hammondville, where she and her husband had both worked for several decades. Now retired, Mrs. Patterson held several educational positions during her lifetime. Mrs. Patterson was contacted for the study during my talk to a women's organization in the Hammondville area.

Quinnell, Helen. Born in the mid-1920s, Ms. Quinnell (an Anglo American) grew up in Hammondville while her family farmed outside of town. She married in 1950 and left to teach school in a county south of Charlotte. Widowed in the late 1970s, she returned to the Hammondville region, where she lives today on her family's former property. Ms. Quinnell had been contacted during my talk to a women's club in the Hammondville area. She is also the cousin of Lucy Wallace.

Randle, Vernon. An African American, Mr. Randle was born on a farm near Hammondville in 1909 (perhaps on the Quinnell family farm) and grew up in a family of sharecroppers and farmers. Married in 1930, Mr. Randle has worked all his life at a series of jobs: at the Hammondville mill warehouse, as a laborer on the railroad, and as a security guard. Now widowed, Mr. Randle still lives in the house he built for his father-in-law in 1932. Mr. Randle was suggested for the study by Mr. Baker.

Sanders, Richard. Born in 1923, this African American has lived all his life in Hammondville, except for a career in the military during World War II. His parents were also from Hammondville, where his father had a service job and his mother worked for area white families. Married, with three sons and grandchildren, Mr. Sanders lives in the same neighborhood as Don Underwood and Vernon Randle. He was referred to the study by Mr. Baker.

Taylor, Gladys. Born in Hammondville around 1915, Ms. Taylor's family originally came from North Carolina to work in the mill, but her father also clerked in the town's stores. An Anglo American, she serves as her church's historian. She was contacted for the study during my talk to an area women's group.

Underwood, Don. Born in the early 1930s in a small town north of Columbia, South Carolina, this African American came to Hammondville in 1947 as a railroad worker and liked the community so much he remained. A neighbor of Mr. Sanders and Mr. Randle, he stopped by to visit during a conversation with Mr. Sanders and was invited to participate in the research.

Vaughn, William and Patricia. Mr. Vaughn and his wife were both born around 1920 and live in Greenville. Both Anglo Americans, they had also lived for a time in New York and New Orleans. Mr. Vaughn is a retired newspaper editor. He and his wife were suggested for the study by Lucy Wallace.

Wallace, Lucy. An Anglo American, Ms. Wallace is descended from one of the "first families" of Greenville. Now retired but active in community organizations, she taught for several years at a local technical school. She is also the cousin of Helen Quinnell, who suggested her for the study.

Yarbrough, Mary. An Anglo-American resident of Greenville, Ms. Yarbrough was born in the second decade of this century and was later educated at a college in New England. The mother's sister of Lucy Wallace, she was suggested for the study by her niece.

ABBREVIATIONS USED

CLCU = Cooper Library, Clemson University, Clemson, SC.
HCYC = Historical Center of York County, York, SC.
MMUSC = McKissick Museum, University of South Carolina, Columbia.
PDHRC = Pendleton District Historical and Recreational Commission, Pendleton, SC.
UNCCH = University of North Carolina, Chapel Hill.
USCC = South Caroliniana Library, University of South Carolina, Columbia.

Introduction

On general folklife references, see John M. Vlach, "The Concept of Community and Folklife Study," in *American Material Culture and Folklife: A Prologue and Dialogue*, edited by S. J. Bronner (Ann Arbor, MI: UMI Research Press, 1985), 63; and Charles Wilson and William Ferris, eds., *Encyclopedia of Southern Culture* (Chapel Hill: University of North Carolina Press, 1989), 451–57. Sauer's comment is cited by Rupert Vance, *Human Geography of the South: A Study in Regional Resources and Human Adequacy* (Chapel Hill: University of North Carolina Press, 1932), 20; Carl Epting, "What Factors in the Social Heritage of South Carolina Are Favorable or Unfavorable to Education?" M.A. thesis (University of South Carolina, 1924, USCC), 23. On regional folklife, see Barbara Allen, "Regional Studies in American Folklore Scholarship," in *Sense of Place: American Regional Cultures*, edited by B. Allen and T. J. Schlereth (Lexington: University Press of Kentucky, 1990), 1, 3, and 2. See also Sauer's comments in Charles Kovacik and John Winberry, *South Carolina: The Making of a Landscape* (Columbia: University of South Carolina Press, 1989), 1–2. Others as well have noted the essential connection between a regional sense of place and the folk expressions of those in that place. See for example Michael Ann Williams, *Homeplace: The Social Use and Meaning of the Folk Dwelling in Southwestern North Carolina* (Athens: University of Georgia Press, 1991), 145, on folk architecture; John M. Vlach, *The Afro-American Tradition in Decorative Arts* (Cleveland: Cleveland Museum of Art, 1978), 148; and Vlach, "The Concept of Community," 63, 71–73, on folk art. On the persistence to Carolina Piedmont folklife, see Gary Stanton, *Collecting South Carolina Folk Art: A Guide* (Columbia: McKissick Museum, University of South Carolina, 1989), 1, 2; Daniel Patterson and Charles Zug III, "Introduction," in *Arts in Earnest: North Carolina Folklife*, edited by D. Patterson and C. Zug III (Durham, N.C.: Duke University Press, 1990), 24. Holly Mathews, "Killing the Self-Help Tradition among African Americans: The Case of Lay Midwifery in North Carolina, 1912–1983," in *African Americans in the South: Issues of Race, Class, and Gender*, edited by H. Baer and Y. Jones (Athens: University of Georgia Press, 1992), 78, argues that some traditions, like midwifery, may actually be deliberately legislated out of existence.

METHODOLOGY

For this methodology, see Jacquelyn Hall et al., *Like a Family: The Making of a Southern Cotton Mill World* (Chapel Hill: University of North Carolina Press, 1987), xii–xiii. Morland's comments come from a talk he delivered at a regional college in South Carolina on January 7, 1949. See also his field notes (1948–49), Field Studies in the Modern Culture of the South, in the Southern Historical Collection of the Manuscripts Department, UNCCH. See also Morland, *Millways of Kent* (Chapel Hill: University of North Carolina, 1958), 7. The actual authorship of these notes appears to be uncertain, but they are cited as they appear in the archives. Ralph Patrick, one of the researchers for the project and evidently the one assigned to study the "townways of Kent," reported in his 1948–49 field notes that there seemed to be a "defensive attitude" about the study and a concern that Kent will "show up well." While two books on Kent were completed (*Millways* and *Blackways of Kent*), the third never appeared. The unpublished manuscript exists as Patrick's dissertation, "A Cultural Approach to Social Stratification" (Ph.D. dissertation, Harvard University, Cambridge, Mass., 1953; HCYC). For my study, about 25 percent (8 of 30) of these recorded informants have been of African-American descent and about 46 percent have been women (14 of 30). As examples of secondary sources, see Rosser H. Taylor, *Carolina Crossroads: A Study of Rural Life at the End of the Horse-and-Buggy Era* (Murfreesboro, N.C.: Johnson Publishing Co., 1966), 1–2, whose observations of the people of eastern and central Carolina are based "on the memory of one who knew them well." See also Lois Mac-Donald, *Southern Mill Hills: A Study of Social and Economic Forces in Certain Textile Mill Villages* (New York: Alex L. Hillman, 1928), 69, who states that she gathered her impressions about "the mind of the workers" from guided, informal interviews. Likewise, Marjorie Potwin's *Cotton Mill People of the Piedmont: A Study in Social Change* (New York: Columbia University Press, 1927) was based on observations of mill workers while she served as a community recreational director (7–8). In contrast, see John McCain's ("Some Small-Town Folk Beliefs of the Carolina Piedmont," *Social Forces* 12, no. 3 [1934]) description of what he termed "folk sociology— . . . popular beliefs [that] were encountered in the course of growing to young manhood in a representative Carolina Piedmont town of some thousand souls" (418). On the other hand, Susan Willis ("A Mill Town in 1934," B.A. thesis [University of South Carolina, USCC, 1985], 8–9) questions the accuracy of many contemporary (i.e., 1920s–1930s) descriptions of mill life, since the authors often received funding from corporate sponsors. Thus, she relied on oral sources. I have also used these various sources critically.

Chapter 1. The Piedmont Region

THE PIEDMONT REGION

For the delimitation of the Piedmont region, see Karen McDearman, "Piedmont," in *Encyclopedia of Southern Culture*, edited by Charles Wilson and William Ferris (Chapel Hill: University of North Carolina Press, 1989), 575. Odum's comments come from a draft of *American Regionalism* (1938), in the Howard Odum Papers, p. 13, and Howard Odum, *Southern Regions of the United States* (Chapel Hill: University of North Carolina Press, 1936), 486. See also William Barlow, *"Looking Up at Down": The Emergence of Blues Culture* (Philadelphia: Temple University Press, 1989), 79, who centered the region in South Carolina. Bob Korstad, "Industrialization in the Piedmont: An Overview" (Southern Oral History Program, Southern Historical Collection of the Manuscripts Department, UNCCH, 1980), 10, divided tobacco from cotton production in central North Carolina. See also the map of textile spindles in Hall, *Like a Family*, xxvi–xxvii. Cf. Robert DeCoin, *History and Cultivation of Cotton and Tobacco* (London: Chapman and Hall, 1864), 29–30, which put the division somewhat more easterly. On dimensions, see W. C. Hendricks, ed., *North Carolina: A Guide to the Old North State* (Chapel Hill: University of North Carolina Press, 1939), 9; M. F. Maury, *Maury's Revised Manual of Geography. Special Geography of South Carolina* (New York: University Publishing Co., 1884), 1. For a geological discussion of the Piedmont plateau, see Vance, *Human Geography*, 26–27. For width and elevation, see Maury, *Revised Manual*, 1; William S. Powell, *North Carolina: A Bicentennial History* (New York: Norton, 1977), 7; Vance, *Human Geography*, 27. On soils, see Kovacik and Winberry, *South Carolina*, 39–40; Mabel Montgomery, ed., *South Carolina:*

A Guide to the Palmetto State (New York: Oxford University Press, 1941), 8. See Kovacik and Winberry, *South Carolina*, 43–44, on pines and kudzu. For the geological origins of the Blue Ridge, see Kovacik and Winberry, *South Carolina*, 16, and Hendricks, *North Carolina*, 10. On geophysical divisions, see Hendricks, *North Carolina*, 9; Montgomery, *South Carolina*, 8; Kovacik and Winberry, *South Carolina*, 18. While the term "Low Country" is still used to describe the coastal area in general and the Charleston/Beaufort area in particular, the term "Up Country" has been replaced by "Upstate." In historical references, the older term will still be used. See also the Emanuel Schumpert interview (WPA File, USCC, 1939), 3.

On the cultural division between the Piedmont and Low Country, see Montgomery, *South Carolina*, 3; Dunlap, "Time Study 'Omnia Mutantus, Nihil Interit,' " in Franklin Ashley, ed., *Faces of South Carolina: Essays on South Carolina in Transition* (N.p., 1974, USCC), 114. On settlement patterns, see Montgomery, *South Carolina*, 3–6; Ralph Patrick and John Morland field notes (Field Studies in the Modern Culture of the South, in the Southern Historical Collection of the Manuscripts Department, UNCCH, 1948–49); "Tar Heels All," in Hendricks, *North Carolina*, 4–5. For descriptions of Charlestonians, see Montgomery, *South Carolina*, 4–5. On Upstate paranoia, see Edmunds, "The Crossroads of the New South," in Ashley, *South Carolina*, 224. For earlier variants of the Charleston/China joke, see Louise Jones DuBose, "Family Reunions in Lay-by Time" manuscript (WPA File, USCC, 1941), 3, and Montgomery, *South Carolina*, 4–5. On the Sand Hills, see Montgomery, *South Carolina*, 3–4. For the symbolic mediation between Low Country and Upstate, see Karl Heider, "The Gamecock, the Swamp Fox, and the Wizard Owl: The Development of Good Form in an American Totemic Set," *Journal of American Folklore* 93 (1980): 20–21. For Piedmont/mountain differences, see Jennings Rhyne, *Some Southern Cotton Mill Workers and Their Villages* (Chapel Hill: University of North Carolina Press, 1930), 66; Potwin, *Cotton Mill People*, 53–56 (the phrase did not originate with her); Anonymous, "Shouting for Heaven" manuscript (WPA File, Southern Historical Collection of the Manuscripts Department, UNCCH, 1939). On state pride, see Ben Robertson, *Red Hills and Cotton: An Upcountry Memory* (Columbia: University of South Carolina Press, [1942] 1973), 5; Hendricks, *North Carolina*, 3.

SETTLEMENT HISTORY

Native-American Settlement   Much of this information may be reviewed in Kovacik and Winberry, *South Carolina*, 52–59. For a more complete discussion of the Southeast's prehistory, see Charles Hudson, *The*

Southeastern Indians (Knoxville: University of Tennessee Press, 1976), 34–97. On European contact and consequences, see Kovacik and Winberry, *South Carolina*, 59–70 and Hudson, *Southeastern Indians*, 97–119.

Euro-American Settlement On European settlement, see W. J. Cash, *The Mind of the South* (New York: Knopf, 1941), 21–3; Powell, *North Carolina*, 9; see also Kovacik and Winberry, *South Carolina*, 80. For settlement reasons, see Louise Jones DuBose, "Contemporary Culture" manuscript (WPA File, USCC, n.d.), 5–6. Gradually, though, larger cotton plantations, some owned by in-migrating Low Country planters and others by prospering Upcountry farmers, replaced some of these "small independent farmsteads" (see Kovacik and Winberry, *South Carolina*, 89). See also Max Revelise, "Scotch-Irish at Williamsburg 1732" manuscript (WPA File, USCC, 1936), n.p.; Schumpert interview, 8; Robertson, *Red Hills and Cotton*, 99, 9; Cash, *Mind of the South*, 32, and Louise Jones DuBose, "Who Is the South Carolinian?" manuscript (WPA File, USCC, 1939), 6.

African-American Settlement On black settlement, see Vlach, *Afro-American Tradition*, 148–9; Velma Childers interview ("Black Heritage in the Upper Piedmont" Project, PDHRC, 1990). Images about the relative difficulty of life under slavery often contrast with those of African Americans who look back almost wistfully on the "good times" of paternalistic care under slavery, compared to the challenges of Reconstructive freedom and the more recent economic difficulties of the Great Depression. Of course, many of the WPA interviewers were white, and thus their racial background and position as interviewers probably influenced most of the positive comments about slavery. See also the Maxine Williams interview ("Black Heritage in the Upper Piedmont" Project, PDHRC, 1989). For white perspectives, see Louise Jones DuBose, "The Negro" manuscript (WPA File, USCC, 1939), 10 and the Warren Flenniken interview (WPA File, USCC, 1937[?]), 4. On the difficulties facing African Americans during Reconstruction, see the Lucindy Brown interview ("Black Heritage in the Upper Piedmont" Project, PDHRC, 1988); Violet Guntharpe interview (WPA File, USCC, n.d.), 1; "Promised Land—Greenwood County, South Carolina" manuscript (WPA File, USCC), 1. See also the "Granny" Cain interview (WPA File, USCC, 1937), n.p.; Henry Ryan interview (WPA File, USCC, 1937), 1. Cash's comment is in *Mind of the South*, 49–50. Mitchner's comment is in Belinda Hurmence, ed., *My Folks Don't Want Me to Talk about Slavery: Twenty-One Oral Histories of Former North Carolina Slaves* (Winston-Salem, N.C.: John F. Blair, 1984), 80.

Chapter 2. Regional Economy

THE DEVELOPMENT OF COTTON FARMING

On the devastation of the Civil War, see Bruce Catton, *This Hallowed Ground* (Garden City, N.Y.: Doubleday, 1956), 370–78. On Reconstruction, see the Robert Gooding interview (WPA File, USCC, 1938[?]), 5; Ben Thomas interview (WPA File, USCC, 1939), 4; Allen Tullos, *Habits of Industry: White Culture and the Transformation of the Carolina Piedmont* (Chapel Hill: University of North Carolina Press, 1989), 56–64. On cotton farming and the development of sharecropping, see Cash, *Mind of the South*, 145–52, 157–8; Vance, *Human Geography*, 187. For a more recent perspective, see Steven Hahn, "The 'Unmaking' of the Southern Yeomanry: The Transformation of the Georgia Upcountry, 1860–1890," in *The Countryside in the Age of Capitalist Transformation: Essays in the Social History of Rural America*, edited by S. Hahn and J. Prude (Chapel Hill: University of North Carolina Press, 1985), 180–94; see also Hahn, *The Roots of Southern Populism: Yeoman Farmers and the Transformation of the Georgia Upcountry, 1850–1890* (New York: Oxford University Press, 1983), 142–202. For associated problems with sharecropping, see Vance, "Cotton and Tenancy" in "Problems of the Cotton Industry: Proceedings of the Southern Social Science Research Conference," 1935, in Odum Papers; see also Montgomery, *South Carolina*, 58–59; Hendricks, *North Carolina*, 59–60; Odum, *Southern Regions*, 491–93. The letters are from Pearson to E. Reeves, Nov. 9, 1884, Elizabeth Reeves and Andrew Reeves Papers (Southern Historical Collection of the Manuscripts Department, UNCCH); see also David Copeland and James Copeland, "Farm Diary" (Southern Historical Collection of the Manuscripts Department, UNCCH); Pearson to E. Reeves, Jan. 8, 1888, Reeves Papers. On the geophysical impact of cotton planting, see the John B. Culberton interview (WPA File, USCC, 1939) and Eugene R. Crow, "Some Effects of Farm Tenancy on Public Education in South Carolina" (M.A. thesis, University of South Carolina, 1924 USCC), 12–13; Robertson, *Red Hills and Cotton*, 268–69. On the devastation to the region, see Tullos, *Habits of Industry*, 135; Kovacik and Winberry, *South Carolina*, 105. For statistics, see Crow, "Some Effects," 2–4; and B. O. Williams, "An Appraisal of Farm Tenancy in South Carolina," B. O. Williams Papers (Special Collections CLCU), 2. For solutions, see Robertson, *Red Hills and Cotton*, 157–58; Thomas Dawley, *The Child that Toileth Not: The Story of a Government Investigation* (New York: Gracia Publishing Co., 1912), 404–6.

THE DEVELOPMENT OF THE TEXTILE INDUSTRY

On the origins of the industry, see Tullos, *Habits of Industry*, 56; Cash, *Mind of the South*, 179–82; Kovacik and Winberry, *South Carolina*, 98. For industrialization, see W. G. Cooper, ed., *The Piedmont Region: Embracing Georgia, Alabama, Florida and the Carolinas* (Atlanta: Chas. P. Byrd, 1895), 57, 95; MacDonald, *Southern Mill Hills*, 5; Kovacik and Winberry, *South Carolina*, 114. For mill expansion, see Hall, *Like a Family*, 24–25; Melton A. McLaurin, *Paternalism and Protest: Southern Cotton Mill Workers and Organized Labor, 1875–1905*, Contributions in Economics and Economic History No. 3 (Westport, Conn.: Greenwood, 1971), 9. For descriptions of the area by the 1920s, see Vance, *Human Geography*, 289–300; August Kohn, "Leads State in Cloth-Making," in *South Carolina: A Handbook*, edited by the Department of Agriculture, Commerce and Industry, and Clemson College (Columbia: South Carolina Department of Agriculture, 1927), 57; MacDonald, *Southern Mill Hills*, 2; and Hall, *Like a Family*, xxvi–xxvii. On the growing gulf between mill and town, see Montgomery, *South Carolina*, 346; Cash, *Mind of the South*, 200–202.

For background information on "Hammondville," see Tullos, *Habits of Industry*, 143–46; Donna Roper, "Documentation of a Building for Historic Preservation Purposes: 'The Piedmont Cotton Mills,'" 1977; Ralph Christian and Donna Roper, "Nomination Form, National Register of Historic Places, Piedmont Manufacturing Company," 1977, 2; see also *The Bridge* [Piedmont: USCC] Oct. 1918.

The Textile Labor Pool   See Montgomery, *South Carolina*, 76; see also Morland, *Millways*, 15–16; Kovacik and Winberry, *South Carolina*, 114. On the ethnic composition of these laborers, see John Gillin, "Forward," in Morland, *Millways*, viii; McLaurin, *Paternalism*, 4; Montgomery, *South Carolina*, 76.

For farm labor sources, see Tullos, *Habits of Industry*, 303, 13; McLaurin, *Paternalism*, 4; MacDonald, *Southern Mill Hills*, 92. See also Morland field notes; Potwin, *Cotton Mill People*, 48–50. Parker's interview is cited in MacDonald, *Southern Mill Hills*, 19. For the perceptions of farmers, see the Paul and Pauline Griffith interview (Southern Oral History Program, Southern Historical Collection of the Manuscripts Department, UNCCH, 1980); Tally Smith interview (WPA File, USCC, 1939), 6. See also Alexander Batchelor, "A Textile Community" (M.A. thesis, University of South Carolina, 1926, USCC), 19; Hall, *Like a Family*, 43.

On mountain-area labor sources, see Rhyne, *Cotton Mill Workers*, 67. On the work of labor scouts see Potwin, *Cotton Mill People*, 57; Harriet Herring, *Welfare Work in Mill Villages: The Story of Extra-Mill Activities in North Carolina* (Chapel Hill: University of North Carolina Press, 1929), 21; Susie Simmons interview (WPA File, USCC, 1938), 8. Captain Smyth is quoted in "South Carolina Industries" manuscript (WPA File, USCC, n.d.), 8; Robert Adams interview (Southern Oral History Program, Southern Historical Collection of the Manuscripts Department, UNCCH, 1979). On African-American labor trends, see DuBose, "Negro," 13; Hendricks, *North Carolina*, 55. For black migration to the North, see Kovacik and Winberry, *South Carolina*, 124. On this attitude about "shiftless" blacks remaining behind, see Morland's field notes. For general changes to work patterns, see Phillip Wood, *Southern Capitalism: The Political Economy of North Carolina, 1880–1980* (Durham, North Carolina: Duke University Press, 1986), 27.

The Fall of King Cotton   On the coming danger signs, see DuBose, "Contemporary culture," 7; the Culberton interview; Thomas interview, 6; Cash, *Mind of the South*, 360, 396; Arthur Raper, "Notes on Union County [SC] 1943," Arthur F. Raper Papers (Southern Historical Collection of the Manuscripts Department, UNCCH), 11. For soil information, see Kovacik and Winberry, *South Carolina*, 41, 112; Brice Latham interview ("Speaking of History: Sounds and Scenes in the Pendleton District" Collection, PDHRC, 1982). For photographs of the devastation, see the Photograph file (South Caroliniana Library, USCC). These comments are from Sauer to Odum (Jan. 23, 1935), Odum Papers. For government intervention, see Kovacik and Winberry, *South Carolina*, 127–8.

THE COTTON PIEDMONT AFTER 1945

For general changes to the area, see Tullos, *Habits of Industry*, 303. For cotton growing changes, see Kovacik and Winberry, *South Carolina*, 167–69. On peaches, see the *Greenville News*, July 11, 1993. On pines, see Kovacik and Winberry, *South Carolina*, 212.

Industrialization   See Kovacik and Winberry, *South Carolina*, 194 on the persistence of the textile industry; Wood, *Southern Capitalism*, 172–3, and *South Carolina Textiles* on industrial consolidation. For corporate consolidation and the manager's quote, see the *Anderson [SC] Independent-Mail* May 5, 1991. On new industries, see John Edmunds, "The Crossroads of the New South," in Ashley, *South Carolina*, 225; Joseph Spengler, "Introduction," in Thomas Steahr, *North Carolina's Changing Population* (Chapel Hill: Carolina Population Center, 1973), 3. For the Upstate's infrastructural development, see "Economic Distress in Our Cities: Spartanburg, South Carolina" (Hearing before the Committee on Banking, Finance, and Urban Affairs, House of Representatives, Serial No. 102–89. Washington, D.C.: U.S. Government Printing Office, 1992), 10. On corporate relocation, see Kovacik and Winberry, *South Carolina*, 212, and "Economic Distress," 105. On foreign corporations, see the *Greenville News*, Sept. 10, 1991. For the development of the furniture industry, see Bob

Korstad, "Industrialization in the Piedmont: An Overview" (Southern Oral History Program, Southern Historical Collection of the Manuscripts Department, UNCCH, 1980), 11; see also Vance, *Human Geography*, 314. On this uneven development, see "Economic Distress," 105, 8, 82, and the opening statement by Representative Henry Gonzalez (Texas), 83. See also the *Greenville News*, Sept. 10, 1991.

On unionization, see Cash, *Mind of the South*, 297, 350–53. Despite the high price, unions did find support in the Piedmont. Willis's thesis presents a personal portrait of one of the leaders of a strike at the Hammond Mill, Clyde Gilreath. Fired from his job, blacklisted, and unemployed for three years, Mr. Gilreath and his family were reduced to abject poverty. Eventually Mr. Gilreath begged the mill's owner for a job in another town, with the promise that he would never join another union. He kept his promise, even writing an antiunion booklet for supervisors. The author of the thesis was Gilreath's granddaughter. See also Kovacik and Winberry, *South Carolina*, 183. For another perspective, see Wood, *Southern Capitalism*, 157–63. Hall, in *Like A Family* (pp. 347–57), notes that many Piedmonters organized into unions. They faced an uphill struggle, however.

CONCLUSION

For these comments, see Kovacik and Winberry, *South Carolina*, 153.

Chapter 3. Contemporary Social Groups

AFRICAN AMERICANS

On white perspectives toward blacks, see "Social Life and Recreation" manuscript (WPA File, USCC, n.d.). Kent informants are cited in Morland's field notes and in Morland and Patrick's field notes. See also Edmunds, "Crossroads," in Ashley, *South Carolina*, 227. On interracial relationships, see DuBose, "The Negro," 15; Childers interview. On the development of these ties, see the Thomas interview, 2; Morland field notes; and Robertson, *Red Hills and Cotton*, 257–58.

On segregation, see Patrick and Morland field notes. Robertson's recollection exists in the Ben Robertson Papers (Special Collections CLCU), 6. On cultural segregation, see Margaret Bethea, "A Family Like Thing," in Ashley, *South Carolina*, 184; Edmunds, "Crossroads," in Ashley, *South Carolina*, 228. I do not wish to imply that social segregation is unique to the South; it is not. On cultural connections, see Hendricks, *North Carolina*, 95.

WHITE ELITES OR THE "ARISTOCRACY"

The Kent groupings are from Patrick's field notes; see also Morland, *Millways*, 173–4; Patrick, "Cultural Approach," ii–iii; William Brockington, "Sparkleberry," in Ashley, *South Carolina*, 217–18; Patrick and Morland field notes. For class divisions, see William Jacobs, *The Cotton Mill Village: A Correct Picture of the Much Discussed Village System of the Textile South* (Clinton, S.C.: Jacobs and Co., 1932[?]), n.p.; Patrick and Morland field notes. Walter Edgar, Director of the Center for Southern Studies at USC, described class awareness as an "intricate minuet" between wealthy and poor; his comments were made at the 1995 South Carolina Humanities Council annual meeting.

MILL VILLAGERS OR "LINT HEADS"

For the divisions between mill and town, see Morland, *Millways*, 262; Patrick, "Cultural Approach," 297. On stereotypes, see the "First Church of God, Concord, N.C.," manuscript (WPA File, Southern Historical Collection of the Manuscripts Department, UNCCH, 1938), n.p. For these attitudes, see Morland, *Millways*, 181, 183–84; Morland field notes. On inferiority, see Rhyne, *Cotton Mill Workers*, 197; the ministers are cited in MacDonald, *Southern Mill Hills*, 99; Morland, *Millways*, 103–4; Ralph Austin interview (Southern Oral History Program, Southern Historical Collection of the Manuscripts Department, UNCCH, 1979). On current feelings, see Adams interview; Brockington, "Sparkleberry," in Ashley, *South Carolina*, 218; Pat Conroy, "Horses Don't Eat Moon Pies," in Ashley, *South Carolina*, 53.

RURAL WHITES OR "REDNECKS"

On comparisons between mill and farm, see Robertson, *Red Hills and Cotton*, 274–75. For the origin and definition of "redneck," see Francis Boney, "Rednecks," in Wilson and Ferris, *Encyclopedia of Southern Culture*, 1140–41.

POOR WHITES OR "WHITE TRASH"

Williams, "The Poor White," 1–2, in Williams Papers. These comments are from Ella Kelly interview (WPA File, USCC, n.d.); Moses Lyles interview (WPA File, USCC, n.d.); Childers interview. See also DuBose, "The Negro," 15; Fred Alexander interview (WPA File, USCC, 1938), 9. See also J. Wayne Flynt, "Poor White," in Wilson and Ferris, *Encyclopedia of Southern Culture*, 1138–39.

YANKEES OR NORTHERNERS

See DuBose, "South Carolinian," 8; Cash, *Mind of the South*, 319–22, 338–39. This quote is from the Patrick and Morland field notes.

While it is acknowledged that other ethnic groups exist in the Upstate, space precludes their discussion.

Chapter 4. General Social and Cultural Values of Piedmont Folk

GENERAL CHARACTERISTICS

For their overviews, see Cash, *Mind of the South*, viii; 428–29; Odum, *Southern Regions*, 498–501; Odum, "Notes and Abstract Basic to Paper on 'Cultural Elements Differentiating the South from Other Regions,'" 20–22; see also Odum's speech to the City Club, Rochester, N.Y., 5 in Odum Papers. Ms. Blue's comments appear in the A. F. Raper Papers.

Heritage   On this characteristic, see Stephen Gardner, "Stopping on the Vacuum Pipe," in Ashley, *South Carolina*, 93; DuBose, "South Carolinian," 5; Robertson, *Red Hills and Cotton*, 28, 31.

Conservatism   For this trait, see Epting, "Factors," 51; the comment about Kent's conservatism is from the Patrick field notes. On these comments, see Williams, *Homeplace*, 35; John Arnold, "Lancaster Observations: Past and Present," in Ashley, *South Carolina*, 202–3.

Family and Relatives   On this aspect of Carolina folklife, see W. Willimon and H. W. Cabell, *Family, Friends, and Other Funny People: Memoirs of Growing Up Southern* (Columbia, S.C.: R.L. Bryan Co., 1980), 61; the Kent observation is from the Patrick and Morland field notes. See also the Jack Delano Farm Security Administration photographs (1940–1941), Arthur F. Raper Papers (Southern Historical Collection of the Manuscripts Department, UNCCH); M. Williams interview.

On the connections between kin, see Robertson, *Red Hills and Cotton*, 31; Patrick, "Cultural Approach," 111. For the young bride's feelings, see Patrick, "Cultural Approach," 135–38.

Religion and Faith   For background, see E. Fronde Kennedy, "Bible Belt and Quite Proud of It" manuscript (WPA File, USCC, n.d.), 1, 3; Hendricks, *North Carolina*, 96; Cash, *Mind of the South*, 80, 130–34, 137–41; Potwin, *Cotton Mill People*, 18; Patrick field notes.

Individualism   For comments, see Epting, "Factors," 43, 29, 31; Potwin, *Cotton Mill People*, 15–16; Robertson, *Red Hills and Cotton*, 45; Tullos, *Habits of Industry*, 188.

The "Lost Cause" of the Confederacy   On this characteristic, see Cash, *Mind of the South*, 296; Epting, "Factors," 33; Willimon and Cabell, *Family*, 81; and Taylor, *Carolina Crossroads*, 23–24. For alternate perspectives of Sherman's conquest of Columbia, see Catton, *Hallowed Ground*, 375–77.

Racism   On the pervasiveness of racial prejudice, see Patrick, "Cultural Approach," 351; Hartwell Ayer, ed., *South Carolina Hand Book* (Charleston, S.C.: Lucas and Richardson, 1895), 6. For these attitudes, see *The Bridge* Sept. 1923; Patrick, "Cultural Approach," 358. On the improvement of race relations, see Brockington, "Sparkleberry," in Ashley, *South Carolina*, 219. On negative attitudes, see the Leon Berry interview (Southern Folklife Collection of the Manuscripts Department, UNCCH, 1980).

Paternalism   On paternalism toward tenants, see the Lillie Westmoreland interview ("Speaking of History: Sounds and Scenes in the Pendleton District" Collection, PDHRC, 1982). For mill village paternalism, see *The Bridge*, May 1919; Eugene Shaffer, "Southern Mill People," *Yale Review* (XIX, 1930): 326. For the origins of this attitude, see Tullos, *Habits of Industry*, 3–4; Cash, *Mind of the South*, 210.

Southern Hospitality   On Southern hospitality, see Patrick, "Cultural Approach," 122 (both quotes from this page); Hendricks, *North Carolina*, 94; Montgomery, *South Carolina*, 7; Tallie Smith and Mattie Smith interview (WPA file, USCC, 1939).

Southern Chivalry   On chivalry, see Patrick, "Cultural Approach," 120, 124–26 (the quote is from p. 45); Robertson, *Red Hills and Cotton*, 10–11. On the honoring of women, see Patrick and Morland field notes. The Blease quote is from a *New York Times* article, July 16(?), 1930, in the A. Raper Papers. Robertson (*Red Hills and Cotton*, 261) has a fictionalized account.

Slower Pace of Life   On the slower pace of life, see the James Johnson interview (WPA File, USCC, n.d.), 2; Epting, "Factors," 34–35, 50; Robertson Papers, 3. For the potential consequences, see DuBose, "South Carolinian," 5; Patrick, "Cultural Approach," 127–28; Cash, *Mind of the*

South, 344–45. On the persistence of this attitude, see Gardner, "Stopping on the Vacuum Pipe," in Ashley, *South Carolina*, 96.

Chapter 5. Folk Speech

SOUTHERN SPEECH

On the general characteristics of Southern speech, see Hendricks, *North Carolina*, 95. The response is quoted in the *Greenville News*, Oct. 20, 1991.

REGIONAL VARIATIONS

Northern and Southern Speech Kendrick's editorial is in the *Greenville News*, Oct. 25, 1992. For pronunciations see the Morland field notes. For Yankee confusion see Bethea, "A Family Like Thing," in Ashley, *South Carolina*, 185.

Low Country, Upstate, and Mountain Variations On Low Country pronunciations, see Patrick and Morland field notes; DuBose, "South Carolinian?," 6; Montgomery, *South Carolina*, 4–6. On Gullah, see for example Montgomery, *South Carolina*, 104; Patrick and Morland field notes.

Intraregional Variation On the similarity between black and white speech, see the Thomas interview, 2. For white pseudo-kin terms for blacks, see Patrick, "Cultural Approach," 76. On the manipulation of names, see the Patrick and Morland field notes. For formal titles, see the Patrick field notes.

GENERAL CONVERSATION PATTERNS

On this habit, see the Morland field notes. On linkages with family, see DuBose, "Contemporary Culture," 9; Powell, *North Carolina*, xvi.

CHARACTERISTIC WORDS OR EXPRESSIONS

On the plural of "you," see DuBose, "Contemporary Culture," 10. For "right" references, see DuBose, "Contemporary Culture," 10; George P. Wilson, ed., "Folk speech," in N. White, ed., *The Frank C. Brown Collection of North Carolina Folklore*, vol 1 (Durham, N.C.: Duke University Press, 1952–64), 584. See Wilson, "Folk Speech," 583, for a reference to "reckon." On lay-by time, see F. W. Bradley, "A Word-List from South Carolina," *American Dialect Society* 14 (1950): 43; and Lucie Platt, "Dialect

Words and Phrases (Sumter County)" manuscript (WPA File, USCC, n.d.), n.p; Wilson, "Folk Speech," 556, offers the verb "lay-by" as in general use. For various food terms, see The Pearls [Mary Collum and Frances Burnet], *According to Grandma* (Lexington, S.C.: The Kivers, 1964), 37, 39; Wilson, "Folk Speech," 516. On pinders, see also Wilson, "Folk Speech," 574; Platt, "Dialect Words" (also on crackers, pie, and hoppin' John). For "nabs," see Ida Moore, "Balfour Mill" manuscript (WPA File, Southern Historical Collection of the Manuscripts Department, UNCCH, 1939). On galluses, see Bradley, "Word-List," 31. On "pine straw" see David Copeland's farm diary of May 22, 1885. Ethel Harmon is quoted by Anne Kimzey in her field notes (Folk Traditions of the Savannah River Valley, Folklife and Oral History Program, MMUSC, 1988). For "giving some sugar," see also the Morland field notes.

PLACE NAMES AS FOLK SPEECH

On place names, see Kovacik and Winberry, *South Carolina*, 80.

Chapter 6. Storytelling and Verbal Artistry

THE SOCIAL CONTEXT OF STORYTELLING

On general mill storytelling, see Morland field notes; Mary Gattis interview (Southern Oral History Program, Southern Historical Collection of the Manuscripts Department, UNCCH, 1979). For mill operative storytelling, see also "Saluda Sam" [Donald Roper], "More Piedmont War Stories" (Interview in the Piedmont, S.C. Footbridge Festival souvenir program, 1992). On African-American storytelling, see the Patrick and Morland field notes. See also Vlach, *Afro-American Tradition*, 150, on improvisation in black speech. For the continuity of storytelling, see the Kimzey field notes.

For southern characteristics in storytelling, see Robertson, *Red Hills and Cotton*, 40.

STORIES FROM THE PIEDMONT

Local Character Stories   For Barbee's story, see Harry Field, "The Bone Buyer" manuscript, Thaddeus S. Ferree Papers (n.d.). Had either of these stories been told by African Americans (rather than about them), they might well fit into the genre of clever slaves outfoxing their masters, as described by Charles Joyner (*Down by the Riverside: A South Carolina Slave Community* [Urbana: University of Illinois Press, 1984], 183–89). However, since the stories had been told by Anglo Americans, they probably represent simply humorous anecdotes. On injustices toward African Americans, see the L. Brown interview.

Rhymes This rhyme also appears in other sources, e.g., Newbell Puckett, *Folk Beliefs of the Southern Negro* (Chapel Hill: University of North Carolina Press, 1926), 73. Puckett's informants from Columbus, Miss., added another verse uncollected from the Piedmont: "Ten's a ten,/Hit's mighty funny;/Ef you cain't count good/You don't git no money" (73). Mattie Harrell, in her WPA interview (WPA File, USCC, 1938), described a children's game called, "there ain't no bears out tonight." Could this be related to Ms. Baker's folk rhyme? The memorials appeared in the *Greenville News,* Aug. 29, 1993, and Oct. 3, 1993.

Folktales The anonymous description of these earlier tale-telling times may be found in the "Speaking of History: Sounds and Scenes in the Pendleton District" Collection (PDHRC, 1982) interviews. For the "Raw Head and Bloody Bones" story, see Hurmence, *My Folks,* 21, who report the same story from earlier generations and from different locations. The story, more magical than frightening, is retold by Leonard Roberts (*South from Hell-fer-Sartin: Kentucky Mountain Folk Tales* [Lexington: University of Kentucky Press, 1955], 54–58). Morland's tale is from his field notes. The oak/acorn story is from the "Speaking of History" interviews. For another version of the tenant/owner story, see C. Grayson Dalton interview ("Speaking of History: Sounds and Scenes in the Pendleton District" Collection, PDHRC, 1982). An anonymous reviewer of this manuscript suggested the tale exists independent of racial associations; however, I have only heard it as a racial injustice.

Stories of Supernatural Phenomena On African-American beliefs, see Puckett, *Folk Beliefs,* 311–12; Charles Joyner, *Folk Song in South Carolina* (Columbia: University of South Carolina Press, 1971), 4; Stiles Scruggs, " 'Ha'nt' and Witch Experiences" manuscript (WPA File, USCC, n.d.). The assumption that African Americans would know more ghost stories, in fact, explained the fieldwork questions of WPA workers, who frequently asked their black informants but rarely their white respondents for examples. On the relationship between black and white beliefs, see Puckett, *Folk Beliefs,* 312; Joyner, *Folk Song,* 4; Hurmence, *My Folks,* 21 (for the Johnson quote). See the Eula Durham and Marjorie Hearne interviews (Transcript on file, Southern Oral History Program, Southern Historical Collection of the Manuscripts Department, UNCCH, 1979) for Ms. Durham's description, and Puckett, *Folk Beliefs,* 312, for a quote explaining the influence of black beliefs on whites.

Jokes and Pranks   Some jokes and pranks are cited in the Patrick field notes and Morland field notes. This joke may be found in the Jimmy Elgin interview (Southern Oral History Program, Southern Historical Collection of the Manuscripts Department, UNCCH, 1979). Mary Elrod's joke is from the Jeptha Elrod interview, "Explaining Ourselves: Tradition and Change in the Old Pendleton District" (Folklife and Oral History Program, MMUSC, 1987). The men's club joke and the Catholic joke are from Patrick and Morland field notes. Ms. Childers's anecdote is described in her interview, and the Horton-directed quip is from the J. Elrod interview.

Mill Pranks   Mill practical jokes are described in the Elgin interview and the Gattis interview. On the meanings behind these pranks, see Douglas DeNatale, "The Dissembling Line: Industrial Pranks in a North Carolina Textile Mill," in *Arts in Earnest: North Carolina Folklife*, edited by D. Patterson and C. Zug III (Durham, N.C.: Duke University Press, 1990), 274–76. Schaefer Kendrick's column appeared in the *Greenville News*, Oct. 25, 1992.

Chapter 7. Customary Beliefs

NATURAL PHENOMENA

Weather Prognostication   On bird flocks indicating bad weather, see also the Nora and Albert Wood interview ("Folk Traditions of the Savannah River Valley," Folklife and Oral History Program, MMUSC, 1988); see Puckett, *Folk Beliefs*, 509; and Wayland Hand, ed., "Popular Beliefs and Superstitions from North Carolina," *Brown Collection*, vol. 7, p. 309, for a related belief about chickens flocking. For the "devil beating his wife" idea, see also Puckett, *Folk Beliefs*, 518; Margaret Bryant, "Folklore from Edgefield County, South Carolina, II," *Southern Folklore Quarterly* 12 (1948): 281; and from North Carolina, Hand "Popular Beliefs," 276–78; Travis Jordan, "Old Folk Superstitions," Folklife material from the Federal Writer's Project (Davis Library, UNCCH, n.d.), 3–4. For changes to traditions, see the N. and A. Wood interview.

Solar and Lunar Influences on Natural Phenomena   On planting by the moon, see also "Dutch Fork Folklore" manuscript (WPA File, USCC, 1937); Hand, "Popular Beliefs," 502–5; A. Wood interview (also for the specific quote). On skepticism, see also the N. Wood interview.

Only one informant, Vernon Randle, provided names for constellations. Those he remembered he had learned from his grandpa, born a slave: "And he could just take you out and . . . show you stuff in that sky—'Yon Job's Coffin, yon the Seventh Star, yon the Dipper.' . . . Well, I ain't seen nothing like that. But now if he could get you, show you, don't you know you could see sense in it." See also Hendricks, *North Carolina*, 98, on Job's Coffin as a constellation.

Beliefs about Human Activities On gender identification, see also the Morland field notes.

FOLK HEALING AND MEDICINES

Traditional Healers For details on paramedical remedies, see Holly Mathews, "Introduction: A Regional Approach and Multidisciplinary Perspective," in *Herbal and Magical Medicine: Traditional Healing Today*, edited by J. Kirkland, H. Mathews, C. Sullivan III, and K. Baldwin (Durham, N.C.: Duke University Press, 1992). For protection from witches, see Scruggs, " 'Ha'nt' and Witch Experiences," 1; George Burris interview (Southern Historical Collection of the Manuscripts Department, UNCCH, 1939). On protective amulets, see also W. N. Harriss, "Negro Conjure," Folklife material from the Federal Writer's Project (Davis Library, UNCCH, n.d.), 1–2. On silver charms, see also Puckett, *Folk Beliefs*, 288, 314; and Hand, "Popular Beliefs," 106–7, 113, 131, 165. It is highly likely, as Puckett (*Folk Beliefs*, 80, 311) argued, that the ideas about conjure protection have direct antecedents in West African cultures. Charles G. Zug III (personal communication) concurs. Sheila Walker, an anthropologist with fieldwork experience in West Africa, mentioned that cowrie shells there serve the same purpose when worn in the same manner. Since silver holds mystical powers in Euro-American tradition, I suggest that the African-American silver dime charms likely represent an acculturative blend of black and white beliefs.

On the importance of traditional healers, see Holly Mathews, "Doctors and Root Doctors: Patients Who Use Both," in *Herbal and Magical Medicine*, 70, 76–80; Gattis interview. On the transmission of power, see Ralph Strickland interview (Southern Oral History Program, Southern Historical Collection of the Manuscripts Department, UNCCH, 1980). On the psychological functions of healers, see Mathews, "Doctors and Root Doctors," 84–86. For variations in belief, see the Berry interview. For a similar doorstep bewitchment, see Patrick and Morland field notes.

On the persistence of healers, see Holly Mathews, "Introduction," in *Herbal and Magical Medicine*, 7–8; Karen Baldwin, "Aesthetic Agency in the Folk Medical Practices and Remembrances of North Carolinians," in *Herbal and Magical Medicine*, 182; Carole Hill, "Reproduction and Transformation of Health Praxis and Knowledge among Southern Blacks," in *African Americans in the South*, 46; Mathews, "Doctors and Root Doctors," 94.

On African origins of these ideas, see Mathews, "Doctors and Root Doctors," 70; on Anglo-American origins, see Mathews, 70, 72. On German American healing, see G. L. Summer, "Personal Knowledge" manuscript (WPA File, USCC, 1936). On Native-American origins, see the Strickland interview. On the religious bond, see Mathews, "Introduction," 3.

Traditional Curing Practices   On blood stopping, see also Mary Hicks, "Love Potions, Charms and Cures Used by Negroes" (Folklife material from the Federal Writer's Project, Davis Library, UNCCH, n.d.), 16. On blood stopping in the Piedmont, see also Morland field notes; Hand, "Popular Beliefs," 126. For talking out fire, see James Kirkland, "Talking Fire Out of Burns: A Magico-Religious Healing Tradition," in *Herbal and Magical Medicine*, 41; the D. A. Rivers interview (WPA File, USCC, 1937); Hicks, "Love Potions," 17; and Hand, "Popular Beliefs," 138.

Traditional Healing Materials   For these citations, see M. F. Maury, *Manual of Geography*, 4; Rosa Kanipe interview (WPA File, Southern Historical Collection of the Manuscripts Department, UNCCH, 1939), 11. On the "backyard drugstore," see the Kimzey field notes; Mathews, "Doctors and Root Doctors," 70, on African-American medicines; Patrick and Morland field notes for the quote. On "black drop" tea, see the Anna Pearsall interview (WPA File, USCC, n.d.), 3; E. Durham interview. Dr. Patti Connor-Greene, a psychologist, has suggested that African Americans might more frequently use laxatives as weight-loss methods; she has speculated that this practice may have cultural roots in the traditional use of purgatives among blacks.

Ethel Hilliard is quoted in Tullos, *Habits of Industry*, 177, 221. Ms. Hilliard's mother also made teas from red oak bark (215). For references to black snake root, see the N. Wood interview.

Midwives   On African-American midwives, see Mathews, "Self-Help Tradition," in *Herbal and Magical Medicine*, 62–63. For personal midwife experiences, see the M. Williams interview; Alice Gassoway interview ("Black Heritage in the Upper Piedmont" project, PDHRC, 1989); Ida Johnson interview ("Speaking of History" interviews). On changes to the tradition, see Albertha Gilchrist interview ("Folk Traditions of the Savannah River Valley," Folklife and Oral History Program, MMUSC, 1988); Mathews, "Self-Help Tradition," 78.

Chapter 8. Social Gatherings and Activities

INFORMAL CELEBRATIONS

Sunday Dinner For an invitation to Sunday dinner, see Willimon and Cabell, *Family, Friends*, 6–8. The Kent reference is from the Morland field notes, as is the concern by children about running short on food. The preacher comment appears in the "Speaking of History" interviews.

Family Reunions On traditional family reunions, see DuBose, "Family Reunions," 1–3, 6. As an anonymous reviewer of this manuscript has noted, family reunions assist in maintaining black family solidarity as well.

Informal Visiting For examples of farm visiting, see the Copeland farm diary; Mamie Smith diary (Mary Alice Sifford Collection, York County Historical Society, HCYC, 1892–93). On family togetherness in mill towns, see also Hall, *Like a Family*, xvii, 20, 141–44. The quote is from the Colie Craft interview (WPA File, USCC, 1938). Kirkpatrick's ideas are found in the Laura Kirkpatrick interview (Southern Oral History Program, Southern Historical Collection of the Manuscripts Department, UNCCH, 1979). On elite socializing, see the Patrick field notes. On family togetherness, see the Gattis interview. See also the interview with Karl Heider, *Greenville News*, June 22, 1994. For the persistence of traditional social interaction, see Edmunds, "Crossroads," in Ashley, *South Carolina*, 233; Roy Elrod interview ("Explaining Ourselves: Tradition and Change in the Old Pendleton District," Folklife and Oral History Program, MMUSC, 1987); Kimzey field notes.

Informal Social Assistance On neighborliness, see Arnold, "Lancaster Observations," in Ashley, *South Carolina*, 198; L. Kirkpatrick interview.

Wakes and Funerals On neighborly assistance, see the Patrick field notes; Morland field notes. For comments about wakes, see the M. Williams interview; Mary Gattis and Helen Howard interview (Southern Oral History Program, Southern Historical Collection of the Manuscripts Department, UNCCH, 1979). For African-American variations, see Vlach, *Afro-American Tradition*, 139. Perhaps this concept might explain, at least in part, the vivid tales of ghosts by African Americans. For African-American recollections, see Puckett, *Folk Beliefs*, 86–87.

On the stopping of clocks, see Lucy Cobb, "Folk Customs" (Folklife material from the Federal Writer's Project, Davis Library, UNCCH, n.d.); Paul Brewster, ed., "Beliefs and Customs," *Brown Collection,* vol. 1, p. 256. On the covering of mirrors, see Brewster, "Beliefs and Customs," 256. For the origins of these ideas, see Puckett, *Folk Beliefs,* 81–82.

For the persistence of funeral traditions, see the Minnie Dunn interview (Southern Oral History Program, Southern Historical Collection of the Manuscripts Department, UNCCH, 1979); the article is from the *Greenville News,* July 18, 1991.

Parties and Folk Musicians Spacial limitations prevent discussion of various types of informal parties such as play parties, box suppers, and other rural gatherings.

For the origins of Piedmont blues, see Barlow, *"Looking Up at Down,"* 81. On instruments, see the Berry interview; James Putnam interview (Southern Folklife Collection of the Manuscripts Department, UNCCH, 1979). On folk musicians, see the R. Elrod interview; Putnam interview.

Folk Dancing On the associations between black and white dancing styles, see the Longstreet Gantt interview (WPA File, USCC, 1937[?]); Putnam interview; Berry interview. For square dancing, see Mary Hicks, "Barn Dance Figures," Thaddeus S. Ferree Papers (Southern Historical Collection of the Manuscripts Department, UNCCH, n.d.), 1, 3. Round dances are those performed by individual couples (*The Dance Encyclopedia,* ed. by A. Chujoy and P.W. Manchester [NY: Simon and Schuster, 1967], 781, 860). On improvisation in African-American dance, see Vlach, *Afro-American Tradition,* 150; Putnam interview; Delano photographs.

Folk Music On the acculturative process in folk music, see Joyner, *Folk Song,* 6, n. 3; see also the comments in the Putnam interview. While this section focuses on the contribution of African Americans to Piedmont musical traditions, this is not to deny that Anglo Americans also produced their own traditions as well as those influenced by black culture. However, in none of my written or oral sources did white informants mention folk songs; the exception was the "Weave Room Blues." One source (J. Elrod interview) discussed his string band, which mixed popular and commercial songs for a regional radio show. Other informants discussed the minstrel shows and string bands that played throughout the mill towns. However, space precludes their discussion in more detail. Her comment may be found in the M. Williams interview. On distinctions between white and black music, see Barlow, *"Looking Up at Down,"* 80–81; Hendricks, *North Carolina,* 114. See also the comments in the Patrick and Morland field notes. On African-American traditions, see Bruce Bastin, *Crying for the Car-*

olinas (London: Studio Vista, 1971), 8; although cf. Barlow, *"Looking Up at Down,"* 81–82, 95. For the relationship between black music and African-American life experiences, see the Putnam interview; the Childers interview; the M. Williams interview; and Ethel Harmon, quoted in the Kimzey field notes. On cotton-picking and the blues, see the Putnam interview; White's song is from Barlow, *"Looking Up at Down,"* 98–99. On work songs, see the James Williams interview ("Speaking of History: Sounds and Scenes in the Pendleton District" Collection, PDHRC, 1982). Howard Odum and Guy B. Johnson, *The Negro and His Songs: A Study of Typical Negro Songs in the South* (Chapel Hill: University of North Carolina Press, 1925), 252; rpt. (Westport, Conn.: Negro Universities Press, 1968), wrote that "the 'Grade Song' is one of the most typical of all Negro songs. Here may be seen the humor and wit of the Negro workman, and his relation to the 'boss:' 'Well, captain, captain, you mus' be blin'/Look at yo' watch! See ain't it quittin' time?' " For additional examples, see also the J. Williams interview (very detailed). On indirect requests, see Odum and Johnson, 252 (n) and 7.

CALENDRICAL HOLIDAYS

New Year's Eve and Day   On special foods, see The Pearls, *According to Grandma*, 2; Bradley, "Word List," 38; Morland field notes.

The Fourth of July   For traditional celebrations, see the M. Williams interview; "Speaking of History" interviews; L. Brown interview; Gantt interview. On Fourth of July barbecues, see also *The Bridge*, June 1920. For changes, see the Gattis interview.

Lay-By Time   For traditional depictions, see DuBose, "Family Reunions," 1; "Speaking of History" interviews. On social activities, see Thomas interview, 3–4.

Christmastime   Several informants have hinted at two other Christmas customs, which may or may not be widespread. As a child, when Helen Quinnell visited her family's farm, she overheard African Americans discussing "paying" Santa Claus; only Arthur Masters (of my black informants) had thought he remembered his father saying something about that. Ms. Quinnell also had heard blacks describe Christmas Day as the "first" day of Christmas. Maxine Williams, during her interview, said that her birthday came "in Christmas" and "after first Christmas Day." There is also a vague suggestion in the Copeland Diary, in entries by James Copeland for December 25 and 31, 1884. This might also be associated with the Anglo-American tradition of "Old Christmas" and "New Christmas" following the colonial calendrical change. On Christmas fireworks, see also Pearsall interview, 2; Hendricks, *North Carolina*, 95.

Chapter 9. Games and Recreations

CHILDREN'S ACTIVITIES

Both Genders   On mill games, see Morland, *Millways*, 93. Note the suggestion by Gary Stanton, *Collecting South Carolina Folk Art*, 11, that "many topics in children's folklore remain virtually undocumented, especially in the upcountry areas of the state." For other children's games, see also the Childers interview; the Gassoway interview; Paul Brewster, ed., "Children's Games and Riddles," *Brown Collection*, vol. 1, pp. 78–80.

Boy Activities   On community warnings against skinny-dipping, see *The Bridge*, June 1919. For references to "mumble peg," see Patsy Ginns, *Rough Weather Makes Good Timber: Carolinians Recall* (Chapel Hill: University of North Carolina Press, 1977), 90. The game may have been less familiar to African Americans. For tobacco tag games, see the Gassoway interview. For folk toys, see the Putnam interview.

Girl Activities   On general pleasures, see Morland field notes; Gassoway interview; the Delano photograph collection. For "poppy shows" from North Carolina, see Brewster, "Children's Games," 153, and his references. The doll comments may be found in the Childers interview. On girls' imaginary play, see the Morland field notes.

FAMILY RECREATIONS

Shopping   On shopping on Saturday, see also the L. Brown interview.

Flea Markets   For the local importance of flea markets, see also Stanton, *Collecting South Carolina Folk Art*, 16. For her discussion, see DuBose, "Contemporary Culture," 20.

ADULT MALE ACTIVITIES

Womanless Ceremonies   On womanless weddings, see also the Pauline Griffith interview. For lip-synching performances, see the Kimzey field notes.

Hunting On the traditional importance of hunting, see Morland, *Millways*, 171; Patrick and Morland field notes. On childhood experiences, see the Alexander interview; Wes Young interview ("Folk Traditions of the Savannah River Valley," Folklife and Oral History Program, MMUSC, 1988). On the importance of hunting dogs, see the Morland field notes; Everet Boney interview (WPA File, USCC, 1938), 3. For the pleasures from hound sounds, see the Young interview.

For fox hunting, see the Young interview. For raccoons, see the A. Wood interview. For possums, see the Morland field notes. On rabbit gums, see also H. W. Corley, "Folklore—Rabbit Catching" manuscript (Folklife material from the Federal Writer's Project, Davis Library, UNCCH, n.d.).

Fishing On the popularity of fishing, see J. R. Glenn interview (WPA File, Southern Historical Collection of the Manuscripts Department, UNCCH, 1939). On seining, see Taylor, *Carolina Crossroads*, 158.

Moonshining For earlier experiences, see the Mary Hammond interview ("Folk Traditions of the Savannah River Valley," Folklife and Oral History Program, MMUSC, 1988); Alexander interview, 11–12. For bootleggers in Hammondville, see *The Bridge*, August 1922. On bootlegging in the area today, see the *Greenville News*, July 19, 1993, and Oct. 9, 1993.

ADULT WOMEN ACTIVITIES

Sewing and Quilting On learning to quilt, see Laurel Horton and Lynn R. Myers, *Social Fabric: South Carolina's Traditional Quilts* (Columbia: McKissick Museum, University of South Carolina, 1984), 27; "Speaking of History" interviews; M. Williams interview; Gilchrist interview. On additional influences, see Horton and Myers, *Social Fabric*, 27; "South Carolina Handicrafts" manuscript (WPA File, USCC, n.d.), 2. On quilting parties, see "Social Life and Recreation," 3; Kate Flenniken interview (WPA File, USCC, 1937[?]), 2. On tact associated with organizing quilting parties, see the M. Williams interview; Childers interview. On contemporary alterations, see Taylor, *Carolina Crossroads*, 158.

POPULAR TEAM SPORTS

On textile mill teams, see Thomas Perry, *Textile League Baseball: South Carolina's Mill Teams, 1880–1955* (Jefferson, N.C.: McFarland and Co., 1993). On the popularity of auto racing, see Edmunds, "Crossroads of the New South," in Ashley, *South Carolina*, 234.

Chapter 10. Religion and Religious Ceremonies

For his quote, see the Joseph Stewart interview (WPA File, USCC, 1938), 2.

DENOMINATIONS

On Upstate church denominations, see also Robertson, *Red Hills and Cotton*, 102, 203; Montgomery, *South Carolina*, 103. For the Kent jokes and the reflection of social class by denomination, see Patrick field notes. For her quote, see the M. Williams interview.

CHURCH SOCIAL FUNCTIONS

On black church/community activities, see the M. Williams interview and Tony Whitehead, "In Search of Soul Food and Meaning: Culture, Food, and Health," in *African Americans in the South*, 107. On African-American church attendance, see also Patrick and Morland field notes.

On the relationship between southern values and religious beliefs, see Cash, *Mind of the South*, 289–90; Morland, *Millways*, 148–51; Herring, *Welfare Work*, 99.

RELIGIOUS SERVICES

On old-time preachers, see the M. Williams interview; Cal and Emma Kincaid interview ("Folk Traditions of the Savannah River Valley," Folklife and Oral History Program, MMUSC, 1988). Traditionally, such congregational ecstasy was believed by whites to be associated with "Negro worship." See for example Mary Hicks, "Negro Worship" manuscript, Thaddeus S. Ferree Papers (Southern Historical Collection of the Manuscripts Department, UNCCH, n.d.). For anecdotes about speaking in tongues, see the Childers interview. On spiritual healing, see the "Speaking of History" interviews.

RELIGIOUS SONGS AND HYMNS

On religious songs as folklife, see the suggestion by Stanton, *Collecting South Carolina Folk Art*, 13; M. Williams interview; Childers interview. On hymn singing (traditional and contemporary), see the Gilchrist interview; M. Williams interview.

On emotionalism and hymn singing, see the J. Williams interview and the M. Williams interview. (Note: the last phrase in the M. Williams quote preceded the "two hundred years" comment on the original tape.)

REVIVALS AND CAMP MEETINGS

On traditional camp meeting grounds, see DuBose, "Contemporary Culture," 17–18; M. Williams interview. Several photographs in the South Caroliniana Library collection depict "Camp Welfare," an African-American camp meeting ground in Fairfield County, S.C. See also Simmie Smith, "Camp Welfare" manuscript (WPA File, USCC, 1939). On revivals in the Upstate, see the E. Kincaid interview.

ALL-DAY SINGINGS AND HOMECOMINGS

For additional references to shape-note singing, see the James Harbin, Jr., interview ("Explaining Ourselves: Tradition and Change in the Old Pendleton District," Folklife and Oral History Program, MMUSC, 1987) and Phil Perrin, "Shape-Note Hymnody," private manuscript. The singing convention comments are from the Childers interview. On the continuity of this singing, see the Harbin interview.

Chapter 11. Foods and Food Traditions

FOODWAYS IN GENERAL

See the John Wigington interview from the *Anderson* (S.C.) *Daily Mail*, edited by Ellie Rice (WPA File, USCC, 1936). On southern foodways, see Whitehead, "Soul Food and Meaning," 106, 99 (the source of the quote); on the privacy of foodways, see Vlach, "Concept of Community," 73. On the association between foodways and class/occupation, see Whitehead, "Soul Food and Meaning," 108. Whitehead refers to his article, "Sociocultural Dynamics and Food Habits in a Southern Community," in *Food in the Social Order*, edited by Mary Douglas, 1984. For class/occupation ties to foodways, see also Vance, *Human Geography*, 428–29, 425–26, and 423–24; MacDonald, *Southern Mill Hills*, 94. On the ties between black and white foodways, see Whitehead, "Soul Food and Meaning," 108. Tony Whitehead, while acknowledging the interlinking of African- and Anglo-American foodways, suggests that further research should be conducted to discover "whether there seems to be a 'core' foodways system among African Americans"; see p. 102 for what those foods might be. For the possible origins of these traditions, see Whitehead, "Soul Food and Meaning," 104–5, 98. Mary Willis is quoted by Willis, "Mill Town," 10.

FOODWAYS ABOUT MEAT

Pork and Pork Products See the George Tanner interview (WPA File, USCC, 1939), 6. For sources on traditional hog butchering, see the

M. Williams interview; L. E. Cogburn, "Hog Killing" manuscript (WPA File, USCC, 1939); Putnam interview. For her comment, see the Childers interview. On fatback and vegetables, see also the Dunn interview. On chitlins, see also Cogburn, "Hog Killing," 5; Dunn interview (also for her comment).

Wild Game   On cooking possums, see the A. Wood interview. On this trait of turtle meat, see also Ethel Harmon, quoted in Kimzey's field notes, and Hand, "Popular Beliefs," 364.

Barbecues   On the popularity of barbecues, see also Hendricks, *North Carolina*, 105; Montgomery, *South Carolina*, 107. See also the Wesley Jones interview (WPA File, USCC, 1937). For the process of barbecuing, see the W. Jones interview, 2. On the serving of the meat, see the photograph in the Delano photograph collection. On hash itself, see W. W. Dixon, "A Picnic Dinner in Fairfield County" manuscript (WPA File, USCC, n.d.), 1–2; Henry Grant, "South Carolina Outdoor Barbecue Pig Dinner" manuscript (WPA File, USCC, n.d.). On the continued popularity of Upstate barbecuing, see Kimzey field notes; Kovacik and Winberry, *South Carolina*, 207–8.

FOODWAYS ABOUT PLANTS AND
PLANT MATERIALS

Grits or Hominy Grits   The comment about grits is from Robertson, *Red Hills and Cotton*, 66.

Peanuts   On the processing of peanuts, see H. W. Corley, "Folklore— Pender Popping" (Folklife material from the Federal Writer's Project, Davis Library, UNCCH, n.d.), 1. On boiled peanuts, see Kimzey's field notes. While I have seen them for sale in Alabama and Georgia, a reviewer for this manuscript felt they were less common in North Carolina. For parched peanuts, see the Miemy Johnson interview (WPA File, USCC, n.d.), 1.

Greens   For references to greens, see Hendricks, *North Carolina*, 104. For collard greens, see the Corrie Wingard interview (WPA File, USCC, 1938).

FRUITS, SNACKS, AND SWEETENINGS

Wild Grapes   For his observation, see the David Copeland farm diary, Sept. 21, 1884. For references to scuppernongs, see DeCoin, *History and Cultivation*, 34; Hendricks, *North Carolina*, 102, 105.

Moon Pies   The quote is from Conroy, "Horses Don't Eat Moon Pies," in Ashley, *South Carolina*, 53. See also the *Greenville News*, May 16, 1993.

Molasses   For the description of molasses, see Hendricks, *North Carolina*, 105. Landreth is interviewed in the "Speaking of History" collection. For details on the preparation, see the Elbridge Wright interview ("Explaining Ourselves: Tradition and Change in the Old Pendleton District," Folklife and Oral History Program, MMUSC, 1987). Collins is quoted in a *Greenville News* story by Anna Simon, Oct. 9, 1991.

BREADS AND GRAVIES

Biscuits   On the popularity of biscuits, see Vance, *Human Geography*, 418.

Cornbread   On the popularity of cornbread, see Hendricks, *North Carolina*, 104; Vance, *Human Geography*, 427. Vance cites W. C. French, "Home Supplies Furnished by the Farm," *Farmer's Bulletin* (1920): 7, 9. For his definition of cracklings, see Cogburn, "Hog Killing," 8.

ICED TEA

On the popularity of iced tea, see the Morland field notes; Whitehead, "Soul Food and Meaning," 100.

TRADITIONAL FORMS OF FOOD PRESERVATION

On the importance of canning and preserving garden vegetables, see the James Miles interview (Tape, USCC, 1986); Childers interview; Delano photograph collection. For descriptions of canning and drying food, see the Gilchrist interview. Mattie Pullin is discussed in Kimzey's field notes. For curing meats, see Cogburn, "Hog Killing," 6–7.

FOOD CONSUMPTION PRACTICES

On big meals, see Morland, *Millways*, 158–59 (the quote is from 159); Dunn interview. On the origins of big meals, see Whitehead, "Soul Food and Meaning," 104–5.

TRANSFORMATION AND PERSISTENCE
OF FOODWAYS

For the persistence of traditional foodways, see Whitehead, "Soul Food and Meaning," 100–1, 97, 108; Pullin in Kimzey's field notes.

CONCLUSION

On the tie between foodways and locations, see Whitehead, "Soul Food and Meaning," 106.

Chapter 12. Traditional Occupational Culture

FARMING

The quote about children carrying water to field workers is from the "Speaking of History" interviews; see also the Tanner interview (WPA File, USCC, 1939), 6. His quip is from the R. Elrod interview. On the difficulty of farm labor, see the "Speaking of History" interviews and the Tanner interview.

Tenant Farming and Sharecropping On tenancy as a caste, see Hendricks, *North Carolina*, 54–55; Cash, *Mind of the South*, 280–82; Robertson, *Red Hills and Cotton*, 288. See also Montgomery, *South Carolina*, 53–59; Vance, *Human Geography*, 200, 203.

On black farm labor, see Jesse Davis interview (WPA File, USCC, n.d.). On women, see the Craft interview; Odell McNeil interview (WPA File, Southern Historical Collection of the Manuscripts Department, UNCCH, 1939). For her quip about poverty, see the Childers interview. For a discussion of the differences between sharecropping and tenant farming, see E. J. Holcomb and G. Aull, "Sharecroppers and Wage Laborers on Selected Farms in the Counties of South Carolina" (Bulletin 328, Clemson Agricultural College, Agricultural Experiment Station, Clemson, South Carolina, 1940), 7, 49. On buying on credit, see the M. Williams interview.

For the ambiguity of prices, see for example W. T. Newell, "Overseer's Day Book of a Small Plantation" (Special Collections, Cooper Library, CU), 64. On exploitation, see Cash, *Mind of the South*, 397–98; Henry Ketchin interview (WPA File, USCC, 1938), 7. For other inequities, see Taylor, *Carolina Crossroads*, 126. On dishonest landowners, see the James Benson interview ("Black Heritage in the Upper Piedmont" Project, PDHRC, 1989). The potential for landholders to take advantage of tenants with no access to the books and with few math skills would be true for whites as well. See the comments by McNeil (p. 4), a white prostitute raised as "the eleventh child of a sharecropper." She noted that "Papa and Mama didn't neither one have a bit of schooling, so they couldn't figure whether he [the landlord] was cheating or not." On the tendency for sharecroppers to break even every year, see the Tanner interview; Manda Walker interview (WPA File, USCC, 1937), 4. For other injustices, see the Burris interview. However, see the Berry interview for a successful black legal challenge to white injustice.

For mill work as a subculture, see Hall, *Like a Family*, 114 ff.

Traditional Types of Workers On mill workers like a family, see the Edna Hargett interview (Southern Oral History Program, Southern Historical Collection of the Manuscripts Department, UNCCH, 1979); Norman is quoted in Tullos, *Habits of Industry*, 133. However, cf. MacDonald, *Southern Mill Hills*, 37, who argued that since workers moved so much, "it becomes harder to establish a sense of community." On mill shifts, see Morland field notes. On child labor, see Batchelor, "A Textile Community," 28. For actual experiences, see Phillips in "Speaking of History" interviews; Miles interview. On the tendency for children to leave high school for mill work, see Tullos, *Habits of Industry*, 185.

Mill Working Conditions On the enjoyment of mill work, see Oliver Wilson interview (WPA File, USCC, 1939), 7. For descriptions of mill work tediousness, see the Craft interview, 6, 12. On physical challenges, see the Miles interview; see also Hardin and Hilliard, cited in Tullos, *Habits of Industry*, 276, 235. For stories of injuries and death, see Thompson, cited in Hall, *Like a Family*, 83.

Mill Worker Attitudes "Tricks of the trade" are described in Tullos, *Habits of Industry*, 13. For general worker attitudes, see MacDonald, *Southern Mill Hills*, 144; Willis, "Mill Town," 21–22; Morland, *Millways*, 232–49, 201. On worker complacency, see also Morland, *Millways*, 50–51, 172 (see also 35). On living for today, see Morland, *Millways*, 46; *The Bridge*, Jan. 1920; Abel Starnes interview (WPA File, USCC, 1939). For his linking of these attitudes to culture, see Morland, *Millways*, 87, 114. On the lack of control over mill workers' lives, see MacDonald, *Southern Mill Hills*, 38; Morland, *Millways*, 50. On mill workers and their recognition of poverty, see Shaffer, "Southern Mill People," 327–28.

Mill Work and Workers Today On brown lung disease, see Tullos, *Habits of Industry*, 331, n. 1.

For white elite attitudes toward manual labor, see Tullos, *Habits of Industry*, 12; Robertson, *Red Hills and Cotton*, 7; Patrick and Morland field notes.

African-American Women   For observations about domestic help, see the Childers interview; L. Brown interview; Dunn interview; Gassoway interview. For a white view, see the Morland field notes. For comments about African-American child-care providers, see the Gassoway interview; M. Williams interview. On the cultural exchange between black and white households, see the Patrick and Morland field notes. On anecdotes about cooking, see the Dunn interview; Gassoway interview. On "toting," see also Taylor, *Carolina Crossroads*, 135; and Wilson, "Folk Speech," 602. For recollections about washerwomen, see the Gassoway interview.

African-American Men   On black male opportunities, see the Simon Gallman interview (WPA File, USCC, 1937), 1; Childers interview. For black work crews, see Patrick and Morland field notes. On learning and practicing such skills as carpentry, see the Childers interview. This is not to imply that all carpenters were black.

Chapter 13. Material Culture

COUNTRYSIDE CULTURAL USE OF SPACE

On the importance of the "home place," see Williams, *Homeplace*, 115, 118; M. Williams interview; Patrick, "Cultural Approach," 39. Rhyne's comment is from *Cotton Mill Workers*, 14. To keep the ties even after death, see Potwin, *Cotton Mill People*, 41–42; Ben Robertson Papers, 6. On the relationship between the home place and family heritage, see Williams, *Homeplace*, 133–35; Culberton interview, 1–2; *Greenville News*, July 21, 1993. For the home place as a family reunion site, see DuBose, "Family Reunions," 1; see also Patrick, "Cultural Approach," 49. On the pattern of children living near parents, see Williams, *Homeplace*, 37, 116–17. See also the "Speaking of History" interviews. On mobile homes, see Williams, *Homeplace*, 36.

Tenant Houses   For historical descriptions, see the Lyles interview, 1; Childers interview. For personal recollections, see the M. Williams interview. On bare yards, see Robertson, *Red Hills and Cotton*, 60. Ms. Landreth appears in the "Speaking of History" interviews. On the clustering of homes in rural areas, see Kovacik and Winberry, *South Carolina*, 106–7.

MILL COMMUNITY CULTURAL USE OF SPACE

For descriptions, see Rhyne, *Cotton Mill Workers*, 25. For alternate views, see William Buchanan interview (WPA File, USCC, 1939), 3. For the spatial arrangement of mill villages, see *The Bridge*, Oct. 1918; see also Jacobs, *Cotton Mill Village*, n.p. On the result of this arrangement, see Herring, *Welfare Work*, 226; Morland, *Millways*, 18. On utilities, see Potwin, *Cotton Mill People*, 45; and Morland, *Millways*, 18. On the arrangement of Hammondville's sidewalks, see Frances Evans and Glenn Shirley, *Mountain Memories: Yesteryear at Piedmont Camp* (Privately printed [available from the Anderson County Library], 1992), 7. For construction descriptions, see Morland, *Millways*, 16; see also Adams interview. For human modification to mill houses, see the Ollie Farrington interview (WPA File, Southern Historical Collection of the Manuscripts Department, UNCCH, 1939). On gardens in mill towns, see also the Pauline Griffith interview. On adjustments to personal space in mill houses, see MacDonald, *Southern Mill Hills*, 21. On supervisors' houses, see *Greenville News*, Jan. 24, 1889.

AFRICAN-AMERICAN URBAN COMMUNITIES

For shotgun house descriptions, see the Mattie Jamison interview (WPA File, Southern Historical Collection of the Manuscripts Department, UNCCH, 1939); Patrick and Morland field notes. For his analysis of this type of home, see Vlach, *Afro-American Tradition*, 123–29 (evolution); 137 (configuration of rooms and origin).

FOLK ARTS AND CRAFTS

Clothing On the use of discarded cloth to make clothes, see the "Speaking of History" interviews and "Uses for the Flour Sack" manuscript (Thaddeus S. Ferree Papers, Southern Historical Collection of the Manuscripts Department, UNCCH, n.d.), 2. For recollections, see Gassoway interview. On head scarves, see the Patrick and Morland field notes; Helen Griebel, " 'Some Wore Rags Round Dere Heads': The African American Woman's Headwrap" (paper presented at the American Folklore Society annual meeting, Jacksonville, Fla., 1992). On African-American improvisation, see Vlach, *Afro-American Tradition*, 3.

Quilting For comments on the social importance of quilting, see Horton and Myers, *Social Fabric*, 3. On the origins of African-American patterns, see Vlach, *Afro-American Tradition*, 44, 55, 67, and 74–75; and Horton and Myers, *Social Fabric*, 30–31. Horton's observations are from a public presentation from January 1992. Ms. Cunningham is quoted in the Kimzey field notes. On quilts as family heritage, see the Hammond interview; "Speaking of History" interviews.

Caning and Basketry On the general folk skill, see the George Briggs interview (WPA File, USCC, 1937). For comparisons between Upstate and Low Country basketry styles, see Dale Rosengarten, "Spirits of Our Ancestors: Basket Traditions in the Carolinas," in George Terry and Lynn Robertson Myers, *Carolina Folk: The Cradle of a Southern Tradition* (Columbia: McKissick Museum, University of South Carolina, 1985), 13–15; Gary Stanton and Tom Cowan, *Stout Hearts: Traditional Oak Basket Makers of the South Carolina Upcountry* (Columbia: McKissick Museum, University of South Carolina, 1988), 3; see also the Berry interview. On making baskets, see Laurel Horton, in Stanton and Cowan, *Stout Hearts*, 3. On learning the skill and on types of baskets, see the Berry interview; A. Wood interview; Horton, in Stanton and Cowan, *Stout Hearts*, 11, 12. For descriptions of the process of weaving, see Horton, in Stanton and Cowan, *Stout Hearts*, 7–10. On the persistence of this folk craft, see Horton, in Stanton and Cowan, *Stout Hearts*, 13, 5, 2, 15; Berry interview.

Pottery and Ceramics   On Carolina pottery, see John Burrison, "Carolina Clay: The Rise of a Regional Pottery Tradition," in Terry and Myers, *Carolina Folk*, 1–5; Vlach, *Afro-American Tradition*, 76–82; see also Charles G. Zug III, *Turners and Burners: The Folk Pottery of North Carolina* (Chapel Hill: University of North Carolina Press, 1986). On contemporary Carolina pottery, see Charles G. Zug III, "Pottery, North Carolina," in Wilson and Ferris, *Encyclopedia of Southern Culture*, 485–86; and Vlach, *Afro-American Tradition*, 96. An anonymous reviewer of this manuscript distinguishes the stoneware traditions of central North Carolina (one Moravian, the other Anglo American) from that in South Carolina. On Native-American crafts, see Burrison, "Carolina Clay," in Terry and Myers, *Carolina Folk*, 6–8; "South Carolina Handicrafts," 3.

Additional Crafts   On male woodcarving, see Kimzey field notes. On ironwork, see the Alexander interview, 13.

Cemetery Inscriptions and Decorations   For references to older African-American grave markers such as stones or slabs, see the M. Williams interview; Vlach, *Afro-American Tradition*, 145.